REFIGURING
THE
HERO

PENN STATE STUDIES IN ROMANCE LITERATURES
Editors, Frederick A. De Armas and Alan E. Knight

REFIGURING THE HERO
From Peasant to Noble in Lope de Vega and Calderón
by Dian Fox

REFIGURING
THE
HERO

From Peasant to

Noble in

Lope de Vega and Calderón

Dian Fox

The Pennsylvania State University Press
University Park, Pennsylvania

Publication of this book has been aided by a grant from the Program for Cultural Cooperation Between Spain's Ministry of Culture and United States' Universities.

Library of Congress Cataloging-in-Publication Data

Fox, Dian.
    Refiguring the hero : from peasant to noble in Lope de Vega and
Calderón / Dian Fox.
        p.   cm.
    Includes bibliographical references and index.
    ISBN 0-271-00737-0
    1. Vega, Lope de, 1562-1635—Criticism and interpretation.
2. Calderón de la Barca, Pedro, 1600-1681—Criticism and
interpretation. 3. Heroes in literature. 4. Nobility in
literature. 5. Peasants in literature. 6. Honor in literature.
I. Title.
PQ6485.F69   1991
862'.3—dc20   90-45893
                                                                         CIP

It is the policy of The Pennsylvania State University Press to use acid-free paper for the first printing of all clothbound books. Publications on uncoated stock satisfy the minimum requirements of American National Standard for Information Sciences— Permanence of Paper for Printed Library Materials, ANSI Z39.48–1984.

CONTENTS

ACKNOWLEDGMENTS

I have profited from the support of many friends and colleagues during the course of this project. Dru Dougherty asked a decisive question at the right time ("Why may these *comedias* be read so differently today?") and aided my search for an answer. Félix Martínez Bonati read drafts of the manuscript provided guidance on technical points and style. Bruce W. Wardropper clarified several important matters of fact.

Others gave their time, interest, and sound advice. They include Frederick A. de Armas, Philip W. Silver, Harry Sieber, Thomas Austin O'Connor, James A. Parr, Marcia Welles, Perry J. Powers, Teresa Gracia, L. Shon Soderquist, Robert Molla, James Mandrell, Donald Hindley, the late Richard L. Predmore, and Benjamin Franklin of the Newport Public Library. Patricia Kenworthy, Eduardo Martínez Bonati, and José Antonio Sánchez facilitated my meetings in Madrid with José

Luis Abellán, Javier Navarro de Zubiyaga, and Ignacio Amestoy.

Research was made possible by Columbia University's Chamberlain Fellowship program and its Council for Research in the Humanities, by the Spanish government's Federico de Onís fellowship program, and by a grant from the Comité Conjunto Hispano-Norteamericano Para la Cooperación Cultural y Educativa, co-sponsored by the American and Spanish governments under the auspices of the Fulbright Program. The *Bulletin of the Comediantes* and *Revista Canadiense de Estudios Hispánicos* have granted permission to reprint material that originally appeared in these journals.

PROLOGUE

The liveliness and charm of seventeenth-century Spanish theater cannot fail to strike anyone encountering Lope de Vega and Pedro Calderón de la Barca for the first time. Readers (or playgoers) who have grown up with Shakespeare will not be disappointed by the wit and lyric of the Spanish stage, its drama of court and kingship, comedy of manners, and stirring tragedy. However, unlike Shakespeare, and unlike Corneille, the Spanish Golden Age dramatists, in a few of the very best and most famous pieces, centered the action around a character of low social class. Hispanists have long hailed such plays as Lope's *Peribáñez* and Calderón's *The Alcalde of Zalamea* (*El alcalde de Zalamea*) as the earliest secular literature in Europe to make a hero, in the positive moral sense, of the common man.

My own initial reaction upon reading these dramas in graduate school was a combination of surprise, pleasure, and discomfort. Although I loved the plays, and although I could sense in them an underlying humane moral concern, I could not embrace with wholehearted enthusiasm the moral characters of Peribáñez or Pedro Crespo any more than I would trust my life to Claudius or Richard III. My suspicion of a peasant who would stab his noble adversary in the back (Peribáñez) or secretly imprison and strangle him (the *alcalde* Pedro Crespo) was complemented by bewilderment at the response of the authority figures who were charged with judging the actions of the formidable peasants. It astonished me that at the conclusions of popular entertainments reaching all strata of society in seventeenth-century Counter-Reformation Spain, stage kings would materialize to bless ex cathedra peasants' actions that were violently inhumane and potentially inducive of explosive social behavior.

My doctoral dissertation, which evolved into *Kings in Calderón* (London: Tamesis, 1986), examined the royal Calderonian figure whose appearances, although sometimes quite brief, are so often crucial to the restoration of order in some of these *comedias* — or as I eventually concluded, fairly often to the further disruption of order. In the historical plays, at least, Calderón frequently cast monarchs famous in oral and written tradition for their bad judgment, to preside over the conclusions. Attention to the interplay between characterization and the Spanish anti-Machiavellian political theory then prevailing indicated that the king's approval would not always necessarily have signified the playwright's.

Since the king does not rule in a vacuum, it was impossible to contemplate kingship without taking into account seventeenth-century attitudes toward citizenship. Ideally, all subjects, no matter what their social rank, ought to have access to the ruler; this indeed is one of the political morals of Calderón's mythical play, *Life Is a Dream* (*La vida es sueño*), as the concluding chapter of *Kings in Calderón* showed. At the same time, that every citizen ought to conduct himself peacefully and respect the social hierarchy, is also a political moral of that piece. The essential religious and political orthodoxy informing Calderón's plays could, I felt, shed some light on the social values of the plays of other seventeenth-century Spanish writers.

Having completed the study on political aspects of Calderón, and after readings in other literatures both previous to and contemporary with that of the Spanish Golden Age, I returned to the peculiar "peasant-honor" plays. Now, equipped with evidence beyond simple intuition, I found myself more convinced than ever that alternative readings of these pieces could legitimately be offered. They could have been (and can be) acted and directed quite coherently in ways that would in fact comply with seventeenth-century social, moral, and religious restrictions on literary heroism. That is, a strong case can be made that these plays censured rather than condoned the actions of the peasants who take revenge.

It is of course to be expected that twentieth-century readers, many of whom are non-Hispanic, should receive the works differently from the ways in which they may have been intended by the seventeenth-century playwrights. The thesis of the present study has to do with the magnitude of the change—due to political, religious, and economic developments in the past 350 years—in our requirements for heroism. Modern consumers of literature tend to accept and expect "heroic" behavior in men and women without regard to social standing. Sometimes the more oppressed the character, the higher our hopes for his or her success in overcoming class barriers. It is perhaps only natural that we should indulge this liberal sentiment by bestowing equal heroic opportunity where it did not used to belong: on characters in literature produced in predemocratic and strictly hierarchical social settings. In other words, we twentieth-century readers are so eager to throw our support behind the social underdog that we cheer on the insubordinate behavior of peasant protagonists in plays of a period that condemned such insubordination.

Granted, even in a contemporary audience not everyone may receive the work the way the author intends it, and it is perilous to discuss an author's intentions. In the case of theater, the orientations of the director and actors may be further variables influencing the transmission of a given text. Without going into the complications of seventeenth-century *comedia* reception at this point, I will note that plays could be experienced in the public theater by a broadly based urban audience, in palace performances by royalty and dignitaries, or in some cases read in private if one had the resources. Wlad Godzich and Nicholas Spadaccini's recent remarks on fragmented reception of Golden Age literature are a healthy caution against the privileging of one monolithic and "correct" reading of a work.[1]

Such a concession does not, however, signify that it is pointless to speculate on likely ways in which the works may have been presented and received, based on what we know about the author and his other works, and on cultural conditions of the time. Indeed, the intrinsically elliptical character of drama, especially when it is *read,* invites the receiver's imaginative collusion in a construction of its meaning, and the meanings will vary as the receivers do. My purpose is to offer a set of readings that are consistent with each other, and whose assumptions and conclusions can find ample justification in Spanish Golden Age culture and history. They are not proposed to be exclusive of other possible constructions.

Chapter 1 builds a frame of reference for later examination of the individual works, with an overview of the idea of the hero in Spanish literature before 1700. One precondition for heroic behavior in Western literature until well into the modern age has indeed been noble blood. Superior lineage seemed automatically to confer upon a character a keener moral awareness, although in general the hero did not live up to his moral potential until he had undergone some sort of test or ordeal. Then, particularly in Spanish Golden Age drama, he frequently faced a choice between a violent response to his dilemma — revenge — or peaceful discourse. Seventeenth-century Spanish playwrights and their audiences inherited a popular legacy of heroism depicted in epic and ballad traditions, and were immersed in Counter-Reformation religious and anti-Machiavellian political norms. The peasant as a heroic figure fell outside this set of values, as did violent revenge for a perceived personal affront.

Succeeding chapters examine the characterization and social context of several of the most famous Golden Age *comedias.* Chapter 2 deals with three that define social roles by explicitly or implicitly juxtaposing heroic and unheroic behavior (Calderón's *Life Is a Dream;* Lope's *The Villano in His Corner* [*El villano en su rincón*] and *The King, the Greatest Alcalde* [*El mejor alcalde, el rey*]). Chapter 3 treats Lope's peasant honor plays, *Peribáñez* and *Fuenteovejuna.* In the first case, the character commonly taken to be the antagonist — a nobleman — may actually be seen not as a villain, but as a type of flawed hero. In the second, the behavior of both the villagers and their aristocratic oppressor seriously transgresses accepted social and religious norms, which are personified in and articulated by the Catholic monarchs, Isabella and Ferdinand. Chapter 4 examines *Luis Pérez, the Galician* (*Luis Pérez, el gallego*) and *The Alcalde of Zalamea,* the only two *comedias* by Calderón with peasant protagonists. The concluding chapter addresses more specifically the conditions that cause us in the twentieth century so earnestly to seek a revolutionary, democratic temper in these seventeenth-century Spanish masterpieces.

Because I am suggesting a reassessment of the place of the Spanish Golden Age theatrical canon within its European context, and since my concerns are at times comparative, I direct this study not only to specialists in Spanish letters but also to scholars and students of other literatures who are less familiar with Golden Age Spain. English translations of foreign language quotations are therefore provided. When referring to Spanish historical monarchs, I use the English spelling of the proper name (Henry III). References to the fictional versions of these characters retain the Spanish spelling (Enrique III).

for Pat and L. D.

Chapter 1

THE FIGURE OF THE HERO
IN SPANISH LITERATURE BEFORE 1700

"I want a hero." Lord Byron's tongue-in-cheek nineteenth-century quest for a great man led him to seventeenth-century Spain's idea of a fourteenth-century rogue, Don Juan Tenorio. Yet the genesis of Byron's hero probably owed more to satires of prose romances, Italian burlesque epics, and Spanish picaresque novels than to Tirso de Molina's Baroque play, *The Trickster of Seville* (*El burlador de Sevilla*) or to medieval Spanish history; and the poet's greatest inspiration came from contemporary British scandals.[1] His *Don Juan* was not really about a foreign civilization of centuries past, but his own nineteenth-century England.

The hero in any age will more likely reflect the values and concerns of his author's, not his (presumed) own, circumstances and culture. The term "hero" can with equally sound justification apply to Homer's semidivine Achilles, to the noble Cid, Rodrigo Díaz de Vivar, to George Eliot's middle-class Maggie Tulliver, to Alexandra Kollontai's proletarian "worker bees," and to Sartre's anti-intellectual intellectual. Often, the character is invested with some distinguishing power or sensibility setting him painfully apart from his fellows. As in the last example, the character may attempt to fulfill himself precisely by shedding any claim to individual distinction, joining a larger, anonymous mass, losing himself in a cause.

The idea of the "hero" and the "heroic" in literature and society has of course evolved continuously since Homer's epics. As Victor Brombert points out, the modern hero "must be socially *representative*": "Certainly the hero in the image of God is not the same as the hero in a Marxist, Freudian, or structuralist perspective."[2] Generally, as I have suggested, the peculiarities in fiction are attached closely to the concerns of the host society. In Spain during the Reconquest, at the height of the Middle Ages, for example, the Cid, great warrior and slayer of the infidel, became the subject of epic and then ballad cycles. When with its success the urgency of this military campaign began to wane, and literary fashions moved into the court, romance elevated more refined knights like Amadís de Gaula, who went questing as much for the sake of private love as for public acclaim.

Northrop Frye presented an often-cited model of the hero's decline in social standing and powers since the classical Greeks in his essay "Historical Criticism: Theory of Modes."[3] In Frye's conception (based on Aristotelian distinctions), the earliest hero-figure, from Greek mythology, is part human, part divine; as such he excels other men in every regard. Chronologically, the demigod is followed by the human hero of romance, "superior in *degree* to other men and to his environment" (33). He is allowed at times to avail himself of supernatural aid. If the hero is better than his fellows but subjected to the laws of nature, he is the protagonist of the "*high mimetic* mode, of most epic and tragedy" (34). The hero who is one of us—a possibility due at least in part to the rise of the bourgeoisie and literacy since the sixteenth century—belongs in Frye's terminology to *low mimetic* fiction. Finally, the character may seem socially inferior to us, as a member of the working class; or inferior in kind, owing to ironic or absurdist treatment, often the case in twentieth-century fiction. Perhaps next, Frye suggested, will be a return to the mythical semidivine in genres such as science fiction. A manifestation of the completion of the large cycle may indeed be lately flourishing in Latin American prose fiction, for example, the *realismo mágico* of such writers as Gabriel García Márquez.

To be sure, within the frame of that trajectory of general decline in the hero's relative social standing and power of action, one can find variations and contrary tendencies. Morton W. Bloomfield determines subcycles of hero/antihero, each period reacting in a Hegelian manner against the ideals of the preceding epoch.[4] While Beowulf, Roland, and the Cid excelled physically and spiritually in the early and High Middle Ages, the later medieval period had no heroes of comparable stature. Bloomfield attributes this paucity to neo-Augustinian and then humanistic reactions against the traditional heroic values of violence and desire for worldly glory. The later Renaissance, with Spenser, Shakespeare, Milton, and Corneille, resurrected the great heroes, now Christianized.[5] Correspondingly, while the eighteenth and twentieth centuries tend to reject the hero, the nineteenth-century Romantics brought him back.

In order to understand better the seventeenth-century Spanish cultural climate in which both aristocratic and plebeian protagonists were produced, we shall examine in greater detail the trajectory of heroism posed by Frye and nuanced by Bloomfield. Following is a brief overview of the conventions and attitudes, beginning with those of the ancient Greeks and Romans, from which the heroes of Lope de Vega and Calderón derived.

Heroic *Desengaño*

According to classical Graeco-Roman tradition, a hero is a great man worthy of fame and imitation, often godlike or semidivine; always a prince or member of the high nobility. And as W. T. H. Jackson points out, central to most Western epic poetry is the conflict between the hero and his king.[6] Seldom is the hero completely successful (the *Odyssey* is exceptional in this respect; Odysseus *is* the king and does recover Ithaca). The *Iliad* ends with the expectation of Achilles' death; *Beowulf* with the hero's solemn funeral. If Roland and not Charlemagne is truly the hero of the *Song of Roland,* this epic too ends with the loss of its hero, although in death he earns redemption.

Generally, we expect the main character in a work of literature to undergo some sort of ordeal that results in a transformation in character or outlook. The advent of the moment of truth may be called "revelation," "epiphany," "anagnorisis," or, in Spanish, *desengaño.*[7] However, the earliest heroes, of the preclassical Greek epic, do not seem to experience anything resembling spiritual development. Despite their thriving inner emotional lives, for Achilles and Odysseus evidence of conscience or willing submission to a higher law is absent.[8] Here are men who obey external necessities, but no strong figure of central earthly authority. Nor do they worry about being called to account in an afterlife; that of the *Iliad* is barely suggested. The Hades of the *Odyssey* is ephemeral, disorganized, and not consistently connected with any concept of justice, of reward or punishment for actions in this world.

Notwithstanding these metaphysical limitations, Homeric heroes do possess a major trait of early heroic stature: political autonomy. Hegel in the *Aesthetics* points out that during the heroic age (meaning that of the Homeric heroes), one's rights were not protected by any state; therefore one had to and could, like Achilles, Orestes, and Odysseus, make one's own laws.[9] Without the constraint of legal institutions, all actions were free to be purely heroic. Hegel sees the Cid, the medieval Spanish epic hero, in the same sort of prelegal independent personal and social situation. Shakespeare's recourse to medieval chronicles and romances as the sources of tragedies can be attributed to the fact that in the early days, unencumbered by social restrictions, true heroism could exist. According to Hegel, the hero *must* emanate from privileged condition

> because of the perfect freedom of will and production which is realized in the idea of royalty. . . . On the other hand, in the figures drawn from the lower classes, if they undertake to act within their restricted circumstances, what we see is subjection everywhere; for in civilized states indeed they are as a matter of fact in every way dependent, straitened, and, with their passions and interests, fall continually under the pressure and compulsion of the necessity outside them. (192)

In contrast to Shakespearean drama, however, Spanish Golden Age *comedias* set in the Middle Ages supply the aggrieved protagonist with an accessible higher authority, so that the freedom Hegel describes should not be expected to apply here. In fact, we are sometimes quite accurately able to identify the exact year of the Spanish play's setting precisely by the identity of the king presiding or appearing ex machina to resolve the central conflict. In *Peribáñez, Fuenteovejuna,* and *The*

Physician of His Honor, Lope de Vega and Calderón furnish prominently (and at times anachronistically) established royal strongholds of power. Therefore, while their sources, like Shakespeare's, may be medieval chronicles, Lope and Calderón obviate the license for "true heroism" that Shakespeare has granted to, say, Henry IV. Consequently, the recourse to violence on the part of the offended protagonists (who are not royal or in some cases even aristocratic) in the historical Spanish *comedias* will be of central concern in later chapters of this study.

The "civilized" circumstances offered by Spanish Golden Age theater are augured in one classical epic hero who obviously did reject personal license and subordinate himself to the ideal of a higher authority. Virgil's portrayal of the hero in the *Aeneid* represents a significant advance over the Greek epic heroes in political awareness; this awareness results, precisely, in a restriction in the scope of activities open to him. Aeneas is now able to foresee the ramifications of his behavior, to make choices, and to accept responsibility for them. His journey is one of transition, the escape from the demolition of one society and its institutions, to the foundation of a new, complex legal system. The *Aeneid,* unlike the Homeric epics, is a sentimental (in Schiller's sense) and learned product of a complicated and sophisticated social structure. The hero changes from son to father, from impulsive youth to pious patriarch accepting a supreme responsibility to the state. Each leg of that journey, and most poignantly the interlude with Dido in Book 4, reminds the hero that his emotions, impulses, and personal desires must give way to national destiny. This epic hero cannot really make his own law.

The visit to his father in the Elysian Fields at the center of the poem invests Aeneas, symbolically and literally, with a conscience. His tour of Hades, in Virgil's rendition a highly developed instrument of justice, is really a revelation of his own conscience, as he meets comrades from his past, and a prophecy of the future. The gods and the parent guiding him (by this point purely metaphorical expressions of conscience) withdraw from active intervention, and the hero, "pious Aeneas," proceeds under the impetus of duty. Yet this piety is ambiguous: even his final violent confrontation with Turnus is morally dubious, as it seems to contain an element of personal revenge sanctioned by greater national purpose, the good of future Rome. A recent revisionist interpretation finds the entire poem the story of the corruption of the hero. At first a man who feels deeply the losses of his wife, mistress, and father, Aeneas learns to suppress his personal life in favor of the state. He becomes a frustrated, violent automaton, the embodiment of fascism: Virgil prescribes for contemporary Rome, torn by a century of civil war, a strong and repressive ruler.[10] The union of moral conscience and state ideology will be found as well in Spanish Golden Age drama, a popular entertainment composed and disseminated during an epoch of strict political and religious hegemony, lending itself to such radically conflicting views of the protagonists and themes.

It would, in any case, be supportable to state that the Spanish *comedia* protagonists operate in a Virgilian rather than Homeric political context. This being the case, their rejection of higher authority and recourse to vigilante justice is all the more interesting—particularly considering that Peribáñez and Pedro Crespo are Christians in an adamantly Catholic environment, are not noble, and yet still claim (openly or secretly) the princely prerogative of epic revenge.

Indeed, whatever Virgil might have intended with his epic poem, he and his hero were embraced by medieval scholars for their visionary and moral natures. The emphasis on civic and religious duty lacking in Homer but pervading the *Aeneid* lent itself to Christian coloring; Reuben A. Brower shows that Renaissance translations of the epic into English, to which Shakespeare would have had access, make Aeneas as much saint as soldier.[11] At the same time, however, the formula *fortitudo et sapientia*,[12] to which the character of epic heroes since Aeneas typically conforms, betrays a fundamental dichotomy in the heroic nature. This dichotomy presented a special difficulty to the medieval poet, especially as St. Augustine's condemnation of worldly glory in *The City of God* gained prominence in the later Middle Ages.[13] The constitutive inner conflict of the Christian warrior-hero continues into Renaissance and post-Renaissance times.

The wronged protagonist's choice between revenge and appeal to a higher authority is a central issue in a number of the best-known Spanish Golden Age plays. Sancho of Lope's *The King, the Greatest Alcalde,* together with Peribáñez, the villagers of Fuenteovejuna, and Pedro Crespo, faced a crisis originating in the collision between Graeco-Roman and medieval European conceptions of admirable behavior. Revenge is a significant motivating force for the classical epic hero. When the epic arises again in the Middle Ages under the auspices of Christianity, the poet must confront the disturbing polarity between the exigencies of portraying the traditional hero—a superior man who wins glory, often violently—and the values of his religion, which reject the desire for fame and call for the imitation of Christ, that is, nonviolence. *Beowulf,* its pagan hero in a poem with a Christian attitude, presents, according to Bernard F. Huppé, a "picture of the inevitable fate of a war-like society governed by the law of revenge; we are shown the uselessness of all things in this world unless they are governed and directed to the end of being useful to salvation."[14] In the French epic, Roland attains truly *Christian* heroic status by reconciling himself to martyrdom for the Christian cause, having stayed, unreinforced, too long in the fighting. The ensuing trial and gruesome execution of the traitor Ganelon "in amazing pain" ("par merveillus aban"),[15] himself moved to treachery by the desire for revenge against Roland, satisfies the demands both of vengeance and justice.

Apart from some aheroic lyric poetry—the kharjas[16]—the earliest Castilian literature in Spain, and the prototype of heroic ethical conflict against which to measure that of the Spanish *comedia,* is the epic *Poem of the Cid (Poema de mio Cid).* The protagonist is Rodrigo Díaz de Vivar, a historical character who lived from about 1043 to 1099. The most recent investigations indicate that the epic was composed by a learned poet, possibly a lawyer from the area of Burgos in northern Spain, about 1207.[17] Although the text of the *PMC* itself was not known in Golden Age Spain, the figure of the Cid and versions of his story flourished in subsequent popular and erudite lore through the seventeenth century. The *PMC* poses a complex rumination on class relations and political requirements for heroism. It contains a frank acknowledgment of the king's fallibility, something unexceptional in epic poetry. However, this work's hero, who could easily settle things on his own, with certain reservations eschews independent remedy to affront and patiently awaits the satisfaction of legal recourse. The Cid's dilemma and his response to it provide a useful paradigm for considering similar difficulties facing the protagonists of several Golden Age plays.

Much of the action of this poem likewise is motivated by the drive for retribution, which coalesces in a denouement unparalleled in epic poetry. Although formally divided into three cantos (*cantares*), thematically the work falls into two nearly equal halves. As the epic opens, Rodrigo, the Cid, must leave Burgos, having incurred the disfavor of Alfonso VI, King of Leon and Castile, due to malicious gossip among envious courtiers. In exile, the Cid undertakes highly effective military campaigns against the Moors, and could easily become a sovereign in his own right. Yet he continues to avow allegiance to Alfonso, sending his estranged king impressive gifts of booty won from the Moors. By the epic's midpoint, Alfonso has recognized his error in blaming such a worthy and successful vassal. He pardons Rodrigo and offers compensation by marrying the hero's daughters to two young aristocrats (*infantes*) from Carrión. While the Infantes are attracted by the Cid's great wealth, they are repulsed by his inferior social standing. For Rodrigo's part, this marriage would be of considerable social and political benefit. Unlike the classical epic hero, Beowulf, or Roland, Rodrigo is neither semidivine, nor a member of the high nobility. He hails from the lower aristocracy. The anonymous poet clearly means the Cid's energetic heroism to contrast with the vestigial indolence of Alfonso's highborn courtiers, including the two young Infantes who would marry Doña Elvira and Doña Sol.

While the first half of the poem fairly exclusively chronicles Rodrigo's military exploits, the second half assumes a more domestic and psychological character. The daughters are wed with catastrophic results: the Infantes prove themselves cowards, and, in shame at their own public disgrace, take irrational reprisal against Rodrigo by beating and abandoning Elvira and Sol in the wilderness at Corpes. Hereafter, the motivating force of the poem becomes the recovery of the Cid's honor, his revenge for the outrage against his daughters at Corpes. Yet it is not Rodrigo who orchestrates the retribution, but his king, Alfonso. As the victims' father, Rodrigo's name has been blackened. As the author of the marriage, the King has also been insulted, by association; as sovereign he is the source of his subjects' honor. He becomes the active protagonist and personally undertakes to restore Rodrigo's honor. Alfonso holds court at Toledo; the Infantes are found guilty; and along with returning the dowries and other gifts to the Cid (the riches, naturally, they have already spent), they and a third brother are ordered to stand in single combat.

Again, the Cid is not principal of the action, but observer. Again, Rodrigo by association extends the disgrace to others, so that the crime must finally be recognized as an attack on the whole of legitimate society, from the King down. Declaring to his men that his affront is also theirs, the Cid delegates the three combats to his three best men. Of course, they triumph, although they refrain from killing their opponents: humiliation will suffice. In the end, the aristocratic family of the Infantes is made impotent and loses all stature at court, while the King marries the Cid's daughters to princes of evident good character from Aragon and Navarre. The hero has chosen to construe the Infantes' crime as a universal affront, and to refer his complaint to available legal structures.

With very little active exertion on his own part, the upwardly noble Rodrigo has institutionalized his "revenge" into what might more properly be called "justice," and succeeded in elevating his family into the highest social stratum.

It is tempting to read the poem as an indictment of privilege earned by birth instead of personal merit, and Alan Deyermond has seen in this epic a satire on the higher nobility.[18] It certainly reflects the historical conditions of its (or rather, the poet's) period: at this point in Iberian history, a monarch's authority was hardly absolute, and constantly subject to challenge from the most powerful feudal lords—hence, Alfonso's special interest in bringing the potent and charismatic Rodrigo back into the fold.[19] Nevertheless, the character of its hero and the nature of his heroics raise several disturbing questions, the least of which concerns Rodrigo's unorthodox social ascent. It has been pointed out that the *Poem of the Cid* is unique among epics because the hero has no flaw and learns little; society changes in response to its encounter with Rodrigo.[20] The King learns to act like a king should, exercising his authority and extinguishing the influence of malicious courtiers, and the social composition alters to assimilate the warrior-hero into its upper class.

The Cid, however, is found by scholars exemplary in every respect, a model of the strength and wisdom expected of the standard epic hero. Rodrigo is hailed as a family man after the fashion of Hector. His departure from Ximena, the wife whom he must leave behind as he heads into exile, will be a poignant contrast to the Infantes' crime and desertion of their wives at Corpes. The first sign of goodwill he begs of Alfonso during the drawn-out "mating-dance" that leads to reconciliation, is that his wife and daughters be allowed to join him in the kingdom of Valencia, which he has won from the Moors. Not only the greatest soldier in combat and strategist in a holy war, he also shows mercy to the defeated after the battles are over. The victory of his men in the judicial duels proves that right (and God) are on his side. While St. Gabriel's visit to him in a dream is a far cry from the active divine intervention of the Greek epic, it too is evidence of supernatural favor. Although it is true that the Cid may appear obsessed with the booty won from battle, Jackson points out (81) that the hero covets these goods not for himself, but to gain back the good graces of the King. All of his campaigns against the Infidel are won in the name of the reluctant monarch. After reconciliation at the poem's midpoint—in which the hero has thrown himself at the King's feet[21]— Rodrigo reacts with misgiving to Alfonso's plan to marry his daughters to the Infantes of Carrión: " 'It is not meet,' replied the Campeador, 'that I should give my daughters in marriage, for they are young and few in days. The princes of Carrión are of high estate and worthy of my daughters and even better.' " Yet immediately he interrupts himself, swallowing his protest: " 'I begot my daughters; you reared them. They and I are yours to command. Doña Elvira and Doña Sol are in your hands, O King. Give them to whom you please and I shall be content' " (79).

> ("Non abria fijas de casar"　　　—respuso el Campeador—
> "ca non han grant heda(n)d　　　e de dias pequeñas son.
> De grandes nuevas son　　　los ifantes de Carrion,
> perteneçen pora mis fijas　　　e aun pora mejores.
> Hyo las engendre amas　　　e criastes las vos;
> entre yo y ellas　　　en vuestra merçed somos nos,
> afellas en vuestra mano　　　don Elvira e doña Sol:
> dad las a qui quisieredes vos　　　ca yo pagado so.")
> 　　　　　　　　　　　　　　　　　(lines 2082–89)

Ironically, it is this determined loyalty that in fact leads to the injury of his cherished daughters: because their unions have been arranged by Alfonso, Rodrigo stubbornly ignores glaring evidence of the mean character and unworthiness of his new sons-in-law. He overlooks their pusillanimity in his court at Valencia, and rejects warnings about them from his men. Alfonso has honored him with these liaisons, and the hero will not question the King's actions under any circumstances, even when the well-being of his own children is at risk. He suppresses his doubts and subordinates his family's safety to a political ideal and the promise of social elevation, trusting his daughters' lives to a monarch with proven poor judgment.

Cedric Whitman finds in the Greek hero an element of self-destructiveness that leads to calamity for characters such as Oedipus, Telemonian Ajax, and Antigone.[22] The Greek audience, versed in the traditional lore and thus foreseeing the consequences of these protagonists' rash behavior, would have perceived them as benighted. I submit that Rodrigo's obsessive loyalty to an undeserving ruler might well have been regarded with similar dramatic irony, with *disapproval* by the audience of the *Poem of the Cid*. I have mentioned elsewhere that during the period of the composition of this epic, on the Iberian Peninsula as in the rest of

Europe, no king's power was absolute.[23] On the contrary, the tradition of elective kingship was a relatively recent memory. Feudal rule prevailed; a king was merely preeminent among powerful lords. Political ties were tenuous, and frequently broken. It was not until the late thirteenth century in Spain that Alphonse X ("the Wise") laid the legal groundwork paving the way for consolidation of the power of the monarchy.[24] In the late twelfth or early thirteenth century, though, when the poem was written, a prudent vassal might judiciously withhold complete submission to a ruler who had yet to demonstrate a competence to govern.

Does the Cid attain illumination (*desengaño*)? The hero of a serious work of literature—especially, one might expect, the hero of a Christian epic, as he is presented as a model for emulation—ought to arrive at some sort of epiphany. Roland understands that pride kept him from sounding the oliphant, and confesses his sins before dying. Does the Cid ever realize that his own unquestioning acquiescence to Alfonso has contributed to the injury of his daughters? Clearly, the King who arranged the marriages bears a measure of responsibility for the unhappy results, but the vassal who accepted the arrangement and continued to support it wholeheartedly, despite compelling evidence of its profound flaw, must share the blame.

Nevertheless, the poet portrays the Cid's attitudes altogether subtly. During the protracted reconciliation in the first half of the poem, Rodrigo's emissaries to Alfonso always carefully conveyed the hero's unqualified respect for and devotion to the monarch; and the King responded with a restraint that gradually warmed to acceptance and, finally, corresponding respect and goodwill. Rodrigo's first contact with Alfonso following the crime at Corpes takes on an entirely new tenor that shifts the balance in their relationship. The Cid's message to the King is uncharacteristically blunt: Muño Gustioz is instructed,

> "tell the good King to weigh in his heart this wrong which the Princes of Carrión have done to us, for he it was who gave my daughters in marriage, not I, and they have been basely abandoned. Some dishonor falls to us therefrom, but, great or small, it is all dishonor for the King" (111).

> ("desta desondra que me an fecha   los ifantes de Carrion
> quel pese al buen rey   d'alma e de coraçon.
> El caso mis fijas,   ca non gelas di yo;

quando las han dexadas   a grant desonor
si desondra i cabe   alguna contra nos
la poca e la grant   toda es de mio señor.")

(lines 2906–11)

The subtext of this unusually bold declaration is that Rodrigo has acquiesced too much in the past, and that things will now change. Alfonso immediately shifts his role to subservient apology and kowtows to the Cid from this point on. While the King actively pursues justice on behalf of his vassal, it is really Rodrigo who pulls the strings, accepting or vetoing Alfonso's procedures throughout the entire second half of the poem. The King convokes the court at Toledo, prepared to disown any who dare not to appear (lines 2993–94). Rodrigo's arrival—an annoying and defiant five days late—is greeted by the worried King not with anger, but with great relief. The Cid declines Alfonso's invitation to enter the city, on the grounds that he wishes to rest and keep an all-night vigil at San Servando. Rodrigo does not add that he will use the time secretly to outfit an escort of one hundred knights with armor and weapons underneath their ceremonial garb. He instructs Minaya,

> "Let [my men] don their quilted tunics, to cushion the armor, and over their tunics their coats of mail, shining like the sun. Above their armor they will wear their ermines and other skins, the latches well fastened so that the armor does not show. And under their mantles let them gird on their sweet-cutting swords. In such wise shall we arrive at the court to demand justice and plead our cause. Then, if those of Carrión seek trouble, well, with a hundred knights like these I shall fear them not!"

> ("Velmezes vestidos   por sufrir las guarnizones,
> de suso las lorigas   tan blancas commo el sol,
> sobre las lorigas   armiños e peliçones,
> e que non parescan las armas,   bien presas los cordones;
> so los mantos las espadas   dulçes e tajadores;
> d'aquesta guisa   quiero ir a la cort
> por demandar mios derechos   e dizir mi razon;
> si desobra buscaren   ifantes de Carrion
> ido tales çiento tovier   bien sere sin pavor!")

(lines 3073–81)

Rodrigo's lack of confidence in Alfonso and his court, which would be patent to the epic's audience, borders on lèse majesté and is a vivid contrast to the hero's previously blind subservience. In short, the hero of the *Poem of the Cid* does change as the result of the private tragedy of his daughters, which he deliberately converts into a communal disgrace. His understanding of political loyalty fundamentally alters, becoming consistent with then-prevailing notions of the proper relationship between king and vassal. The truly wise subject, in accordance with the unsettled political conditions in early thirteenth-century Spain, reserves the right to entertain doubts about the policies of his king, and to except himself from that ruler's authority should circumstances warrant.

The nascent defiance evident in the Cid's attitude at the end of the *Poem of the Cid* became a prominent trait of his character later in the poems of the epic cycle. Typically, subsequent lore on the same subject tends to focus on the hero's youth, family, and minor events in his life not treated in the original story; often, some corruption in his character occurs. In the late fourteenth-century epic *Youth of Rodrigo* (*Mocedades de Rodrigo*) and in some surviving ballads, the hero's insubordination becomes his salient trait. He strikes his own father, draws his sword without apology in the presence of the King, and commits other acts of blatant disrespect.[25] Since the *Poem of the Cid* was probably composed by a learned poet and then diffused by traveling players (*juglares*), this literary epic entered the public domain of learned and illiterate alike as it passed into the oral tradition. By the fifteenth century the legend of the Cid and all aspects of his life, military and domestic, had become the most popular historical subject in Spain's ballad tradition.[26]

In any case, the epic vision of heroism contained in the *Poem of the Cid* holds up for admiration the blossoming of this enterprising nobleman's political awareness. The hero perceives his earlier blindness, and attains not only restitution but social advancement, through his consummate yet qualified personal restraint (*mesura*). Although a military man with the means to correct with force a personal affront, Rodrigo allows the fledgling judicial system of Alfonso's government to address the issue. He achieves a most satisfying settlement through appeal to a flawed but finally effective higher authority. In political terms, then, the poem expresses a qualified affirmation of a monarchic order.

Such finely nuanced fictional ruminations on revenge, restraint, and chary recourse to higher authority survived quite surprisingly intact through several succeeding centuries, even when historically the king's position was growing ever stronger. During the Middle Ages and Renaissance, the Spanish ballads (*romances*) carrying the tale of the Cid and other public and private dramas flourished to a degree unique in Europe. Furthermore, as distinct from the rest of the Continent, Britain, and Ireland, this popular genre was enthusiastically appropriated by educated poets throughout the sixteenth and into the seventeenth centuries. The ballads, which gained favor among all degrees of society, were often probably fragments of earlier lost epics and chronicles; therefore many *romances* narrated acts of heroism originating in history that had passed into folklore. Some, called "border" ballads ("romances fronterizos"), dwelt on events along the frontiers of the Reconquest. Others drew from chivalric subjects, such as those found in the Carolingian cycle.

   In nearly all of these songs, the acts of heroism or love feature aristocratic or royal characters; many deal with disagreements between king and vassal.[27] Colin Smith points out that two prevailing themes are justice, that is, "a proper revenge for wrongs committed," often involving feuds between noble families; and "simply that life is tragic."[28] The *romances* with tragic themes frequently show a famous public figure or local hero meeting a sad end due to the treachery of others, not to any fault of his own.[29] For example, Don Alvaro de Luna (1390?–1453), who had been the favorite of King John II (1406–1454), abruptly fell from grace and was executed. Second in number only to historical ballads about the Cid, the songs treating Don Alvaro made him a Christ-figure doomed by envy. The ballads acted as a cultural conduit for heroism; both the Cid and Don Alvaro were to become popular protagonists of Spain's seventeenth-century drama, as did many other subjects and scenes from the oral tradition. In turn, "the Spanish heroic theater," Ramón Menéndez Pidal writes, "constituted a kind of dramatic epic" ("La comedia heroica española se constituyó a modo de una epopeya dramática").[30] It is to be expected that the theatrical scenes influenced by the historical or pseudohistorical oral tradition, as in Lope's *Knight of Olmedo* or Calderón's *Physician of His Honor,* concern not the predicaments of farmers and peasants, but famous champions (or villains) of noble when not royal blood.

   "Novelesque" ballads, on the other hand, could portray private dramas at almost any social level. One familiar variation which also exerted considerable influence on the seventeenth-century stage was the encounter in the wilderness between a *caballero,* usually mounted, and a young girl on foot, the *serrana*. These poems, *serranillas*, and their close relations the *pastorelas*, composed by cultured poets but with a popular tone, were not confined to the ballad verse form. They could be humorous or serious, and described the seduction or attempted seduction of one or the other, most often the innocent victim being the peasant girl. *Serranillas* gained acceptance thanks in part to their inclusion in the *Book of Good Love* (*Libro de Buen Amor*) by Juan Ruiz, Arcipreste de Hita (1283?–1351?). They were subsequently a favorite kind of *poesía de tipo tradicional*, traditional-type poetry, much of which was actually produced by learned poets. Variations on the encounter between the amorous *caballero* and simple rustic girl became a typical plot element in Spanish Golden Age theater, and indeed are central to this book's discussions of Lope de Vega's *The Villano in His Corner, The King, the Greatest Alcalde, Peribáñez,* and *Fuenteovejuna;* as well as Calderón's *Life Is a Dream* and *The Alcalde of Zalamea.*

Once the popularity of the ballads and other traditional-type poetry had reached its zenith, parody naturally followed: protagonists of the earlier, serious verses began to receive ironic treatment. Not long into the seventeenth century, Francisco de Quevedo y Villegas (1580–1645), among others, wrote some scathingly witty lampoons of heroic themes that had passed their prime.[31] Another subject in poetry and prose that underwent this type of deflation at the turn of the seventeenth century was the pastoral. Imported along with sophisticated verse forms into Spain from Italy in the early sixteenth century by Juan Boscán (c. 1490–1542) and Garcilaso de la Vega (1501–1536), the pastoral of course presents an idealized portrait of life among shepherds. The characters, who happen to be highly literate, sing sophisticated love complaints while their neglected flocks listen in sympathy. Although these literary shepherds are essentially and sometimes literally aristocrats in disguise, their tears are hardly heroic; in his *First Eclogue* Garcilaso explicitly rejects the epic model as he exhorts his patron, Don Pedro de Toledo, Viceroy of Naples, to lay down his arms and listen to "the sweet lament of two shepherds" ("el dulce lamentar de dos pastores").[32]

The pastoral poem and novel (see especially Jorge de Montemayor's *Diana* [1559] and Miguel de Cervantes's *La Galatea* [1585]) thrived through the midsixteenth century, joining other idealistic genres, the chivalric and sentimental romances. If the driving force of epic verse had been revenge, that of romance was love, and the plots of these tales tended to complexity, lack of direction, and, in the case of the pastoral, inaction. The popularity of these "drawing-room" genres would conform to Bloomfield's theory that the high heroics of *Beowulf,* the *Nibelungen-lied,* the *Song of Roland,* and the *Poem of the Cid* are followed by a period of works with less dominant and vigorous protagonists. Tristan, Lancelot, Gawain, Troilus, and in Spain, Amadís de Gaula, are motivated at least as much by love as by glory; their tales are episodic; and sometimes a work's heroics are diffused among several protagonists, a technique called *entrelacement.*[33] They bequeath to Golden Age theater a plot that nearly always complicates centrally (e.g., *The King, the Greatest Alcalde*) or peripherally (*Life Is a Dream*) with obstacles to the protagonist's romantic love. Another device that gained favor and is "anti-heroic," Bloomfield asserts (35), is making the author of a work its main character. Witness Dante's pseudo-autobiographical "I" (who often cowers, weeps, and faints) in the *Divine Comedy.* Chaucer's *Canterbury Tales,* the *Romance of the Rose,* and the *Book of Good Love* are all first-person narratives.

Vittore Branca points out that the Italian *novelle* of Boccaccio in the fourteenth century went so far as to lionize the merchant and banking classes, which in effect controlled political and financial dealings in Europe in the late Middle Ages.[34] But it must be kept in mind that the hero's transformation from vengeful epic warrior to refined and sophisticated gentleman was, as Bloomfield describes it, generally not so much in social standing as in his motivation and power. While on occasion even a squire may be the protagonist in a chivalric romance, none of these works actually narrates the deeds of a truly plebeian subject.

The romance genres, in any case, although not heroic in the concentrated, strictly classical sense—that is, not occupying their characters always in the most glorious of pursuits, of honor, revenge, and so forth—still idealize their protagonists. These are beautiful people, aristocrats untroubled by everyday concerns, primarily consumed with feelings of romantic love and its consequences. As such, and despite any dialectical movement with respect to heroic portrayals in literature, the characters populating these genres are indeed, by the late sixteenth century, ripe for parody. By the time the "peasant-honor" dramas reached the Spanish stage in the seventeenth century the pastoral was in fact passé, primarily the object of ridicule in literary circles rather than imitation. Nevertheless, modern *comedia* criticism inclines to see eulogies of bucolic simplicity in plays dealing with peasants.

It is true that, perhaps thanks partly to the legacy of the pastoral genre, together with religious developments in the sixteenth and seventeenth centuries, the protagonist in certain types of Spanish fiction took several steps down the social ladder. Conditions for deflation of the idealizing romances are particularly favorable in Spain of the Counter-Reformation, in the aftermath of the Council of Trent (1545–1563). The prose genre we call picaresque is prefigured in the anonymous *Lazarillo de Tormes*,[35] whose beginning, Walter L. Reed notes, plays on the opening of the *Aeneid*,[36] as well as on that of *Amadís de Gaula*.[37] *Lazarillo* was soon translated into many languages, and by the 1590s was a significant influence on English prose. Thomas Nashe's *The Unfortunate Traveller* (whose scurvy protagonist is nevertheless a gentleman) is clearly indebted to the Spanish tale.

Mateo Alemán officially inaugurates Spain's picaresque in the two-part *Guzmán de Alfarache* (1599 and 1604). This type of novel is also presented in the first person, since, as Maurice Molho points out, "the 'I' of the picaro is simply the life story of a protagonist so base that third-person narration is out of the question: it could occur to no one but the picaro himself to record such a life" ("el *yo* del pícaro no es sino el tema personal de un protagonista tan ruin que la tercera persona de las historias le es vedada: a nadie sino a él mismo se le puede ocurrir escribir la gesta de su vida").[38] The picaresque novel describes the disreputable career of its generally illegitimate and sometimes *converso*[39] protagonist. The picaro always strives greedily for at least the appearance of honor and social status that the circumstances of his birth have denied him. Pablos in Quevedo's *The Rogue* (*El Buscón*) (1604?) is the obverse of the traditional epic hero with paradoxically similar motivation: born in shame, he craves not only fame, but also revenge against the society that excludes him.[40] While the picaro dons many disguises and plays many roles, and his sham is inevitably exposed, "legitimate" society's hypocritical esteem for appearance over genuine worth is the true object of ridicule. In its often grotesque exaggeration, the picaresque novel paints only the seamy side[41] of Spanish society and cannot be called truly realistic.

Alexander A. Parker, in *Literature and the Delinquent*, suggests that the picaresque is patterned in Spain after such books as Pedro Malón de Chaide's *Conversion of Mary Magdalene* (*La conversión de la Magdalena*) (1588); these books belong among "the religious writings of the last thirty years of the sixteenth century [which] are the influence that . . . can alone explain the transition from idealism to realism in the novel" (21). The preface of the *Conversion* contains an indignant attack on Montemayor's *Diana,* whose tales of worldly love might lead young girls astray.[42]

Like Malón de Chaide's book, Alemán's story, Quevedo's *Rogue,* and other picaresque novels are always narrated in retrospect, after the protagonist's real or suggested reform; these tales of criminal lives are, paradoxically, highly moral ones intended in part to show by contrast the didactic failings of the earlier idealistic genres. And, like the *Conversion of Mary Magdalene,* the picaresque novel follows the dictates of Counter-Reformation sensibilities in showing human nature at its nadir in order to depict the potential for spiritual redemption in even the most depraved among us. The lowborn and usually illegitimate scoundrel's origins by definition (according to the contemporary outlook) impose an inclination to reprehensible character and conduct, but nevertheless can always be overcome by the use of free will. At least theoretically, the possibility of attaining *desengaño,* of recognizing and renouncing immorality, should be within the range of even the picaro's experience. Therefore, the character, noble or not, who knowingly persists in wrong behavior merits the audience's rigorous censure.

While Miguel de Cervantes's *Don Quixote* is sometimes incorrectly identified as a picaresque novel, a self-styled picaro does appear in both volumes (1605 and 1615) of the work. Ginés de Pasamonte is in Part 1 a galley slave who claims to be composing the history of his exploits. " 'It is so good,' " he boasts, " 'that it means trouble for *Lazarillo de Tormes* and for all that has been written or ever shall be written in that style' " (" 'Es tan bueno . . . que mal año para *Lazarillo de Tormes* y para todos cuantos de aquel género se han escrito o escribieren' ").[43] In the sequel he is revealed as the culprit in the robbery of Sancho's dapple and appears as Master Pedro, the crafty owner of a puppet show that is demolished by Don Quixote.

More than his status as rogue, it is Pasamonte's role as artist and controller of the action that sets him in a special class of Cervantine characters, the "satanic surrogate poets."[44] These figures—including in the *Quixote* the pseudonarrator Cide Hamete Benengeli; Andrés in the exemplary novel, *The Little Gypsy Girl* (*La gitanilla*); and Chanfalla and Chirinos in the dramatic interlude *The Marvellous Pageant* (*El retablo de las maravillas*)—tend to be knaves or conmen on the fringes of society who delight in concocting fictions perhaps only incidentally in order to profit from the gullibility of the audience. An air of lighthearted good humor seems always to surround these Cervantine rascals: unlike Lazarillo or Pablos, Cervantes's picaros maintain a detached perspective on the events that subjugate and sometimes confuse other characters. The "artists" who succeed in their scams and seem cheerfully exempt from poetic justice are so favored, Forcione speculates, because Cervantes counts himself among them.

Don Quixote purports to discredit the novels of chivalry for their lack of verisimilitude and abundance of stylistic excesses, which have driven the protagonist insane. Yet the *Quixote* itself is also filled with impossibilities, among them the narrative's chronological disorder and the reappearance of Don Quixote and Sancho Panza in Part 2 following their demise at the end of Part 1.[45] The work thus simultaneously parodies and assimilates the idealistic genre it pretends to deplore.

The book also contains several pastoral episodes, and near the end of the sequel Don Quixote and Sancho decide that now might be the moment to shed their chivalric identities and become shepherds, "Quixotiz" and "Panzino" (Part 2, chap. 67, 1025). Cervantes himself had published the first part of his own long pastoral novel *La Galatea* in 1585, and for the next forty-one years until his death continued to promise a continuation. Several of his short exemplary novels may rightly be called quasi-pastoral (*The Little Gypsy Girl; The Illustrious Kitchen Maid* [*La ilustre fregona*]),[46] while others, *The Dogs' Colloquy* (*El coloquio de los perros*) and *Rinconete y* [*and*] *Cortadillo,* explicitly attack or parody the absurdities of that genre. The approach to pastoral in *Don Quixote* marries admiration to the product of the Counter-Reformation, disapproval. This ambivalence toward the genre following its sixteenth-century apogee manifests itself also in Golden Age theater, which at times casts an ironic light on that ideal bucolic vision.

Often in pastoral literature, urban characters for sentimental reasons disguise themselves and hie to the wilderness, to escape love or to tend flocks and berate the cruel mistresses who have disdained them. *Don Quixote* has its share of pseudoshepherds, whose bucolic folly parallels the chivalric one of the protagonist. These characters, and chiefly among them the beautiful and militantly chaste Marcela, may rate criticism because like the novel's protagonist, they refuse to play their proper roles in Spanish society, to "*be* who they *are*" ("ser quienes son"[47]). Like any woman in seventeenth-century Spain, Marcela ought to choose either matrimony or the convent. Instead, she rejects both and flees any encounter with her fellows. In traditional pastoral, the aristocrat in disguise eventually returns to civilization following his amorous retreat to the country, having attained some sort of perspective during the period of contemplation. Renato Poggioli calls Marcela's story a "pastoral of the self," a misanthropic variation that denies Christian charity, or love of one's neighbor.[48] The apparent intent not to return to society also suggests Joseph Campbell's hero, who resists reintegration.[49] Marcela repudiates her social obligations, as does Don Quixote in choosing the quest for adventure over the life of an average country gentleman.

Don Quixote is a work of fiction that is itself essentially occupied with historical changes in the conception of what constitutes heroic behavior. Its militant, mad protagonist fails in his chivalric guise because he wants to live out a medieval romance, where the sword avenges injustice, instead of the quiet routine of a modest seventeenth-century country gentleman born in a society with institutions established to address legal complaint. Alonso Quijano finally attains the only type of heroism available to a man of his restricted circumstances when he renounces his extravagant folly, entrusts the righting of wrongs to established higher authority, and, having at last mastered a graceful self-restraint, meets a quiet Christian end.

In any case, this complex novel simultaneously imitates and ridicules the chivalric and pastoral romances that precede it. Although *Don Quixote* is far from realistic, it contains numerous realistic scenes. Many of these focus on the relationship between the protagonist and his "squire," Sancho Panza, the illiterate countryman who ignorantly subscribes to his master's folly. The story of Don Quixote is nearly as much the story of his companion, both being major characters who undergo significant changes during the course of their adventures. Don Quixote's quest is at bottom one for his sanity, which he recovers. At first, Sancho Panza, an inarticulate laborer, believes he wants to be governor of an island. By the time he attains his goal, Sancho has traveled much and learned a great deal. He governs well but understands that he was meant to farm, that his wife and children were not meant to wear silk and ride in carriages, but to adhere to the class and circumstances into which they had been born. *Don Quixote* can be seen to contain, among many other marvellous things, a highly imaginative argument for preserving seventeenth-century class distinctions. But its strong social conservatism notwithstanding, this novel joins the picaresque in focusing to an exceptional degree on the life of a common man. It surpasses the picaresque, in deeming its humble character worthy of a third-person narrative. The *Quixote* treats Sancho Panza with a considerable amount of depth and often, dignity, and finally offers this rustic as a character meriting our affection and respect.

In the early seventeenth century, *Guzmán de Alfarache* actually exceeded the *Quixote* in volumes sold both in Spanish and in translations abroad; the two books' immense popularity throughout Europe inspired picaresque-type tales such as Grimmelshausen's *Simplicissimus* (1669), Lesage's *Gil Blas* (1715–35), and Defoe's *Moll Flanders* (1722).[50] During the generations preceding the Industrial Revolution and Romanticism, these Spanish works helped make possible a view of the man of humbler circumstances as worthy of respect. In that sense and in its many instances of at least psychological if not physical realism, *Don Quixote* is the most significant antecedent of the modern novel. Whether this book's comparatively dignified treatment of the lowborn Sancho Panza was matched on the contemporary stage will be explored in subsequent chapters.

Hero or Saint?

"Tell me now, which is the greater thing: to bring a dead man to life, or to kill a giant?"

"The answer is obvious," replied Don Quixote. "To bring the dead to life, of course."

"Ah," said Sancho, "that is where I've caught you. Then, the fame of those who resurrect the dead, who give sight to the blind, who heal cripples and bring health to the sick, who have lamps burning in front of their tombs, and whose chapels are thronged with devout people kneeling and adorning their relics will be a better one in this life and in the next than the fame of all the heathen emperors and knights-errant in all the world."

"What do you want me to infer, Sancho, from all that you have said?" asked Don Quixote.

"I mean to say," replied Sancho, "that we might set about becoming saints. Then we shall get the good name we're after all the sooner. . . . [I]t's better to be a humble little friar of any order you like than a valiant knight-errant. A couple of dozen lashings will carry more weight with God than a couple of thousand lance thrusts, whether they be given to giants, dragons, or other monsters."

(Part 2, chap. 8, 582–83)

("Y dígame agora: ¿cuál es más: resucitar a un muerto, o matar a un gigante?

—La respuesta está en la mano—respondió don Quijote—: más es resucitar a un muerto.

—Cogido le tengo—dijo Sancho—. Luego la fama del que resucita muertos, da vista a los ciegos, endereza los cojos y da salud a los enfermos, y delante de sus sepulturas arden lámparas, y están llenas sus capillas de gentes devotas que de rodillas adoran sus reliquias, mejor fama será, para este y para el otro siglo, que la que dejaron y dejaren cuantos emperadores gentiles y caballeros andantes ha habido en el mundo.

—¿Qué quieres que infiera, Sancho, de todo lo que has dicho? —dijo don Quijote.

—Quiero decir—dijo Sancho—que nos demos a ser santos, y alcanzaremos más brevemente la buena fama que pretendemos. ... [M]ás vale ser humilde frailecito, de cualquier orden que sea, que valiente y andante caballero; más alcanzan con Dios dos docenas de diciplinas que dos mil lanzadas, ora las den a gigantes, ora a vestiglos o a endrigos.)

(Part 2, chap. 8, 595–96)

The humble (and practical) Sancho Panza in effect champions restraint over revenge in the quest for public acclaim. Cervantes here speaks comically to a potentially painful dichotomy in heroic values, one that received serious treatment in the Golden Age *comedia*. The difficulty in fact had begun to develop during the Middle Ages, and the trend gained impetus during the flowering of Renaissance humanism and the dissemination of the Counter-Reformation. The long-held view that prowess in battle was a major part of heroism went hand in hand with an esteem for personal reputation. The high regard for name was bound to collide with the Christian ethic that condemns acts of violence and exhorts imitation of Christ, especially once the holy war of the Reconquest was completed. Spanish Golden Age playwrights, who recognized in the conflict between the desire for honor and Christian teaching a fertile ground for drama, produced the "honor plays," among the most poignant and controversial masterpieces of the period.

Yet if such dilemmas were the complications of many seventeenth-century dramatic pieces, including the lighter "cape-and-sword" ("capa y espada") intrigues as well as the fewer tragedies, the propriety of violence is not doubted in the medieval epic. As Christian as the *Song of Roland* and the *Poem of the Cid* claim to be, they are military epics composed and disseminated during the Reconquest. The cause is divine and at stake is the Faith itself. Two of the most interesting characters in these epics are in fact Roland's colleague the Archbishop Turpin, and Rodrigo's Bishop Don Jerónimo. Both of these men of the cloth are also fierce warriors who take great pride in slaying Moors: Jerónimo requests the honor of the first blow against the Infidel at Valencia, and after the battle "cannot count the Moors he has slain" (70) ("non tiene en cuenta los moros que ha matados" [line 1795]). Turpin's anatomically detailed Homeric-type battle victories beg for the exaggerated treatment which Rabelais will be happy to supply during the height of humanist pacifism in sixteenth-century France.

In terms of years, Douglas Bush observes, the (English) Renaissance is of course far nearer to us than to classical antiquity. "[B]ut the Renaissance hero is far closer to Achilles and Agamemnon, Odysseus and Aeneas, Orestes and Oedipus, than he is to Leopold Bloom or Kafka's K or Frederic Henry or Isaac McCaslin or Willy Loman."[51] Bush's remark is, if anything, still truer for Spain, where in his seventeenth-century dictionary Sebastián de Cobarruvias defines "heroic" ("eroico"): "As in an heroic action, read illustrious, great; from the word *heros, herois,* which for the ancients referred to men who, even if they were mortals, their deeds were so magnificent that they seemed to partake of divinity" ("Como hecho heroico, vale ilustre, grande; díxose de la palabra *heros, herois* que cerca de los antiguos sinificava tanto como hombres que, no embargante fuesen mortales, eran sus hazañas tan grandiosas que parecía tener en sí alguna divinidad").[52]

In 1734, the first dictionary published by Spain's newly minted Royal Academy (Real Academia) preserves the authority of "the Ancients," entering under "hero": "The illustrious and great man whose deeds made him worthy of immortal fame and memory. The Ancients called so those who by their great actions were taken for deities by the populace, and (as Lucian says) for a composite of god and man" ("El Varón ilustre y grande, cuyas hazañas le hicieron digno de immortal fama y memoria. Los Antiguos llamaban assi à los que por sus acciones grandes los tenia el vulgo por deidades, y [como dice Luciano] por un compuesto de Dios y hombre").[53] Characters like Sancho Panza, the picaro, or Peribáñez, lacking illustrious origins, would not qualify for heroic status according to these definitions.

Significantly, the most recent edition of the academy's *Dictionary of the Spanish Language* (*Diccionario de la lengua española*) preserves the essence of the earliest definition of "hero"[54] but adds four variations: "2. An illustrious man famous for his deeds or virtues. 3. He who carries out a heroic action. 4. The principal character of any poem in which an action is represented, and especially of the epic. 5. Any of the characters of elevated caliber in the epic" ("2. Varón ilustre y famoso por sus hazañas o virtudes. 3. El que lleva a cabo una acción heroica. 4. Personaje principal de todo poema en que se representa una acción, y del épico especialmente. 5. Cualquiera de los personajes de carácter elevado en la epopeya").

Now, heroic status may be earned by "deeds or virtues," or simply by being the main character of a narrated action—meaning that a humbly-born citizen could rate the designation of "hero." The definition of "heroine" ("heroína") is still more contemporary and, with respect to literature, socially neutral. Besides "An illustrious woman famous for her great deeds" ("Mujer ilustre y famosa por sus grandes hechos") and "She who carries out an heroic action" ("La que lleva a cabo un hecho heroico"), the academy adds, "Protagonist of a play or of any other similar work of fiction; such as the novel" ("Protagonista del drama o de otro poema análogo; como la novela" [ibid.]).

For the present consideration of the figure of the hero in Spanish literature before 1700, then, it must be kept in mind that by the seventeenth century, the hero was officially at least still a titular descendent of the semidivine classical Greek and Roman epic protagonist. However, the descent was far from direct, so that by the time the Spanish Golden Age *comedia* reached the public playhouse, that hero and those great deeds emanated from a Catholic Christian house. The leading man ("primer galán") in a serious drama was and represented a character thoroughly immersed in the Peninsular Counter-Reformation ethic, regardless of the time or setting of the action. Although neglected or tacitly understood in then-contemporary definitions, the religious factor traces its own ancestry at least back to the times of the Cid himself, and the lives of saints after which, according to recent research, his own epics may be patterned.

W. T. H. Jackson has stated that the *Poem of the Cid* is only nominally Christian; its and its hero's overriding concerns are political, material, and social. The Cid fights his battles not so much for the Faith, but for the power, booty, and respect he will win. The King strives so vigorously to appease Rodrigo in the second half of the poem not out of conscience and concern for justice, but out of fear: the Cid is now a potentially dangerous rival (116, 123). In this reading, neither Rodrigo nor Alfonso really changes during the course of events.

At the opposite pole of interpretation, but agreeing that the Cid's character remains static, is Geoffrey West. His study of the Latin *History of Rodrigo* (*Historia Roderici*), a work composed before the *Poem of the Cid* and probably by the midtwelfth century, shows that the anonymous Latin poet relied heavily though perhaps unconsciously on the lives of saints for his chronicle's idealizing tone and structure.[55] Until Franciscan and other orders began to exalt poverty, saints normally came from upper-class families. In the effort to bring glory to its hero, the *History of Rodrigo* contradicted other sources by placing the Cid's origins in the high nobility. Guillén de Castro's seventeenth-century Spanish *comedia*, *The Youth of the Cid* (*Las mocedades del Cid*), and Corneille's *Le Cid* do likewise.[56]

In any case, "the vital elements in the *Historia*'s narrative that link it to the hagiographic texts," West writes, "are, on the one hand, the fury and lack of moderation of the king, the violence of his speech and his false accusations and, on the other, the patient, long-suffering behavior of the hero" (103). In this account, if Rodrigo changes at all, it is only to become more saintly (88). His unquestioning and submissive relationship to the King, West asserts, parallels that of the saint to God (103).

It is generally agreed that the *History of Rodrigo* is an important source of the *Poem of the Cid,* and as West has shown elsewhere,[57] there are many hagiographic elements in the vernacular epic. At this point in Peninsular history, the "saintly warrior" or "warrior-saint" are not contradictions in terms: Don Jerónimo announces before battle, " 'He who dies here facing the enemy, his sins will I take upon me and God will take his soul' " (67) (" 'El que aqui muriere lidiando de cara / prendol yo los pecados e Dios le abra el alma' " [lines 1704–5]). After his death on the battlefield where he and Turpin have slain the entire Moorish host, Roland is borne up to heaven by angels (*laisse* 120). Jorge

Manrique's fifteenth-century *Verses on the Death of His Father* (*Coplas por la muerte de su padre*) recognize death in battle as a guarantee of salvation, and find desire for worldly glory a legitimate Christian goal.[58] Spain's patron saint, James (Santiago), who was an emblem central to the formation of national identity during the Reconquest, is always pictured on a white steed wielding a sword, a pose merging the spiritual with the militant. In the late seventeenth century, the soldier who fights for a holy cause and may die a martyr is still held up for admiration.[59] These are heroes who covet "revenge," but always in behalf of a higher cause, not inconsistent, as C. A. Jones shows, with St. Thomas Aquinas's assertions that honor is the "best of all earthly possessions, since it is nearest to being a spiritual possession. These earthly possessions, in any case, are only the third in the order of life's possessions, the first and second being spiritual possessions and the body itself."[60]

Furthermore, the medieval lives of saints often relied on military language used metaphorically: these were soldiers of Christ arming themselves for the battle against sin, hearkening back to St. Paul's *miles christianus*.[61] Yet in Spain as elsewhere in Europe, especially during the later Middle Ages, the rift between classical heroic values of military prowess and glory and the Christian ethic led to some interesting transformations. Whether to imitate Achilles or Christ? In some cases, and most notably in Spain's Golden Age drama, a form of that dichotomy evolves into the subgenre of the honor drama, several of which will receive attention in later chapters.

"Hero or saint?" Huppé, in "The Concept of the Hero in the Early Middle Ages," believes that the two are necessarily mutually exclusive: the saint is simply too perfect; and imitation of Christ by definition entails a rejection of revenge (2–6). The military rhetoric in saints' lives borrowed from epic was merely the means by which the poet could speak to his audience in terms with which they would already be familiar. During the crusading High Middle Ages, and especially in the *Poem of the Cid*, the inconsistency does not appear to trouble the poet and perhaps would not even be evident to him. At least in the end, the truth will out: fame and conscience will concur; the evil men and the good will be clearly revealed to all. Recourse to the judicial duel testifies to that belief. But Bloomfield points out that in the *City of God*, St. Augustine distinguishes between *fame* and *conscience*. "Fame," Bloomfield explains, "is the approval of men, whereas conscience is the approval of God" ("The Problem of the Hero," 43). He who covets fame is fatally attached to this world; the man of conscience, happily to the next.

Bloomfield believes that as Augustine gained prestige during the late Middle Ages, the traditional values of heroism eroded; hence the period of lesser protagonists who quest out of love, not desire for glory, and who cultivate *bienséance,* or courtesy.

Death or misfortune's power to overcome the mighty as well as the meek became the religious theme of the French *Danse macabre* (*Dance of Death*). In Spain, the grim *Dança general de la muerte* (c. 1500) finds a dignified variation in Jorge Manrique's pensive and elegiac *Verses* in memory of his father. Another genre stressing the ephemeral nature of wealth and stature was born in Boccaccio's collected stories of great men brought down by moral failure, usually pride. Certainly the ancestry of *De casibus virorum illustrium* (*From the Fall of Illustrious Men*) can be traced back to Herodotus and the Greek tragedies. Such cautionary tales, along with treatises on the constitution of the perfect prince or gentleman with examples from history—for instance, Petrarch's *Africa* and *Of Men* (*De viris*) and Tasso's *On Heroic Virtue and Charity* (*Della virtù eroica e della carità*)—were translated and imitated throughout Europe.[62] In the early sixteenth century, Castiglione's influential *The Courtier* (*Il cortegiano*) reached Spain almost immediately.[63]

Humanists led by Erasmus seconded the tendency away from the violence of classical heroism; at the same time, the courtly life was also found wanting. The medieval soldier of the Lord, who literalizes St. Paul's metaphor, is converted back into a figurative soldier, the man who "fights" by imitating Christ. Erasmus's influential *Handbook of the Christian Soldier* (*Enchiridion militis christiani*) (1503) explicitly condemns war and its glories. While military conflict materially benefits the leaders, it can only hurt the common man, who may lose everything, including his life. The soldier is lured into joining the ranks with the carrot of glory. As Raymond R. Bolgar puts it, instead of the great warrior, we should, following Erasmus, esteem

> the unromantic private citizen, sturdy and conscientious, but eager to be quit of his task at the first opportunity: a figure not unlike the artisans, shopkeepers and small farmers who were to fight for their beliefs in the Protestant armies of the next two centuries.[64]

The "new Christian hero" touted by Erasmus and his follower in Spain, Juan Luis Vives (1492–1540), is, in Bolgar's words, "humble, practical,

studious, devoted to the Bible, soberly wedded, zealous in the performance of good works" ("Hero or Anti-Hero?" 136). Understandably, Vives
detested the romances of chivalry.

The student of Spanish Golden Age theater might be justified in
viewing such famous, industrious peasants as Juan Labrador, Peribáñez,
and Pedro Crespo as descended from this Erasmian new Christian hero.
Erasmus and his disciples did have a lasting influence in Spain. However, among the common people the requirement of literacy to be a good
Christian was discarded, and the ideal of *sancta simplicitas* took a
non-Erasmian turn. Sancho Panza and many commoners in Golden Age
drama boast of the fact that they cannot read or write. Furthermore,
their illiteracy, it was popularly believed, acquitted them of any suspicion of impure blood: Jews, expelled at the conclusion of the Reconquest
in 1492, had been known for, among other things, scholarship.[65] As for
Vives, who wrote several treatises on women and marriage, and may in
spite of himself have been influenced by the elevation of passionate love
in the romances, he also helped put matrimony on a pedestal. Although
the humanist movement was superseded and officially condemned in
Spain later in the sixteenth century, it managed to bequeath that legacy
of respect for simplicity and domesticity to later generations.

Renaissance humanism, then, rejected the ideal of the hero offered
not just by classical antiquity, but that of medieval epic and romance as
well. In the *Dialogue of Mercury and Charon* (*Diálogo de Mercurio y
Carón*) by the Erasmist Alfonso de Valdés (d. 1532), the exemplary king
warns his son against the evils of war, and describes the type of fame a
prince ought to seek: that which will bring honor to God, not "that
which . . . Alexander the Great acquired, nor Julius Caesar, because
theirs caused so much destruction in the world. Good fame is obtained
with good, not evil, works" (la que . . . adquirió Alejandro magno ni Julio
César, pues fué con tanto daño de todo el mundo. La buena fama con
buenas, no con malas obras se alcança").[66]

Another way in which some Renaissance thinkers dealt with the
pagan-heroic tradition was to regard classical figures and stories that
might seem on the surface violent and immoral, not to mention unchristian,
as Christian allegory. A favorite mythological character who underwent
this metamorphosis was Hercules, beginning in Italy in the late fourteenth century. Eugene M. Waith shows that he became a model of
Aristotelian moderation whose victories were really over vice, in paint-
ings as well as in literature (*The Herculean Hero*, 43). At times he was

represented as an analogue of Christ. This powerful figure, portrayed in all his might and wrath (wrath justified by Aquinas as *ira per zelum*[67]), would succeed in arousing wonder (*admiratio*) among the public. At the same time, according to Waith, he would communicate a more profound message to the more sophisticated consumer of art:

> If learned readers looked well beneath the surface of the mean-ings of the old tales and legends, it was partly because they believed the poet should conceal his special insights from the rude gaze of the many. Boccaccio, in his *Life of Dante,* says that poetry is like Holy Scripture in revealing its mystery to the wise but protecting the simple from more than they can or should comprehend. (49)

Such elitist aspirations may have contributed to the humanists' discom-fort with art arousing wonder and depicting impossibilities: it would be read or heard or seen wrongly by those less enlightened among its public.

In the seventeenth century, Spanish royalty proudly claimed Hercules as a symbol of the Hapsburg line.[68] But the spiritual melioration of classical heroes was hardly confined to Hercules. Virgil had always been held in high regard by medieval Christian scholars, in part thanks to his seemingly prophetic *Fourth Eclogue* (which was mistakenly thought to predict the birth of Christ), as well of course as his authorship of the *Aeneid.* Hence Virgil's poignant if insufficient authority in the *Divine Comedy.* Aeneas's combination of strength, wisdom, and moral vision—his sacrifice and suffering for a higher purpose—would naturally appeal to medieval Christian writers. Apparently as much saint as soldier, moved by conscience, this hero paved the way for the chivalric heroes, and those of Spenser's, Milton's, and Camoens's Renaissance Christian epics[69]—and, I would add, for Lope de Vega's ultimately principled Comendador of Ocaña.

Spanish composers of Renaissance literary epic tended to imitate Virgil and Tasso. The outstanding epic poem of the period, *La Araucana,* by Alonso de Ercilla (1533–96), immortalized New World wars with the Indians. This work, which has more the air of chronicle than fiction, lacks a single true hero and tends to idealize the aboriginal enemy. It does, nevertheless, insist that the exemplary soldier must temper his valor with clemency:

That victor deserves renown
who dominates his own anger;
and the triumph of the merciful man is the greatest,
for he also wins over souls.

(El vencedor es digno de memoria
Que en la ira se hace resistencia;
Y es mayor la vitoria del clemente,
Pues los ánimos vence juntamente).[70]

Influenced by the Counter-Reformation, Lope de Vega among others wrote verse dealing with heroic moments in Christian history; his *La Jerusalén conquistada* was published in 1609.[71]

At any rate, the combination of Platonic, Stoic, and Christian values perceived in Virgil during the Middle Ages was also projected back on Greek literature. By the Renaissance, Greek heroes had been "Virgilian-ized," and these "Virgilian" heroes Christianized. As Brower shows, in *Hero and Saint,* much of the transformation came about in England — and it might be supposed, in Spain as well, possibly to an even greater degree — through the zeal of contemporary translations of Homer, Virgil, Ovid, Seneca, and Plutarch.

In this wedding of the classical and Christian, the hero had gained a conscience without losing his drive for worldly glory. If the two dispositions are not at odds in the *Poem of the Cid,* ultimate material and social success being evidence of God's favor, the dilemma of their conflict often became the central focus in subsequent literature, most notably in Renaissance drama. Love or conscience versus the demands of honor rends the hearts of Corneille's Cid and Cinna; Shakespeare's Hamlet and Othello; and numerous protagonists of Spanish Golden Age drama.

The Hero and the Peasant

It is generally supposed that Spanish drama, like that of the rest of Europe, originated in the liturgy. Eventually leaving the church for the public square, the themes often became as secular as the sites of performance. During its apogee in Madrid, from the late sixteenth century through the seventeenth, public performances of Golden Age drama were still held outdoors, in yards (*corrales*) surrounded by private homes and converted into theaters. While royalty sometimes attended these performances incognito, the king and his retinue were regularly feted privately at the royal palace (*Alcázar*), and after 1640 at the new theater on the grounds of the Buen Retiro, where Madrid's Retiro Park stands today.[72]

Unlike medieval drama in the rest of Europe, however, of which there is evidence before 1000, texts of early vernacular drama in Spain are virtually nonexistent.[73] In the monasteries, on the other hand, readings of Roman comedies, and eventually imitations of them in Latin persevered throughout the Middle Ages in Spain as they had in Italy and elsewhere. This university tradition had its impact on later drama and comedy, but perhaps its most spectacular and singular offspring in Spain was the *Tragicomedy of Calisto and Melibea* (*Tragicomedia de Calisto y Melibea*) (1499 and 1502), later known for its protagonist as *La Celestina*. Although it did not quite spring up sui generis — the prologue, for example, plagiarizes Petrarch[74] — this lengthy work is unique in its time. The first version with sixteen acts, the second with twenty-one, it is variously called a novelized drama and a dramatic novel. Fernando de Rojas, a university student who claims to have found the first act already written, is the supposed continuator.

La Celestina is both antiheroic and classical in nature. It tells the story of an aged Spanish bawd, her lowlife cronies, and the aristocratic, illicit lovers they abet, ending in disaster for all. Yet its many comic elements show clearly the influence of Plautus and Terence. Dialogue is by turns realistic and charged with classical erudition,[75] and nearly always ironic, so that although lacking a narrator, we can usually imagine the implied author's judgment of his characters. *La Celestina* also parodies courtly love in the exaggerated rhetoric of the young Calisto, who has probably spent, as Don Quixote will spend, too many hours with his head in books. This dialogue is partly a deflation of courtly love; like the picaresque genre that follows, it offers an acerbic antidote to the romances of chivalry then in vogue.

Celestina as the main character is hardly heroic in any classical sense, except possibly for her charismatic intelligence. She is greedy as well as shrewd. Herself illegitimate and a prostitute in her younger days, she now arranges liaisons, restores young women to physical maidenhood, and to ensure the success of her "business," engages in witchcraft. The

diabolic power of her character is probably most effectively conveyed in
the conjuring scene at the end of the third act, where she challenges
Satan himself, in case he fails to assist in her pimping:

> If thou do it not, and quickly, thou shalt have me for thy mortal
> enemy; I shall strike thy dark and gloomy dungeons with light,
> make public thine endless lies, and cover thy horrid name with
> curses! Again and yet again I conjure thee, trusting in my great
> power, and thus I depart with my thread, in which I do believe I
> have thee now entangled.

> (Si no lo haces con presto movimiento, ternásme por capital
> enemiga; heriré con luz tus cárceles tristes y escuras; acusaré
> cruelmente tus continuas mentiras; apremiaré con mis ásperas
> palabras tu horrible nombre. Y otra y otra vez te conjuro; así
> confiando en mi mucho poder, me parto para allá con mi hilado,
> donde creo te llevo ya envuelto.)[76]

One senses that of the two collaborator-adversaries, Celestina is the
more dreadful. Yet this authoress of illicit liaison and moral debauchery
will, nevertheless, lose control of her work and die at the hands of
characters whom she herself has corrupted.

The weak, pusillanimous, pretentious lover Calisto is never presented
in anything approaching a flattering light until the nighttime scene
immediately preceding his death. As he visits Melibea in her garden,
their dialogue becomes uncharacteristically pure and lyrical; that cyni-
cal authorial irony vanishes for the moment, or becomes poignantly
condolatory as emblems of death loom over the union.[77] Hearing a
disturbance outside the garden, Calisto rushes (unnecessarily) to aid his
servants keeping watch, and falls to his death from the wall. Only at this
point could he be said to approach dignity. It is Melibea afterwards who
might claim the reader's awe, if not respect. Her father, Pleberio,
summoned by the noise, listens in uncomprehending agony as she
declares her passion and its fatal consequences. Regretting only that she
waited so long to enjoy the fruits of that passion, and with a defiance
and stateliness befitting Shakespeare's Brutus, she throws herself from
the tower to her death.

La Celestina ends with Pleberio's ringing declamation of sorrow. The
father has been regarded by scholars as everything from noble victim to

self-consumed materialist.[78] Evidence in his lament is marshaled to suggest that he is a wealthy merchant, possibly a forced convert from Judaism; Rojas was himself a *converso*. Whether any character in this work attains any sort of personal or Christian *desengaño* remains open to debate. The figurative and literal falls of so many characters, and the warnings in the prologue against excessive passion, imply the efficacy of a resigned, Christian-stoic attitude toward adverse fortune of the type implicit in the fall-of-princes genre.

At all events, *La Celestina* is a masterpiece and an anomaly in Spanish literature. As it stands, it is far too lengthy for staging,[79] but the epilogue offers directions on how the parts are to be read aloud, indicating it is a performance text. While not itself an orthodox play, it owes much to the Latin dramatic tradition, and exerts extensive influence over subsequent theater and prose in Spain. "Celestina" joins the *Book of Good Love's* "Convent-Trotter" ("Trotaconventos") as a generic name for the go-between in Spanish literature. *La Celestina* on the whole conforms to the antiheroic vein in late medieval literature identified by Bloomfield (in "The Problem of the Hero").

Vernacular staged theater in Spain is probably only sporadic until the latter half of the fifteenth century. The *officium pastorum*, a traditional Catholic Christmas rite, is behind Gómez Manrique's *Representation of the Birth of Our Lord* (*Representación del Nacimiento de Nuestro Señor*), performed in 1480. This play is an intricate elaboration of the Nativity, meant to be performed at the convent where Manrique's sister was a nun.[80] In 1492, Juan del Encina (1468?–1529?) composed a series of short plays, *Eclogues* (*Eglogas*) for the court of the Duke and Duchess of Alba. These plays, some celebrating Christmas, feature naive and comical shepherds. In one eclogue they are transformed from bucolics speaking *sayagués* (a literary version of rustic dialect) into the four Evangelists, Matthew, Mark, Luke, and John. The actors were probably servants and members of the court; possibly Encina himself played the part of John.

Encina's *Eclogues* are indebted to a number of traditions, religious and secular. The New Testament and the *officium pastorum*, along with Virgil's *Eclogues*, medieval courtly entertainments involving banquets, tournaments, dance, and mummeries, and aristocratic perceptions of the rustic stereotypes, all contributed to these festive occasions.

Encina and Bartolomé de Torres Naharro (d. 1520?) visited Italy in

the early sixteenth century, where they came into contact with translations and imitations of Latin comedy (the *commedia erudita*), as well as
the more popular and improvisational *commedia dell'arte,* supported
there by elaborate court patronage. Torres Naharro wrote the first
"comedias" in Spanish, a term which he used to refer to any five-act
"ingenious artifice of noteworthy and finally happy events, spoken by
actors" ("artificio ingenioso de notables y finalmente alegres acontecimientos por personas disputado").[81] Concerned about proper decorum, he
specifies in his prologue (*prohemio*) that "the servant neither speak nor
act like the lord, and vice versa" ("el siervo no diga ni haga actos del
señor, *et e converso*") (64). There are, Torres continues, two types of
comedia, "a noticia" and "a fantasía." "*A noticia* signifies something
truly noted and seen . . . , *a fantasía,* an imaginary or feigned event, that
has the appearance of truth, although it is not true" ("A noticia se
entiende de cosa nota y vista en realidad de verdad . . . , a fantasía, de
cosa fantástiga o fingida, que tenga color de verdad, aunque no lo sea")
(64). In addition to other influences, Torres's *Comedia Himenea* shows a
certain debt to *La Celestina* in plot, character, and diction. The work's
concern with familial honor and revenge earns it the designation of the
first "honor drama" in Spain.

Several of these plays, along with many by Gil Vicente (1470?–1536?)
and Lucas Fernández (1474?–1542), are populated by two types of
shepherds, in major and minor roles. As in the pastoral poem and novel,
the stylized erudition and noble carriage of many shepherd-protagonists
give the impression that they are courtiers in disguise, while secondary
characters may be comic, rustic buffoons whose silly behavior and
sayagués-type diction place them distinctly lower in the social hierarchy.
The comic shepherd, often ingenuous, lazy, a braggart, and fond of
drink, becomes by the midsixteenth century a stock character in Spanish
theater, and must certainly be considered a literary ancestor of Sancho
Panza, as well as of Pelayo of *The King, the Greatest Alcalde,* Blas of
Peribáñez, and Mengo of *Fuenteovejuna.*

During this period, then, both popular and classical schools exerted
their effects on Peninsular theater. Not long after the plays of Lope de
Rueda (1510?–65) showed the influence of the traveling Italian *commedia
dell'arte* troupes—with formulaic comic lowlife characters—the Portuguese Antonio Ferreira (1528–1569) introduced serious dramas set in
classical antiquity or scenes from Peninsular history.[82] Cristóbal de
Virués (1550?–14), Lupercio Leonardo de Argensola (1550?–1610), and

Juan de la Cueva (1543–1610) wrote tragedies with prominent Senecan strains.

In the first part of *Don Quixote* (chap. 48, 484–85), the Canon of Toledo cites approvingly Argensola's adherence to classical precepts, in protest against violations of the unities of time, place, and action in which then-contemporary dramatists regularly indulged. Unlike in seventeenth-century France, where the academy quite successfully imposed classical rules on drama, such reactionary remonstrations— generally on the part of neo-Aristotelian theorists such as Alonso López Pinciano (1547–1627) rather than dramatists—had scant effect on the Spanish theater itself. While Corneille's works played to an aristocratic audience in France, Spanish and English drama was for the most part a public affair, for the illiterate as well as the learned.[83] In both countries, flagrant violence was done to the unities and to classical decorum of character. In the *New Art of Writing Plays* (*Arte nuevo de hacer comedias*) (c. 1609), Lope de Vega explains with some equivocation that to earn his daily bread he must write for the rabble (*vulgo*), and that in order to please them, "one must speak in the language of fools" ("hay que hablarle en necio").[84]

Lope and many contemporaries also offend classical precepts by featuring royalty and peasants in the same plays. Lope takes this outrage a step farther by occasionally giving major roles to socially inferior characters, a development possibly presaged in the young Cervantes's *Siege of Numantia* (*Cerco de Numancia*) (1580). The four-act play is set during the second-century B.C. Roman siege of the Peninsular Celtic-Iberian city. In defiance of the Roman General Scipio, the town refuses to surrender to imperial rule. Starving, the entire population finally commits mass suicide. There has been a good deal of debate among modern critics over whether the play means to exalt the Romans (Philip II, in 1580 at his imperial height, was marching off to claim the throne of Portugal). Willard F. King sees in Scipio "something of the dignity of the classical tragic hero."[85] On the other hand, the citizens of the town are themselves portrayed with gravity and dignity; over the centuries the play has often been staged to rally in the Spanish public patriotism and opposition to oppression.[86] In any event, despite a characteristically Cervantine ambiguity, the collective protagonist of this play, undifferentiated by considerations of bloodline, has been seen to foreshadow the humble citizens of Lope de Vega's *Fuenteovejuna, Peribáñez,* and *The Villano in His Corner,* among several others.

Certainly no French dramatist of the seventeenth century gave major serious roles to humble characters. Nor did Shakespeare (lowlife, yes; the ill-fated *Sir* John Falstaff or "John Paunch" had been a page at court in his youth [*Henry V*]). Hispanists have singled out a small number of plays from the Spanish Golden Age theatrical tradition for their unique sympathy and respect for the common man. The works of Lope de Vega, himself of humble origins, exhibit a lyricism and spontaneity usually confined to popular poetry, and feature peasants or townspeople in major roles. While Calderón's pieces are distinctly more aristocratic in tone and subject matter, he too is hailed as a democrat at heart for elevating above socially more noble characters the peasant Pedro Crespo as hero of *The Alcalde of Zalamea.* In an essay aimed for the general reader, Duncan W. Moir writes,

> The Spanish drama's greatest contribution to the European tragic tradition is, precisely, its demonstration, in such plays as *Fuenteovejuna, Peribáñez,* and *The [Alcalde] of Zalamea,* that even the peasant may be a truly tragic hero or heroine. For the Spanish dramatists of this period, all men are, as moral beings, equal in the sight of God.[87]

In 1632, three years before he died, Lope de Vega claimed to have written 1,500 *comedias.*[88] Roughly 400 of these remain extant, along with over 100 texts by Calderón. Out of these many hundreds, the plays cited by Moir are, along with Lope's *The Knight of Olmedo* (*El caballero de Olmedo*) and Calderón's *Life Is a Dream,* and several others by Tirso de Molina, the most prodigiously studied and frequently staged in the twentieth century. This very narrow focus on a very small fragment of an enormous corpus is due perhaps partly to the fact that these plays are technically the most accomplished in structure, diction, and dramatic effect. However, other features contribute to their popularity, and chapter 5 will deal more extensively with those nonaesthetic aspects of these plays that would especially appeal to the sensibilities of the modern scholar, reader, and, in the rarer case, audience.

Certain scholars, most notably among them the French Hispanist Noël Salomon, have recognized that the plays with peasant protagonists that we tend to admire are not representative. In his influential *Investigations of the Peasant Theme in the "Comedia" during the Times of Lope de Vega (Recherches sur le thème paysan dans la "comedia" au temps de Lope de Vega*), he writes, "The type of the free and dignified peasant, made possible by the idea of an uncorrupted rural life, does not appear, to tell the truth, except in an extreme minority of the plays[.]"[89] However, their anomalous character is precisely the justification for singling them out:

> But the exception represented by [this free and dignified peasant] merits, for that very reason, a profound analysis; not to mention that the plays in which the peasant exerts himself with all his might to vindicate, in the face of the nobleman who denies it to him, the right to honor are the most celebrated of the Spanish dramatic repertoire: *Fuenteovejuna, Peribáñez and the Comendador of Ocaña, The King, the Greatest Alcalde, The Alcalde of Zalamea.*

> (Le type du paysan libre et digne, préparé lui aussi par l'idée d'une campagne non corrompue, n'apparaît, à vrait dire, que dans une extrême minorité de pièces; mais l'exception qu'il représente mérite, pour cette raison même, une analyse de fond; aussi bien le pièces où le paysan se dresse de toute sa taille pour revendiquer, face au noble qui lui refuse, le droit à l'honneur sont parmi les plus célèbres du répertoire dramatique espagnole: *Fuenteovejuna, Peribáñez y el Comendador de Ocaña, El mejor alcalde, el rey, El alcalde de Zalamea.*) (xxiv)

Salomon's is a masterly and exhaustive study, to which my own analysis, as well as those of many other Hispanists, is indisputably indebted. However, the following pages will quarrel with two aspects of the proudly optimistic and widely embraced view of the peasant protagonist exemplified by his and Moir's statements. In the first place, it cannot be overemphasized that the critical concentration on a few favorite plays has indeed given the erroneous impression that the Golden Age *comedias* focusing on peasants are the rule, not the exception. For example, out of more than 100 plays by Calderón, only two, *The Alcalde of Zalamea* and *Luis Pérez, the Galician* (*Luis Pérez, el gallego*) have peasant protagonists. The percentage of commoners as major characters in Lope and Tirso is also small. Further investigation into the lesser-known playwrights is necessary before conclusions about the social status of their protagonists can be drawn.

Second, as will become apparent in the following chapters, those well-known plays that do feature peasants in central roles can be said to reflect the same social attitudes underlying the other more "aristocratic" and conservative *comedias.* Granted, Spain's Golden Age is exceptional in Europe for allowing rustics to be the protagonists or major characters in some drama, just as the picaro may claim a pioneering role in the evolution of the novel. Moreover, Don Quixote and Sancho Panza, who inhabit relatively low rungs on the social ladder, do distinguish themselves and their creator by attaining that all-important *desengaño* usually reserved for nobler types. However, these characters, who are truly exceptional, cannot be taken to represent the norm. At that time persistent value was still placed on high birth as a precondition for bravery and the profound moral or political introspection resulting in the *mesura* of a true hero—the Cid being the prototype of this virtuous restraint. In this conventional literary context governed not by Graeco-Roman but by Counter-Reformation Catholic principles of admirable behavior, it is, then, quite another matter—in fact, it defies the trajectory of Spanish and Western literary history—to maintain that in seventeenth-century Spain, Lope de Vega and Calderón make serious tragic heroes of any character, let alone a rustic, who resolves his dilemma violently.

It is nevertheless important to acknowledge that the vestigially militant seventeenth-century Spanish culture had never satisfactorily reconciled the glorification of violence marshaled for the Reconquest, with the Christian deference to submission, an incongruity embodied in the figure of St. James. No wonder then, that the two major Spanish playwrights, both of whom during the course of their careers had been soldiers, and both of whom took holy orders, should not only recognize but seize upon the drama of that monumental moral conflict, to test the mettle of their protagonists—a number of whom fail the test. It is, after all, possible for the main character of a play to be morally reprehensible: we are surely not supposed to take Richard III or Macbeth as models for future conduct. In *L'Arte Poetica* (1564), Minturno diverges from Aristotle when he writes, " 'Whoever suffers a marvellous thing, if it is horrifying or causes compassion, will not be outside the scope of tragedy, whether he be good or whether he be evil.' "[90] According to José Pellicer de Tovar, in his *Idea of the Castilian Play* (*Idea de la comedia de Castilla*) (1635), the *comedia* should cause its public to extract "a warning against and not an inducement to follow wicked deeds; an inducement to follow and not a warning against good deeds" ("escarmiento y no ejemplo de las acciones malas, ejemplo y no escarmiento de las acciones buenas").[91]

It is also possible for the same play to have several major characters, only one of which is the hero (in the positive moral respect), and that modern sensibilities may have brought us to bestow our sympathies on the one who fits our requirements for heroism, but not those of the seventeenth century. My intent is hardly to deny Lope's affinity for the common man, or to restrict our understanding of the plays to one reading. I would, however, like to approach social aspects of the *comedia* with attention to their reflection of seventeenth-century attitudes. The chapters that follow may properly be taken as efforts at excavating the themes of the plays without disturbing their archaeological contexts. I shall consider these celebrated works as they might have been presented to a Spanish public immersed in the classical and Renaissance erudite and oral traditions and Counter-Reformation Catholic ideology: a public nurtured on the expectation of personal growth, spiritual strength, and noble blood in its literary heroes.

Chapter 2

PARADIGMS FOR
CONDUCT AND MISCONDUCT

Rank and Rabble in *Life Is a Dream*[1]

It is appropriate to initiate the consideration of "heroism" and class
distinctions in seventeenth-century Spanish dramatic literature with
attention to the most famous play in the Spanish language. No *comedia*
is without its controversy, and Pedro Calderón de la Barca's *Life Is a
Dream* inspires a type of critical disagreement that is particularly ger-
mane to the present study. Is the play's prince a hero or a beast? Is its
rebel soldier a thug or a hero? Does its female lead behave heroically? I
would like to survey those aspects of the work that incite modern critics
to debate these questions and that move modern directors to alter the original text. A scrutiny of the attitudes toward "rank and rabble" contained
in Calderón's seventeenth-century script will help identify some of the
modern predispositions that help to make the play such a problem.

For example, many twentieth-century readers are perplexed by, and inclined to reject, the social conservatism affirmed by the aristocratic characters at the end of *Life Is a Dream*. It offends modern egalitarian sensibilities to witness the final scene's perpetuation of the perceived oppression of the rebel soldier, an emblem for Poland's common people. In fact, in *Life Is a Dream* there are three disenfranchised civic entities striving for recognition: Prince Segismundo, Rosaura, and the rebel soldier. Attention to Calderón's treatment of these three figures, who span the social spectrum, will pave the way for studies of the potentially subjugated but finally victorious peasants of Lope de Vega's *Peribáñez* and *Fuenteovejuna* and Calderón's own *Alcalde of Zalamea*. In the cases of Peribáñez and Pedro Crespo, their "victories"—their successes in achieving goals despite aristocratic opposition—need not be viewed as moral triumphs. The Epilogue of *Refiguring the Hero* will offer a more detailed exploration of historical changes in social standards reinforcing the inclination to see heroes in the *villanos*.

The three-hundredth anniversary of Calderón's death was marked in 1981. Hispanists commemorated the occasion with conferences, collections of essays, and book-length studies dedicated to deepening and broadening the appreciation of the Spanish playwright. Productions of Calderón's plays that would be accessible even to the general public were mounted. *Life Is a Dream,* as the most widely known and generally highly regarded of Calderón's *comedias,* was presented that year by at least four companies in New York City alone. First performed in 1635, frequently translated into other languages, and projecting a mythical, universal character, this work in particular would appeal to an audience untutored in Spanish language, literary history, or criticism.

Life Is a Dream shows a man coming to terms with his own passions, conscience, and with certain metaphysical (Catholic) truths. The play takes place in an imaginary Poland, where the aged King Basilio is about to step down from his throne. His Russian nephew Astolfo and his niece Estrella vie with each other for the right to succeed, until King Basilio reveals to them and to members of the royal court that the political situation is actually not so simple as it would appear. The King has a twenty-year-old son who has been kept secretly imprisoned because of omens that he would one day destroy his father and the kingdom.

Basilio informs his court that he has decided to give the son, Segismundo, a chance to prove that he can govern the nation. The King's councillor Clotaldo drugs the Prince, changes his clothing from animal skins to royal attire, and removes him from his tower-prison. Segismundo awakens in the palace but acts like a beast with his new freedom. He therefore fails the King's test and is drugged, sent back to the tower, dressed again in animal skins, and told that his palace experience was only a dream. At the end of the second act, it appears that the niece and nephew, Astolfo and Estrella, will marry each other and together accede to the Polish throne.

However, Estrella has from the start had a rival for Astolfo's hand. Astolfo had come to Poland from Russia, where he had seduced Rosaura with a promise of marriage, and then abandoned her. At the beginning of the play Rosaura arrives in Poland, accompanied by the clown, Clarín. She is disguised as a man and intent on finding Astolfo. She comes upon Segismundo in the tower just as, in a lengthy, moving soliloquy, he laments his lack of freedom. Clotaldo, Segismundo's jailer and the King's councillor, takes Rosaura under his wing and she becomes a lady of the Polish court. Rosaura does not know that Clotaldo is her father, who had also (like Astolfo) deserted a woman (Rosaura's mother) in Russia, many years before.

In the third act, Segismundo, back in the tower, is set free by a rebellious Polish mob that has learned of his existence. They want the Prince to rule, not Astolfo or Estrella. A civil war ensues between the forces of Prince Segismundo and those of King Basilio. Finally the Prince wins but forgives his father. At the end of the play, order is restored: Astolfo will marry Rosaura; Segismundo will marry Estrella; and one of the rebel soldiers is sentenced to prison for life when he intrudes upon the courtly reconciliation scene.

Modern readers are often troubled by the seemingly unenlightened denouement, which domesticates Rosaura and incarcerates the common man, the rebel soldier who liberated Segismundo and made possible the restoration of his princely prerogatives. In one of the 1981 New York productions of the play, Rosaura, finally offered Astolfo's hand in marriage after all her exertions to that end, declined and marched away to fight in the wars. A second adaptation that year dealt with the most controversial figure of *Life Is a Dream*, the rebel soldier, in the simplest way possible: by eliminating him altogether. There were, consequently, no gestures of gender or class repression to mar the neat congeniality of the occasions.

Undoubtedly, these were concessions to a modern American audience indoctrinated in equal rights and a democratic ideology. After all,

Rosaura's transformation seems defensibly rooted in the character Calderón created. In the original, she is active, clever, and willing to take risks, at least, until that last scene. There, as her colorful and energetic maneuvering to regain or gain a good name finally reaches fruition, she absorbs without comment her delivery to the insultingly reluctant Astolfo. Her only evident emotion is expressed a few lines later, where she endorses Segismundo's imprisonment of the rebel soldier: "How wise and prudent!" (480) ("¡Qué discreto y qué prudente!" [3.1113]).[2] The tempting rhetorical silence during the interim would, however, afford a director considerable latitude for choreographing movements, gestures, or expressions to convey some sense of Rosaura's response to the resolution of her own difficulty. Indeed, in a more recent production, which adhered strictly to Edwin Honig's translation,[3] Rosaura reacts to Astolfo's patrician misgivings to marrying a putative commoner by rushing at him with a sword. Once Clotaldo settles the matter of her paternity and the two are betrothed, she and her fiancé retire to the nether regions of the stage space in ardent embrace. It is unlikely that a seventeenth-century director ("autor") would have been quite so graphic, but these kinds of visual activities are not entirely inconsistent with the character of Rosaura as written in the virgin text.

The fate of the rebel soldier presents an even greater problem to anyone reading, performing, or writing about *Life Is a Dream*. It hardly seems fair to students and to many scholars that while all the others involved one way or another in the civil war are finally reconciled and rewarded, the rebel soldier must spend the rest of his days in prison.

Broadly speaking, whether we view this play as a comedy (moving from disorder to order) or a tragedy (order to disorder) can be gauged by our response to the final treatment of Rosaura and the rebel soldier. For one thing, *Life Is a Dream* ends, as do so many other Golden Age *comedias* and comedy in general, in a flurry of nuptial engagements, a convention traditionally taken by scholars as an assurance that everyone lived "happily ever after." Formally, at least, it satisfies the restoration of order.

The latest generations of Hispanists, however, have begun to reassess the conclusions of many works previously regarded as unambiguously positive. For example, often a royal character presides over or even arranges the distribution of couples; sometimes that monarch is a character out of history whose persona would be freighted for the author's contemporary audience with special and not always favorable connotations. Seventeenth-century Spaniards did not unanimously hold all past rulers in the highest regard, and we see now that the playwright may set the work in the reign of a king who, historically, was renowned as a man of poor judgment, whether weak, corrupt, or tyrannical. Any decree or action of his would be open to question by a public familiar with the historical tradition, through chronicles, ballads, proverbs, and other legendary commonplaces associated with that particular figure.

Among Hispanists, the most frequently cited examples of *comedias* with such dubitable ex machina resolutions are Calderón's "wife-murder" plays, especially *The Physician of His Honor* (*El médico de su honra*) and *Secret Vengeance for a Secret Insult* (*A secreto agravio, secreta venganza*), in which Kings Pedro of Castile and Sebastián of Portugal approve murders of wives suspected (but innocent) of infidelity. Since these were monarchs of notoriously questionable character (Peter was called "the Cruel" more often than "the Just" and died by assassination; Sebastian died in a disastrously ill-advised military campaign), their approvals of uxoricide would not be taken as the playwright's. In the case of *The Physician,* Pedro even bestows a new bride on the homicidal husband, suggesting to the spectator not future wedded bliss, but more woe to come.[4] Consequently, we now feel entitled legitimately to scrutinize any deus ex machina denouement for an irony that might completely contradict the standard interpretation. Some works previously disparaged as inconsistent or misunderstood as "problem plays" are now made comprehensible; others have become more complex, challenging, and rewarding as a result of our more sensitive view to irony and historical context.

In any case, the newly acquired license to doubt an apparently tidy ending has contributed to the credibility of those critics dissatisfied with the conclusion of *Life Is a Dream.* Edward M. Wilson, while viewing Segismundo's development in a generally positive light, thought the imprisonment of the rebel soldier excessive.[5] On several occasions stronger objections have been registered by H. B. Hall, who sees in the reformed Segismundo a "calculating, cruel Machiavellian." The prison motif opening and closing the *comedia* betrays a "cyclical movement [which] hints that injustice and blind oppression are inevitable: Segismundo escapes them only to inflict them on others."[6] T. E. May agrees that a pardon of the soldier would have been in order here, and that his incarceration is Segismundo's first mistake; the Prince in his fear of future disturbances will repeat his father's error.[7] According to Donald McGrady, playwright and protagonist "chastise a scapegoat who incarnates for them the sense of guilt that they bear for overturning society."[8]

Ruth El Saffar has considered the rebel soldier and Rosaura in tandem. In view of the social and psychological demands of his era, at the end of this play Calderón had to suppress the two symbols of passion: sexuality and emotion constitute a threat to the patriarchal social structure and must be excluded from the rigid society of seventeenth-century Spain.[9] El Saffar explains along the same lines the elimination of the female in the wife-murder *comedias,* observing that it is a decision whose psychic toll is paid by character and playwright.

Unless we see, as El Saffar does, a tragic choice mandated by the times, a problem with the negative view of Segismundo's final decree is its complete incompatibility with the trajectory of his character up to that point. All of *Life Is a Dream* has chronicled the protagonist's growing humanity, the tempering of his violent impulses by experience combined with reflection. If, as C. Christopher Soufas demonstrates, in the first act Segismundo's poignant monologue reveals a superbly developed faculty of reasoning,[10] the famous soliloquy ending the second shows a newly acquired ability to doubt. Segismundo puts to good use this skepticism in the third act; his lengthy, probing aside rejects the classical heroic values (and the violation of Rosaura), and opts instead to aid his petitioner, demonstrating the birth of a conscience. That in the end he offers to forsake the power won by force, that he forgives precisely those who would have deprived him of his birthright, and that he gives up the woman he loves, shows that he has learned the lesson well: life *is* but a dream, the world a stage, and these worldly goods we enjoy are not truly ours, but on loan from the Lord. It is the path of *desengaño* traversed by so many other rulers in Calderón's drama, from King Eduardo in *Love, Honor, and Power* (*Amor, honor, y poder*), to Alfonso in *To Know of Good and Evil* (*Saber del mal y del bien*), to Alejandro in *To Give All and to Give Nothing* (*Darlo todo y no dar nada*). To claim then that an abruptly selfish purpose dictates the imprisonment of the rebel soldier at the close of *Life Is a Dream* is tantamount to accusing its author of sloppy work—surely out of character for Calderón.

The directors who want to appeal to modern audiences by altering the text and the scholars who are so exasperated by the final scene, I think, exercise the prerogative and the practice of any recipient of art by bringing their own sets of values and sensibilities to bear on their understanding of the object. Their Calderón is not the one that lived in the seventeenth century, attentive to Catholic Christian skepticism, free will, and the political problems related to the divine right of kings and legitimate succession to the throne, but one born into an epoch concerned with feminism, democracy, and violations of human rights, a society that covets the freedom of the individual to become whatever he can make of himself, rather than insisting that he be what his father (or her mother) was. Such socially engaged approaches to a seventeenth-century script can and do result in its modification or in allegations of the Prince's (or the playwright's) inhumanity.

On the other hand, whoever attempts to re-create the view of the seventeenth-century public faces admittedly insurmountable obstacles and will never completely succeed in such a Sisyphean undertaking. The effort may, however, help redeem the playwright or his protagonist from those imputations of slipshod work or barbarity, and it is to the tradition of close reading combined with attention to historical context that this study is indebted.

That close reading entails especially a consideration of character development or the lack of it. In *Life Is a Dream,* Segismundo most fully matures; the well-meaning Basilio comes to terms with his earlier mistakes; Clarín learns late the fatal flaw in his own conduct—but the clown does learn. Rosaura epitomizes a favorite Golden Age theatrical ploy, the *mujer vestida de hombre,* the woman who dresses as a man in order to cleanse her soiled honor. Lope de Vega recommends the device in the *New Art of Writing Plays,* "because the male disguise is a real crowd-pleaser" (296) ("porque suele / el disfraz varonil agradar mucho" [lines 282–83]).[11] (As distinct from English theater of the period, women were actually permitted to play women on the Spanish stage.)

Rosaura is colorful, vigorous, and determined. But two aspects of her character exclude her from the status of "female protagonist" to which she has been elevated. In the first place, the disguise and the mission to Poland are not her own idea. It is her mother Violante, in her own *desengaño,* who sends Rosaura off to recover her good name. Violante, who vainly trusted to "the slow cure of time" (471) ("al tiempo fácil" [3.641]) to right the wrong of Clotaldo's desertion, sees in retrospect the futility of such a passive tactic. "Learning from her own experience" ("escarmentando en sí misma" [3.639]), Rosaura explains, Violante plotted out her daughter's strategy:

> she bade me follow [Astolfo] to Poland here
> and with prodigious gallantry persuade him
> to pay the debt to honour that he owes me.
> So that it would be easier to travel,
> she bade me don male clothing, and took down
> This ancient sword which I am wearing now.
>
> (471)

> (... que le siga, y que le obligue,
> con finezas prodigiosas,
> a la deuda de mi honor;
> y para que a menos costa
> fuese, quiso mi fortuna
> que en traje de hombre me ponga.
> Descuelga una antigua espada
> que es ésta que ciño ...)
>
> (3.645-52)

Rosaura, then, is the personification of her mother's *desengaño:* that hopeful inactivity accomplishes nothing, that confrontation might attain better results.

But what does Rosaura learn for herself during the progress of the play? In Golden Age drama, another favorite device is the physical fall, especially from a horse. It should suggest to an audience well-attuned to literary conventions a character's confusion of moral values. Rosaura begins the first scene by falling; she arrives in Poland ominously "blind and desperate" (409) ("ciega y desesperada" [1.13]), and is ruled throughout the play by her passion for revenge, if not restitution. In the third *jornada* she attempts to induce Clotaldo treacherously to murder Astolfo: she envisions the scene of retribution in the garden, where the unsuspecting Astolfo will be found awaiting an assignation with Estrella. When Clotaldo demurs, Rosaura confesses herself overcome by "madness" (467) ("locura" [3.452]) which she cannot control ("no podré" [3.454]), by rage and anger ("es rabia, es ira" [3.460]); she then sets off to appeal instead to Segismundo. That she rides up to the Prince amidst his troops without falling off her horse does not signify that Rosaura is now in command of her passions.[12] In the ensuing conversation, the woman goads Segismundo to further violence in behalf of her private complaint, that is, to disrupt the wedding of Astolfo and Estrella. The greater national cause never appears to interest her.

In the end, having achieved the restoration of her honor — not with Astolfo's death, but with his promise of marriage — her only comment is the one admiring the change in *Segismundo*. Rosaura is the executor of her *mother's* epiphany; and the agent and commentator of Segismundo's. She is an (admittedly attractive) medium, not a heroine.

In short, Rosaura's only evident interior change in *Life Is a Dream* is that she calms down. She has satisfied honor according to seventeenth-century Spanish dramatic standards, but Calderón shows no soul-searching. While her story is hardly a "frivolous subplot," we who read or watch the play should not be too captivated by Rosaura, except as a lively and illuminating foil to Segismundo, and a catalyst for his development.

Calderón does, however, stimulate the awakening of Segismundo's conscience through Rosaura's frequent *outward* changes, in costume. It is her enigmatic appearances dressed as a man at the tower in the first act; as a lady at court in the second; and as a woman armed like a man in the third that induce Segismundo to that all-important Christian skepticism. Her sartorial transformations, matched by those of Segismundo, and complemented by the frequently self-referring theatrical dialogue,[13] would remind the audience as well that they are not only at a theater, but in one, the world.

The theater along with the dream, as Jackson Cope has shown, are in fact the two prevailing metaphors in the Europe of that period.[14] Works like Cervantes's *Don Quixote,* Velázquez's *The Spinners* (*Las hilanderas*), and Shakespeare's *Taming of the Shrew* seem deliberately to obscure the border between fiction and reality by leaving out part of the frame that sets off the illusion from its audience. One effect of this violation of the frame is to draw the viewer into the work, so that he will extrapolate his own participation in a fiction: that is, he, like Segismundo, will doubt his own reality, and take refuge in eternity ("acudamos a lo eterno" [3.791]). In a way, then, the spectator is the true hero of Golden Age fiction.

At any rate, the spectacle of Segismundo's and Rosaura's appearances together as cast-off civic entities — both deprived of their birthrights by their fathers, both locked out of rank and recognition because their presence in the world of Basilio, Clotaldo, and Astolfo threatens disorder, and both armed like soldiers for combat in the civil war — would underline their communion of cause in the third act with the rebel soldier, who has himself been excluded from participation in the political life of

Poland. I have shown elsewhere[15] that Basilio errs consistently by ignoring the common people always in favor of the aristocracy: the King reveals his experiment on his son to the court of Poland; the rest of the population, throughout described or self-described deprecatingly as "rabble" ("vulgo"), "bandits and plebeians" (459) ("bandidos y plebeyos" [3.101, 116]), and so forth, learns about the Prince through the force of rumor. The three offended factions—Segismundo, Rosaura, and the people—make their cause a common one.

Why is it, then, that Segismundo gets what he wants (the kingdom); Rosaura what she wants (Astolfo, and a noble bloodline into the bargain); while the rebel soldier must finish out his days in prison? But perhaps the first question should be, What is it that the soldier really wants? In that final scene, observing the rewards heaped upon these aristocrats who in their own ways acted selfishly, in personal instead of national interests, it is only natural for him to speak up, reminding Segismundo,

> If thus you treat him who has not served you,
> What about me, who caused chaos in the realm
> And took you out of your dungeon in the tower?
> What will you give me?
>
> (479)

> (Si así a quien no te ha servido
> honras, ¿a mí, que fui causa
> del alboroto del reino,
> y de la torre en que estabas
> te saqué, qué me darás?)
>   (3.1101–5)

The impulsive appeal nets him life in prison. T. E. May asserts (in "Segismundo y el soldado rebelde," 72) that the soldier originally let Segismundo out of the tower expecting that the Prince would be a tyrant and would reward his accomplices with an ample share of the booty. According to Soufas, the soldier sees "rebellion as an end in itself" and not as a solution to political injustice ("Thinking in *La vida es sueño*," 295b). These assessments are accurate if what the character blurts out impulsively at the end is really what he wants. However, I think that he has been surprised by Segismundo's generosity and speaks up simply because from his standpoint it would be stupid not to. More important,

for the first time in his life and in the lives of his countrymen, all of
whom had been ignored and excluded by the previous regime—for the
first time, this citizen has access to a figure of authority who will listen to
him. What the rebel soldier really wants, what he and his peasant
comrades had been pleading for since they *peacefully* approached Basilio
before the rebellion, is, first, adherence to the law, to legal succession to
the throne.[16] In the tower, having taken Clarín for the Prince, the second
soldier explains,

> All of us told your father himself
> that we recognize you alone
> as prince,
> not the fellow from Muscovy.
> . . . .
> It was our loyalty that made us tell him.
> (458)
>
> (Todos a tu padre mesmo
> le dijimos que a ti solo
> por príncipe conocemos,
> no al de Moscovia.
> . . . .
> Fue lealtad de nuestro pecho.)
> (3.66–69, 72)

Obviously, this civilized petition fell on deaf ears, but the soldier's
request to the new King at the end will not. In Segismundo the people of
Poland attain the two things that Basilio had all along denied them: a
nation of laws, and recognition as citizens of that nation. Like the other
characters assembled after the war, the rebel soldier gets what he really
wants. Like Segismundo and Rosaura, he achieves enfranchisement.

Traditionally in literature, as Daniel L. Heiple has shown[17] and
Segismundo himself remarks, "no traitor is necessary after his treason"
(479) ("el traidor no es menester / siendo la traición pasada" [3.1109–10]).
Symbolically, as Eileen Connolly points out,[18] the imprisonment of
the rebel soldier indicates Segismundo's final domination of his own
unruly passions. But politically, the action is just as significant: Segismundo
institutionalizes for life—registers officially—a previously outlawed party,
which includes the majority of the population of Poland. Segismundo
institutes universal (male) suffrage—and expands his constituency—in

thus at last imposing the law on the rebel soldier. A pardon or an
execution would have added up to further exclusion of the masses from
the political life of Poland, perpetuating Basilio's original mistake.

The integration of the rebel soldier into the civic and legal structures
of this mythical Poland is entirely consistent with the prevailing theory
of statecraft in seventeenth-century Spain. Beginning shortly after the
appearance of Machiavelli's *The Prince* (*Il principe*) in 1513, a long line
of Spanish commentators felt compelled to counterattack the Italian's
pragmatic political science with resounding declamations of the people's
supremacy over the head of government. The Jesuit theorists, most
conspicuously Juan de Mariana and Francisco Suárez,[19] insisted that a
king's power is bestowed upon him by the people, who themselves
originally received it from the Lord. Mariana insisted that any sovereign
who became a tyrant was subject to removal from office, and even to
assassination, provided that the people had met in assembly, that wise
and learned men had properly deliberated over the decision, and that
before undertaking any action they had given the errant monarch due
notice and opportunity to reform.[20] Although Mariana's views were
considered scandalous in northern Europe, they had a good deal in
common with those advanced by George Buchanan in England and
Philippe du Plessis-Mornay in France,[21] and were not new at all, but
developed from classical, Germanic, and medieval feudal attitudes toward
the same problem. Both Jesuits and Calvinists, R. M. Frye notes, con-
curred in asserting that a "prince of royal blood could legitimatize
resistance" (*The Renaissance Hamlet*, 65). The Huguenot apologist
du Plessis-Mornay states that while the private citizen on his own
initiative cannot take up arms—that would constitute sedition—resistance
to tyranny not only can but should be initiated by one " 'born to set it
right,' " meaning the heir apparent or some other member of the royalty
or high nobility, following rigorous self-examination and extensive
deliberation.[22]

The Spanish theorists, however, braced by the Counter-Reformation,
most consistently opposed Machiavelli's pragmatism and the principle of
the divine right of kings. Calderón's theater (in plays such as *Absalom's
Locks* [*Los cabellos de Absalón*], *The Physician*, and *In This Life All Is
True and All a Lie* [*En esta vida todo es verdad y todo mentira*])
consistently supports the slightly more moderate stance of Domingo de
Soto, Luis de Molina, and Francisco de Vitoria, endorsing peaceful
resistance to poor rulership.[23] The public at the *corral*, then, whether

learned or not, had probably seen earlier plays by Calderón and other dramatists, perhaps including *The Star of Seville* (*La estrella de Sevilla*),[24] which express similarly anti-Machiavellian political attitudes. They would regard with approval the peaceful delegation to Basilio requesting Segismundo's accession. However, Alexander A. Parker correctly states that while the people of Poland had grounds to form a "Segismundo party," they had no legal right to undertake the violent overthrow of a legitimate king.[25] Segismundo, having been "born to set it right," might conceivably do so, at least according to the most radical views, Jesuit and Calvinist. But in *Life Is a Dream*, private citizens started the rebellion and only afterwards recruited the Prince: it was not Segismundo's initiative, but that of the "army of bandits and plebeians," who had to persuade their prince to join them. Again, according to Parker, while Segismundo should be free, Basilio should not be deposed, and the rebel soldier deserves punishment "for choosing evil means to achieve a professedly good end" ("Calderón's Rebel Soldier," 125).

On the personal level, Segismundo continually examines his conscience, especially during the third act. Rosaura seeks him out amongst his plebeian army as he contemplates the ramifications for himself of the rebellion. At first, he is inspired by the thought of the fame this revolutionary exploit will gain him:

> If Rome in the triumphs of her early age
> Could see me today,
> Oh, how she would take delight in seeing
> A wild beast in command of mighty armies,
> A wild beast, to whose fiery aspirations
> The firmament were all too slight a conquest!
>
> (468)

Now he interrupts himself, to doubt this essentially classical pre-Stoic rendition of the heroic ideal:

> But let's stoop our flight, my spirit. Let us not
> Be puffed to pride by these uncertain plaudits
> Which, when I wake, will turn to bitterness
> In that I won them only to be lost.
> The less I value them, the less I'll miss them.
>
> (468)

(Si este día me viera
Roma en los triunfos de su edad primera,
¡oh, cuánto se alegrara
viendo lograr una ocasión tan rara
de tener una fiera
que sus grandes ejércitos rigiera,
a cuyo altivo aliento
fuera poca conquista el firmamento!
Pero el vuelo abatamos,
espíritu; no así desvanezcamos
aqueste aplauso incierto,
si ha de pesarme, cuando esté despierto,
de haberlo conseguido
para haberlo perdido,
pues mientras menos fuere
menos se sentirá si se perdiere.)
(3.469–84)

Rosaura soon appears in her third enigmatic costume, provoking an extended aside in which the Prince proceeds in his rejection of the primitive heroic ethic in favor of the Christian refuge in eternity:

Who has known heroic glories,
That deep within himself, as he recalls them,
Has never doubted that they might be dreams?
... [T]hen let us seek
That which endures ...
(473)

(¿Quién tuvo dichas heroicas
que entre sí no diga, cuando
las revuelve en su memoria:
sin duda que fue soñando
cuando vi?
... [A]cudamos a lo eterno ...)
(3.782–86, 791)

Segismundo finally wins his own internal civil war when, victorious in the national arena, he prostrates himself at his father's feet.

We have no evidence of this kind of searching introspection and self-scrutiny in the rebel soldier or his companions, I suspect in part, because neither Calderón nor his contemporaries would have believed the masses capable of such sensitivity. The political writer Diego de Saavedra Fajardo, a member of Philip IV's court during Calderón's service there, writes in his treatise on proper Christian kingship that

> the stupid and blind rabble don't recognize the truth unless they bump into it, because they form their opinions rashly, without reason interfering in the process, having to touch things with their own hands to comprehend the actual event, schoolmaster of the ignorant; and thus, whoever would propose to part the rabble from their opinions by arguing will waste his time and energy. No better method than forcing them to set eyes on their mistakes, and touch them, as one does a skittish horse, compelling it to recognize the insubstantiality of the shadow that frightens it.

> (. . . el vulgo torpe y ciego no conoce la verdad si no topa con ella, porque forma ligeramente sus opiniones, sin que la razón prevenga los inconvenientes, esperando a tocar las cosas con las manos para desengañarse con el suceso, maestro de los ignorantes; y así quien quisiere apartar al vulgo de sus opiniones con argumentos perderá el tiempo y el trabajo. Ningún medio mejor que hacelle dar de ojos en sus errores, y que los toque, como se hace con los caballos espantadizos, obligándoles a que lleguen a reconocer la vanidad de la sombra que los espanta.)[26]

Throughout *Life Is a Dream,* this *vulgo,* while not officially recognized, is regarded as a powerful, unprincipled force greatly to be feared. To Astolfo, it is "astrólogo cierto" (1.556), an infallible oracle whose rumors predict his union with Estrella. After the common people learn through hearsay of Segismundo's existence, the army of "bandidos y plebeyos" wrests him from the tower with a commotion moving Basilio to cry out,

> Astolfo, whose prudence can rein in the fury of a bolting horse?
> Who can restrain a river's current rushing to the sea, proud and
>   precipitate?
> Whose valour can withstand a crag dislodged

And hurtling downwards from a mountain peak?
All these are easier by far than to hold back
A crowd's proud fury, once it has been roused.

(463)

(¿Quién, Astolfo, podrá parar, prudente,
la furia de un caballo desbocado?
¿Quién detener de un río la corriente
que corre al mar, soberbio y despeñado?
¿Quién un peñasco suspender, valiente,
de la cima de un monte desgajado?
Pues todo fácil de parar se mira,
más que de un vulgo la soberbia ira.)

(3.241-48)

While the rabble's native recklessness evidently precludes moderation, the aristocrats in the play are finally able to restrain themselves at the crucial moment. Clotaldo will decline to turn traitor, explaining that he has been "born noble" (466) ("habiendo noble nacido" [3.431]); Segismundo's noble blood (477; 3.986-87) brings him to reconcile with his father; the wedding of Astolfo and Rosaura is eventually suitable because she is, after all, noble.

In short, Calderón recognizes the common people's intrinsic right to citizenship, while his rhetoric (and perhaps the imprisonment of the rebel soldier) betrays patrician reservations about their ability to fulfill unaided their civic obligations. To the end, the peasant in this play acts on impulse. If Segismundo learns that life is a dream, and Basilio that he should have trusted to his son's free will, the rebel soldier learns the wrong lesson. His request for a reward shows that by watching the misguided actions of his "betters" and by observing the happy results, he has gotten the wrong message, misconstruing forgiveness for applause. Apparently lacking the capacity for *desengaño* through abstract reasoning, he is led like a frightened horse to the tower, forced to bump into the revelation being imposed upon him.

Apart from Segismundo and Basilio, the other characters—Estrella, Clotaldo, Astolfo, and Rosaura—do not appear to have assimilated much at all, right or wrong, and presumably will now settle into their roles as courtiers: precisely what ought to lead to "happily ever after," or harmony, in the seventeenth-century cosmological outlook, as described by Tillyard

and Heninger.[27] If we perform well our assigned social roles, if we are
who we are ("somos quienes somos"), order will prevail in the macrocosm.
If but one of us disturbs that fragile chain of being, chaos will reign for
all.

The only other unseemly (or unstable, or un-being) element in the
realm is paradoxically the superconformer, Clarín. Among other errors
(including his wish to elude God's will), his pliability, his persistent
violation of identity, lead to his own downfall. At first in the tower, out of
fear he urges Rosaura to misidentify herself as Clotaldo. Later in the
palace he becomes "a great pleaser of all Segismundos" (436) ("un
grande agradador / de todos los Segismundos" [2:353–54]), bootlicker to
a tyrannical prince, and perhaps a parody of Clotaldo's unquestioning
subservience to Basilio. Back in the tower, this man of fluid character
allows the soldiers to believe he is Segismundo; finally, while all others
are engaged in defending their respective causes, he is a man of no
cause, other than himself. He evades enfranchisement and its concomitant obligations, deliberately excepting himself from the society into
which the rebel soldier has so passionately fought to be admitted. His
desengaño is late and costly, but he does attain it, and not incidentally
without profit for the King.

Life Is a Dream, therefore, is very much of its century, and not a tract
for the Age of Revolution, much less the Nuclear Age: the play makes no
causes célèbres of Rosaura or the rebel soldier. The dramatist, himself a
"don" and frequenter of the royal court, underwrites contemporary
political theory — at bottom this constitutionalism being basically medieval and conservative — and social attitudes. *Life Is a Dream* prescribes
among other things a highly circumscribed acknowledgment of the
citizenship of the common man. Although in this play the populace has
reversed the roles and arrived ex machina to liberate its own king, that is
not the end of the story. At the end, all parties are integrated into a new,
and considerably transformed, political order, which accords the peasant
of Poland a place that ideally would have been his from the beginning.
No reasonable person would claim that Calderón foresaw 350 years in
advance a sort of Solidarity union arising to expel the Russian specter
from Poland, although a director with a cause might choose to play the
comedia that way. The text contains the most aristocratic and traditional
social attitudes. In Calderón's social scheme of things (or at least that
conveyed in *Life Is a Dream*), the common man — the unreflective rebel
soldier — is shown to be constitutionally unfit for heroic status.

The Villano in His Corner:
Supercorrection
of
the Pseudohumanist

During the Renaissance, as Wardropper points out, Spain's real-life heroes were the soldiers and explorers who ventured abroad to risk their lives for the Faith, glory, and financial gain.[28] Nevertheless, in the late sixteenth and early seventeenth centuries, Spaniards found themselves facing a serious economic crisis that could partly be blamed on short-sighted governmental fiscal policies, exacerbated by the public's unwillingness to belong to a mercantile class. Spain had applied income from her colonies in the New World toward financing foreign military action instead of internal economic development: Philip II meant to fight off the Moorish infidel in the Mediterranean and to reclaim all of Europe for Catholicism, preferably under the direction of a Spanish monarch whose empire already included much of the Americas. The calamity of the loss of the Armada in 1588 opened the eyes of some, including possibly Cervantes, to whom was entrusted for several years the unpleasant and dangerous task of attempting to collect taxes from an already overtaxed population in Andalusia, and who himself suffered while trying to collect back wages from the government for his own foreign service in the military.[29]

Furthermore, the expulsion of the Moors and Jews from the peninsula following the Reconquest, which effectively constituted "a decapitation of mercantile Spain" ("una decapitación de la España mercantil"),[30] left behind a legacy of aversion to any economic activity that might be construed as indication of *converso*-status. As stated in chapter 1, it was a fact of life that having to work with one's hands had in the opinion of many become disgraceful. A class of idle minor nobles (*hidalgos*) stubbornly refused as a point of honor to work, even if they were starving, although they did exert much of their energy to maintain appearances. They became the objects of ridicule and despairing parody in works such as *Lazarillo de Tormes, Don Quixote,* and *The Rogue (El buscón)*. Despite the perils of belonging to this class, it was invaded by many, and numerous others adopted the "don" without clear title to it. Those who, like Sancho Panza, eschewed such pretensions and worked the land, felt compelled to insist on their "Old Christian" ancestry.

In any case, economics in collusion with historical circumstance had bled agriculture of its workers, who were attracted by fashion and opportunity to the cities and the colonies. National revenues from New World silver, which had allowed Spain to carry on the wars and import the goods she should have been producing herself, dwindled while expenditures increased. Some farmers ("labradores," who worked the land) had become wealthy, bought titles of nobility, and joined aristocratic landowners in the city. But their prosperity was not the rule. By the end of the sixteenth century the crisis had forced itself into the consciousness of a concerned intelligentsia, who set about considering alternatives for revitalization, especially of agriculture, and who were besieged by professional schemers (*arbitristas*) with often farfetched inventions and grandiose plans to save the realm. These characters, too, earned their place in the satirical fiction of the period.[31]

The more sober and practical thinkers could, however, see that the depopulation of the countryside was a major impediment to economic recovery. Farming and manual labor must be reinvested with prestige, and, according to Salomon (*Recherches sur le thème paysan,* 306), one vehicle of pro-bucolic propaganda in this campaign was the *comedia* which makes a hero of the peasant farmer.[32] This dramatic subgenre is perceived to follow the pastoral or *beatus ille* traditions by idealizing countryside and country people, at the expense of city-dwellers and courtiers. The plays of this type most studied by literary critics, most often taught in the classrooms, and occasionally even brought to life on the stage, are Lope de Vega's *The Villano in His Corner, The King, the Greatest Alcalde, Peribáñez and the Comendador of Ocaña,* and *Fuenteovejuna;* and Calderón's *The Alcalde of Zalamea.*

While Calderón's dramatic opus is technically correct, religiously orthodox, and in its politics unrelentingly anti-Machiavellian, Lope's work has traditionally been regarded as less governed by staunch artistic or moral principles than by the whim of the moment or the exigencies of flattering a patron. This apparent lack of internal or external fixed constraint may contribute to the naturalness and appeal of many works — the lovely simplicity of the verses in *The King, the Greatest Alcalde* and the virtuoso meters of *The Knight of Olmedo* (*El caballero de Olmedo*) come immediately to mind — but it makes judging the plays' themes and the social attitudes they convey a riskier business.

Lope's treatment of social classes is nothing if not equivocal. His biographers describe his lifelong wish to please and associate with, if not

join, the nobility;[33] at the same time, in numerous *comedias* his dramatic persona is Belardo, generally a clown and always of peasant stock.
Lope's frequent references to the *vulgo* in the *New Art of Writing Plays*
seem by turns deprecating and affectionate,[34] while in the "Prólogos" to
the printed collections of his *comedias* the *vulgo* is always regarded as a
nuisance.[35] To Salomon, Lope exalts the peasant; José Antonio Maravall
and José María Díez Borque believe that politically, Lope's plays support
absolute monarchy.[36] In Spanish, the word "villano" proceeds from
"villa," or village. During the Middle Ages, it first applied to one who
inhabits a village and is not a member of the nobility. Joan de Corominas
explains that as time passed the term gradually acquired negative
connotations.[37] To the previous, semantically neutral definition, *Autoridades* adds "rustic or discourteous" ("rústico o descortés") or "vile,
unworthy, or indecorous" ("ruin, indigno, ú indecoroso") (3:488a). In
Life Is a Dream, the exasperated Rosaura and Estrella both hurl the
epithet "villano" at highly aristocratic Astolfo.[38] According to Cobarruvias,
"From 'villanos,' comes 'villainous deed,'" meaning a discourteous and
crude action" ("De villanos se dixo villanía, por el hecho descortés y
grosero" [*Tesoro de la lengua castellana,* 1009a]). Louis Combet finds
that Spanish proverbs often impugn one's behavior and ethics with the
term "villano," which connotes "ingratitude, meanness, avarice, lack of
generosity of heart, vanity and petty pride upon personal enrichment,
distrust, etc." ("l'ingratitude, la bassesse, l'avarice, l'absence de générosité
de coeur, la vanité et la gloriole lorsqu'il vient à s'enricher, la méfiance,
etc.")[39] Salomon notes that these negative qualities often also apply
when "villano" is used in the *comedia* (*Recherches sur le thème paysan,*
762–63).

Lope's *The Villano in His Corner* (*El villano en su rincón*) appeared
in print in 1617.[40] Scholarly speculation has fixed the date of composition at between 1611 and 1616.[41] The play tells the story of the wealthy
plebeian Frenchman, Juan Labrador ("John Farmer"), who, at age sixty,
is content in his prosperity and proud of the fact that he has never
ventured far from the village where he was born. He has not been to
nearby Paris, nor set eyes on the King, and even hides when the
monarch Ludovico is in the vicinity: for the peasant, as in the proverb,
"he is king who sees no king" ("Ese es rey, que no ve rey").[42] Juan is so
satisfied and so certain of continuing in this comfortable condition for
the rest of his life, that he has already had his epitaph engraved in stone
in the village church:

"Here lies Juan Labrador,
who never served an earthly lord,
or saw court or king,
who never feared nor frightened;
nor lacked anything,
nor was injured or imprisoned,
nor in his many years
saw in his home an unhappy event,
envy, or illness."

("Yace aquí Juan Labrador,
que nunca sirvió a señor,
ni vio la corte ni al Rey,
ni temió ni dio temor;
ni tuvo necesidad,
ni estuvo herido ni preso,
ni en muchos años de edad
vio en su casa mal suceso,
envidia ni enfermedad.")[43]

On an outing, young King Ludovico comes upon the church and the epitaph. His curiosity and envy piqued, he contrives, disguised, to meet the man who is so happy and self-sufficient, in the farmer's own home. Later, after romantic intrigues involving Juan's ambitious children, the King summons them and their reluctant father to court, where he confers a title of nobility on Feliciano, marries Lisarda to the distinguished Marshal of Paris, and appoints Juan Labrador as his royal steward in perpetuity.

The play is viewed, rightly I think, as a contest of wills between the farmer and the King. Juan Labrador, who has the habit of calling himself "king in his own small corner" ("rey en [su] pequeño rincón" [1.476]), even forgoes mass in the village church because the King plans to attend. Although this *villano* has the reputation for humility,[44] he takes such evident delight in his vast wealth and independence that his boast not only gainsays his reputation, but mocks precisely those countrymen who make his comfort possible:

I laugh at the soldier
who, as if he had

a thousand legs and a thousand arms, sets out to lose them;
and the other unfortunate soul,
who, as if there weren't
enough land, clutching Fortune's locks,
and dangling from them
in his ambition,
ploughs the open sea,
and stops not even at the sea,
but presumes as well to consume the winds.
Oh, Lord! What great folly
for a man to seek an uncertain grave!

(Ríome del soldado
que como si tuviese
mil piernas y mil brazos, va a perdellos;
y el otro, desdichado,
que como si no hubiese
bastante tierra, asiendo los cabellos
a la fortuna, y dellos
colgado el pensamiento,
las libres mares ara,
y aun el mar no para,
y presume también beber el viento.
¡Ay Dios! ¡Qué gran locura,
buscar el hombre incierta sepultura!)

(1.412–24)

Juan Labrador's isolationism flies in the face of the "real-life" heroism
described by Wardropper. The farmer's complacent view of his own
future is the obverse of the pessimistic tunnel vision that in *Life Is a
Dream* causes Basilio to abuse Segismundo; the two philosopher-parents
subscribe to narrowly deterministic conceptions of events and human
nature. Juan Labrador's disdain for his society's soldiers and explorers
only superficially accords with that Erasmian disapproval of war and
praise of the "unromantic private citizen" who wishes just to do his
Christian duty: this *villano*'s social egotism amounts, like the pastoral of
the self, to a denial of *caritas*. One of the themes of *The Villano in His
Corner*, as Everett W. Hesse, Wardropper, and J. E. Varey have shown, is
the necessity in a healthy commonwealth for brotherly love.[45] Juan

Labrador's obsessive attachment to his "simple" life and his ungraceful submission to its disruption violate the gentle spirit of Erasmian humanism, so that this peasant will be shown to remain unheroic by any standard.

In *Life Is a Dream,* the common man had to battle for access to his king and the political life of Poland. Here, the imbalance tilts in the other direction: King Ludovico goes to great lengths to reach and enfranchise Juan Labrador. The pastiche of monarchical symbols in the third act—scepter, mirror, and sword—is meant to convey visually the need for the farmer's engagement in national and not just personal affairs: he is a citizen; he must acknowledge subordination to his king; and he has the privilege and the duty to look to the king for justice. However, the shaken peasant has heard the call to court as a decree for his own demise (3.780–83), and even after claiming to understand his political error (3.844), repeats twice (3.845–47; 923–24) his expectation that he is about to be put to death. This super-*desengaño,* which not only concedes the King's supremacy, but acknowledges his absolute right to dispose at will of the subject's life, is as misconceived as Juan Labrador's illusion of complete self-sufficiency had been. The farmer in his self-imposed ignorance has distorted legitimate royal authority into divine right. Like the rustic clown Salvano in the first act, who learns to his stupefaction that kings have beards too—this one's is red (1. 691–92)—Juan Labrador must finally learn to *see* that his King is human, too.

And like the surprised rebel soldier in Calderón's play, Juan Labrador is sentenced to life in society; this time the "torre" is the palace of the King of France. To a point, the political moral of *The Villano in His Corner* complements that of *Life Is a Dream.* Here, the ruler takes and pursues the initiative of awakening the citizen, and absorbing him into the political structure. Both plays affirm the principle of universal male suffrage. Both plays extol the necessity of the subject's enlightened contact with his king. However, where Calderón's play succeeds in realizing that goal, Lope's only pretends to: here, King Ludovico's political moral will be shown to be at serious and potentially fatal cross-purposes with the play's economic one.

Victor Dixon maintains that the King of France should be considered a protagonist of *The Villano in His Corner.*[46] The young monarch, naturally curious and humanly envious of Juan Labrador's way of life, finds himself cast in the plot of a *serranilla*-type adventure that he himself has helped to devise.[47] Knowing the farmer will not willingly see him, Ludovico rejects at first the logical recourse, a summons to the

royal court: this young man must "touch with his own hand" ("to[car]
con la mano" [3.251]) Juan Labrador's bucolic worthiness. Besides, the
peasant has a lovely daughter, and a visit in disguise might lead to some
diversion (at least, that's the way it happens in poetry). Ludovico,
faithful to countless literary antecedents, disguises himself as a *caballero*
lost while hunting and takes refuge for the night in the farmer's home.
His own knowledge of rustic life until now probably based on literary
stereotypes, he expects help from Lisarda, Belisa, or Costanza in taking
off his boots[48] and is brusquely undeceived by their curt responses.

In any case, the King's revealing firsthand experience of "real" and
not "poetic" rural life ought to qualify him to govern his constituency
with intelligence. His generous comportment toward Juan Labrador and
the young lovers upon his return to the court testify to the effect on him
of this rustic interlude.

Nevertheless, *The Villano in His Corner* remains, in Marcel Bataillon's
words (*"El villano en su rincón,"* 329), a singular and disconcerting text.
Frances Day Wardlaw states that in *comedias* with peasant protagonists,
usually the commoner solves his own problem, receives his king's blessing,
and life returns more or less to the status quo.[49] In *The Villano in His
Corner,* however, the peasant must abandon his old life and take up an
entirely new one. Furthermore, scholars have wondered, why the setting
in France, and what if anything does that tell us about Franco-Hispanic
relations of the time?

The characters themselves depart in so many small ways from the
literary norm that taken together, they compose a strangely addled
community. None, from Otón, to Lisarda, Feliciano, Costanza, or Juan
Labrador, will be shown to qualify by word or deed during the course of
this play for the adjectives "generous," "wise," "virtuous," or "humble"
that are so often conferred upon them.[50] We tend to overlook their
questionable behavior because of our own susceptibility to the idealizing
literary stereotype, in league with the propaganda they themselves have
put out: we assume that Juan Labrador is humble because that is what
Fileto tells the King; Costanza must be a virtuous girl because Feliciano
says so (2.205–6)—although before long we learn that this high-minded
young man has impregnated his wholesome sweetheart.

Juan Labrador's adamantly anti-aristocratic stance seems monstrous
to his children, who aspire to insinuate themselves into courtly society.
Lisarda treats the disguised visiting King (whom she recognizes) with a
modest restraint that she does not always display toward noble men.

When the aristocrat Otón first meets Lisarda, she is in Paris disguised as a lady, in fact, a "pescadora" (1.199-200), or "angler for men," as the sharp-eyed Finardo guesses. That is, she is typical of many women of questionable character and social standing, out to hook a title and usually wealth by deceptive means (also a stock figure in the fiction of the period).[51] Having spotted a likely catch, without even knowing Otón's name she accepts expensive jewels from him, and offers him, perhaps symbolically, one of her own. She only departs from the stereotype in that her wealth is genuine.

Although the besotted Otón gives his word not to follow Lisarda, as soon as she is out of earshot he reneges and sends Marín on her trail. The servant pursues her to a room in an inn where, he reports, he got quite an eyeful:

> I looked in the room, and watched
> the woman take her clothes off
> and dress herself, bit by bit,
> as a peasant.
>
> (Miro al aposento, y veo
> desnudarse la mujer
> y vestirse poco a poco
> de labradora.)
>   (1.235-38)

Otón is neither disturbed at this peeping lackey's overintimate narrative, nor discouraged by Lisarda's social status from planning his own seduction of her. In fact, since she lacks a husband and standing, it will be easier to get away with.[52] And Otón later phrases his elegy of pastoral retreat in such a way as to suggest that either he has just reread Góngora's *First Solitude* (*Primera soledad*), or that he is no stranger to country dalliance:

> How ill, Finardo, you know [rustic life]
> if you've never chanced
> to arrive at night soaked through,
> or during the siesta with the sun,
> or, lost in the wood,
> from far off a shepherds'

fire has drawn you,
or the sound of dogs
baying hoarsely
reached you,
and you entered the poor hut
protected from above by a canopy
of oak trees bathed in smoke . . . !

(¡Qué mal, Finardo, conoces,
si nunca te sucedió,
llegar de noche mojado,
o a la siesta con el sol,
o perdido por un monte,
si de lejos te llamó
el fuego de los pastores
o de los perros el son,
después que de voces ronco
te dieron alguna voz,
y entraste en pobre cabaña
que tiene por guardasol
robles bañados en humo . . . !)
                              (2.952–67)

Until nearly the end of the play, and despite Otón's protestations to Lisarda to the contrary, the courtier has no intention of marrying the peasant girl. Otón's confidante Finardo informs the King,

He told me
the long story,
by which he came to merit the love
of the discreet peasant girl,
whom he wants to deceive now
with the promise of marriage. . . .
. . . [T]here's no reasoning with love. . . .
Nothing is more inconstant
than a man.

    (El prolijo
discurso a mí me contó,

con que vino a merecer
la discreta labradora,
que quiere engañar agora
a título de mujer. . . .
. . . [A]mando, no hay razón. . . .
No hay cosa más inconstante
que el hombre.)
(3.190–95; 202; 208–9)

The lovers' first tête-à-tête is to be at midnight, "in the garden"; Lisarda instructs Otón to enter through the door "by four cypress trees" ("en la huerta"; "[hay] entre cuatro cipreses una puerta" [2.378, 380]). The symbols of carnal knowledge and death tip Lope's idyll further off-balance, and Casalduero notes (559) in the setting and the hour a reminiscence of the fatal trysting spot in *La Celestina*. Otón is only moved in the third act to declare openly his love for Lisarda, and to accept her hand in marriage, because the King has shrewdly led him to believe he is in competition for the girl. As the saying, and the title of another Lope play goes, "Jealousy gets more results than love" ("Más pueden celos que amor"). This affair—founded on mutual deception, cemented by ambition and jealousy—is hardly one from the heart.

Lisarda and her brother Feliciano both scorn country life. While she admits to frequent "fishing" trips to Paris, he also visits the capital disguised as an aristocrat. Feliciano's favorite "noble" activities are gambling and jousting (1.601–10). Still, he is willing to marry the poor peasant girl, Costanza. The young man, anxious for the summer to pass, prefers an early-winter wedding date (2.405–7). Before the middle of the third act, however, it has become public knowledge that the virtuous, unwed Costanza is going to make Juan Labrador a grandfather, and the nuptials are expedited.

But neither of the farmer's children thinks any peasant good enough to marry Lisarda. From Juan del Encina's *Eclogue Dramatizing a Plea for Love* (*Egloga representada en requesta de unos amores*) (1494) and Lucas Fernández's *Farce or Comedy about a Maiden, a Shepherd, and a Gentleman* (*Farsa o quasi comedia de una donzella y un pastor y un caballero*) (1496 or 1497)[53] to Tirso de Molina's *The Timid Man at Court* (*El vergonzoso en palacio*) (published in 1621), the love of a social inferior for a courtier has been a favorite complication on the Spanish stage. Generally, though, either the love is destined to be unrequited, or the "rustic," who has all along exhibited inordinately sophisticated behavior for his apparently lowly status, is eventually discovered to have been born noble. Both children of Juan Labrador are literate and feel naturally suited to life at court. They are so different from their father that their perplexed discussion of him and their persistent questioning of their relationship with him should produce the usual doubt in the audience. Because the farmer resolutely refuses to set eyes on the King, his son catalogues for comparison the most prodigious barbarians in history (1.537–48), concluding, "Is such great meanness possible?" ("¿Hay tan grande villanía?"). Shortly afterwards he adds, "He doesn't even deserve to be a man" ("Ni aun hombre mereció ser" [1.634]). Lisarda and Feliciano spend much of the intervening one hundred lines earnestly impugning their own paternity:

> FELICIANO.   Is it possible that we were born
> of this monster?
> LISARDA.   I don't know.
> FELICIANO.   If he is our father, why
> did we turn out so differently?
> I'm dying to see the court
> and go about dressed as a man of honor;
> this lowly business wearies me,
> although it's important to please him. . . .
> I don't know how he [could have] sired me.
> LISARDA.   Well what about me?
> I never went to court
> looking like my true self.
> My clothes—overskirt and cloak,
> glove and gilded shoe—
> are fit for the Dauphin's eyes.
> FELICIANO.   I am shocked at [Juan Labrador's] crudeness.
>
> (FELICIANO.   ¿Es posible que nacimos
> deste monstruo?
> LISARDA.   No lo sé.
> FELICIANO.   Si es nuestro padre, ¿por qué
> tan diferentes salimos?
>   Yo muero por ver la corte
> y andar en honrado traje;

<blockquote>
cánsame este villanaje,
aunque a darle gusto importe. . . .
¡No sé cómo me engendró!
</blockquote>

LISARDA.
<blockquote>
Pues ¿qué te diré de mí?
Jamás a la corte fui,
que allá pareciese yo.
Mi ropa—basquiña y manto,
guante y dorado chapín—
puede mirallo el Delfín.
</blockquote>

FELICIANO.
<blockquote>
De su rudeza me espanto.)
</blockquote>

(1.587–94; 611–18)

Such emphatic and repeated insistence on the disparity between parent and offspring so early in the play ought to awaken in the audience suspicion, and perhaps the expectation that in the end these children will by some twist of the plot turn out to have been foundlings of noble blood—rather like Rosaura's "surprise" aristocratic paternity at the end of *Life Is a Dream*. In the meantime, their speculation casts a shadow over the character of their apparently deceased mother[54] and paints horns on Juan Labrador. When the end of the work does come, however, Lope does nothing to dispel these doubts—doubts which would scarcely occur to twentieth-century readers in the first place because they do not conform to our preconceptions about the play: that it idealizes this rustic family. In fact, the flagrant social climbing of Juan Labrador's children is in direct violation of *ser quien se es*, yet in the end they are rewarded, not castigated, for their presumption. Lisarda has appealed to Fortune to stop turning her wheel (3.700–706),[55] and for the first time in history and literature, apparently, the goddess obliges.

We do see that Juan Labrador is in need of some humility and some serious political education, but I think his character flaw extends as well to such small-minded defects as parsimony and pusillanimity, that in the end they must exclude him from any heroic status. Although ostentatious in his charity to the less fortunate—like Cervantes's Knight of the Green Cloak, Juan Labrador's left hand knows (and proclaims) what the right hand is doing[56]—he scolds Fileto for wanting an embroidered cloth to cover a gift of grapes for the village doctor:

JUAN.
<blockquote>
Aren't you foolish? Don't you know
that you might accidentally leave
</blockquote>

the cloth there?
FILETO.   People with integrity
            return dishes and cloths.

(JUAN.   ¿No eres más necio? ¿No sabes
                que a peligro el paño está
                de que se te quede allá?
FILETO.   Entre personas muy graves
                platos y paños se vuelven.)
                                        (1.333–37)

When the King's arrival incognito at night causes a commotion, Juan's
first concern is not that a traveler might need help, but that some idler
might want to pilfer something (2.614–16). He boasts of his willingness
to sacrifice all for his king, but when the time comes, he reacts not with
heroic grace, but with noisy complaint, about what he calls "such harsh
torture."[57] For one who claims so little attachment to the world, Juan
Labrador raises quite a fuss. Although he calls himself a philanthropist,
he is at heart a selfish man. Like Clarín in *Life Is a Dream,* he exempts
himself from personal participation in human affairs on the grander
scale.

Calderón may have set *Life Is a Dream* in Poland for a number of
reasons, including contemporary political conditions there,[58] the fact
that Catholicism continued to prevail there, and perhaps because Poland's
distance would endow it with a mythical, and thus universal character
for the Spanish public. That distance would also allow the playwright
the freedom to dilate on weighty metaphysical and national themes
without danger of direct insult to any living Spaniard. Lope's rationale
for setting *The Villano in His Corner* in apparently contemporary France
is more puzzling, and has evoked a great deal of plausible if unprovable
speculation on the part of scholars. Bataillon (in *"El villano en su
rincón"*) was the first to draw some illuminating parallels between the
imminent wedding of the Infanta in the play and the two royal unions
negotiated and realized between Spain and France during the years in
which Lope most likely wrote the piece, although the correspondences
are not always exact. *The Villano in His Corner* would be, then, a
celebratory bouquet to the French (332–36). Bataillon also shows (339–44)
that one of Lope's sources probably was the story of "The Coalman and
the King" ("El carbonero y el rey"), which takes place in France.

In the midseventeenth century, Juan de Matos Fragoso (d. 1692) rewrote the *comedia* and called it *The Wise Man in His Retreat and the Villano in His Corner* (*El sabio en su retiro y el villano en su rincón*).[59] As Bataillon puts it, Matos "purifies the work of its extravagances" ("purific[a] la obra de las extravagancias" [368–69]). Now the courtier is forced to wed the woman he seduced with promises of marriage; now there are no references to royal weddings—which would of course have lost their topicality. Now Beatriz (née Lisarda) is so much in love with her courtier that she wishes *he* were of a *lower* station (205b); and Costanza, outraged, flatly rejects Montano's (né Feliciano's) suggestion of premarital relations (203a). Now the emphasis is on Juan Labrador's *limpieza de sangre*; and now the setting is Spain.

During the Golden Age, relations between Spain and France were severely strained when not openly hostile, and the disposition of Spanish citizens toward their French counterparts reflected the animosity. Miguel Herrero García has examined Spain's literature of the period for its social attitudes. Works such as Carlos García's *Antipathy of Spaniards and French* (*La antipatía de españoles y franceses*) (1617) and Baltasar Gracián's *Fault-Finder* (*Criticón*), agree that the French are greedy and mercenary; superficial and inconstant—their word of honor is worthless; they are repeatedly called "demonios."[60] Gracián writes, " 'Caesar was certainly right in his *Commentaries* to say that the Frenchman is as bold and proud in prosperity as he is weak-kneed and abject in adversity' " (" 'Bien dijo César en sus *Comentarios* que el francés es arrojado y soberbio en la prosperidad como flojo y abyecto en la desgracia' ").[61] Zamora Vicente notes (lii) that the protracted negotiations for the royal weddings during the period in which *The Villano in His Corner* was written did nothing to abate the animosity between Spain and France. In *Jealousy Gets More Results than Love*, Lope himself writes,

> The Spanish and the French,
> Two belligerent nations,
> Never let the opportunity escape
> To get in a row,
> For although royal blood
> Joins them through marriages
> They are always, like the elements,
> By nature conflicting.

(Nunca faltan ocasiones
Sobre algunos intereses
A españoles y franceses,
Dos belicosas naciones;
Que aunque la sangre real
Los junte por casamientos,
Siempre están como elementos
En contienda natural.)[62]

Because of the sensitivity to blood purity in seventeenth-century Spain, one of the worst insults possible was an allegation of Semitic descent. Despite the gravity of such a charge, playwrights often used that sensitivity to comic effect; Cervantes's interlude *The Marvellous Pageant* (*El retablo de las maravillas*) is an engaging example. In a number of Lope's *comedias,* characters — usually commoners — who wish to assail the integrity of others — usually *hidalgos* — cast doubt on their adversaries' blood purity by calling them Jews. At the beginning of the third act of *The Villano in His Corner,* as the party of courtiers converges on the village, the rustics call out such taunts, although here the courtiers give as well as get. To Bruno's insolent "Where are the Jews going?" ("¿Adónde van los jodíos?" [3.110]), Marín is quick on the uptake: "To look for you, *my kinsmen,* / to make friends" ("A buscaros, *deudos míos,* / para haceros amistad" [3.111-12; italics mine]). The courtier's deft riposte is uncharacteristic in Lope: usually on such occasions, as in *Peribáñez,*[63] the *hidalgos,* who are made to look anemic and ridiculous, can come up with no answer to such needling.

In any case, here Bruno and Fileto proceed in crude denunciation of their "deudos," with garbled references to Sodom and Gomorrah (3.115), Easter, Saint John, and the Eucharist (3.121-23). Salvano's salvo concludes, "and you are going to dine with Judas, / in perpetuity, amen ("y vais a cenar con Judas, / por *seculorum amén*" [3.139-40]).

Although, like Marín's rhetoric toward the villagers, the King's rhetoric toward Juan Labrador stresses universal blood ties, the monarch does not intend it to be taken as an insult. In the third act, Ludovico underlines national brotherhood, figuratively inducting Juan Labrador into his own family by, on four occasions, calling the peasant "relative" ("pariente").[64] Such brotherly love is the basis of national well-being, and one of the themes of *The Villano in His Corner* is precisely that. Nevertheless, I should think that no seventeenth-century Spaniard in his right mind watching this play would take consanguinity with this king as a compliment. Popular and literary tradition of the era regard the man of red whiskers as particularly inimical and ill-omened, suggesting, according to Cobarruvias (*Tesoro de la lengua castellana*, 207a), "malicious, extraordinary and harmful cunning" ("agudeza maliciosa, extraordinaria y perjudicial"). Jews, or Christians of suspect blood were in literature often made redheads, since Judas was supposed to have had red hair: the repulsive and miserly Don Cabra in Quevedo's *The Rogue* had "red hair (and that says it all)" ("pelo bermejo [no hay más que decir]").[65] In a letter to a friend, Francisco Cascales grumbled bitterly after having been cheated by a redhead. But he should have expected treachery; after all, classical literature is full of cruel redheads, as well as poisonous animals of that color: "It is common knowledge that people marked by nature are plagued, and God marked them thus so that we would keep away from them. . . . Truly, this color is for executioners and traitors" ("Es voz del pueblo que las personas señaladas por naturaleza vienen apestadas, y que Dios les puso aquellas señales para que nos guardásemos de ellas. . . . Realmente este color es para verdugos y traidores").[66] According to Herrero García, who discusses that trait and blondness (it applies only to men) in Golden Age works of fiction and in particular, the drama,

> From all these cited texts and from many others that I omit, because it would simply repeat the same idea, it is clear that seventeenth-century writers did not distinguish between blond and red hair. Furthermore, it seems that we can infer that the traits of duplicity and fraud were limited to the beard and did not extend to the hair on the head.
>
> (De todos estos textos aducidos y de otros muchos que omito, por ser mera repetición del mismo concepto, se saca en claro que los escritores del siglo XVII no distinguían entre rubio y bermejo. Además, parece que podemos inferir que la condición de doblez y falsía estaba circunscrita a las barbas y no se extendía al cabello de la cabeza.)[67]

The King of France, and Juan Labrador's "pariente," according to *The Villano in His Corner,* is "aquel mancebo rojo," "that young man with the red beard."

Perhaps, then, Lope sets the play in France not only for its topicality and the source material's Gallic origin, but because in its supposedly idealized characters the multitude of "extravagances"—deceitfulness, broken promises, blatant and rewarded social climbing, innuendos of widespread sexual license, avarice, pride in prosperity and spinelessness in adversity, and suspect lineage in king and commoner alike—would amount, despite an apparently happy denouement, to a resounding denunciation of the French character, and would thoroughly discredit this "perfect prince's" (3.490) purportedly wise and just antidote to Juan Labrador's excessive pride. The King's conscription of the highly success-ful farmer, his heirs, and apparently even the servants, off the land and "por *seculorum, amén*" into a life of privilege and luxury at court, makes the children happy, the servants puffed up, and contributes to Juan Labrador's enlightenment. But what does it do for France? The King's solution violates social decorum; more to the point, at the end of the play, Ludovico embarks on what is in effect a catastrophic fiscal policy by depriving the nation of its most valuable asset, the successful and productive farmer, and that farmer's successors as well. The King wrests the landowner from his estates and forces him and his retinue into court. In the third act, Fileto remarks almost in passing what may in fact be a central theme of the play:

> If the gentlemen,
> clerics, and military men didn't need
> so many servants,
> there would be more men to work the land.

> (Si no hobieren los señores
> los clérigos y soldados
> menester tantos criados,
> hubiera más labradores.)
>
> (3.664-67)

If to the rustics in the village, courtiers are "devils" ("diablos" [1.920]), by Juan Labrador's definition, "villano" is "that good man / who lives in a village" ("aquel hombre / bueno, que en la villa vive" [1.295-96]). His daughter's dictionary adds the more modern, negative nuance: "being villagers, these people are malicious" ("como villana [esta gente] es maliciosa" [2.376]). But in act 2, the King understands that Juan is the semantically neutral *labrador,* one who works the land, and a "labrador

. . . es un carro finalmente" (2.112), that is, a sturdy vehicle suited to carrying heavy burdens.[68] "John Farmer" is the archetypal *labrador,* the representative of a class of workers upon whose activity on the land the nation's prosperity rides. In the third act, the King would correct the presumption of his "carro," and he more than succeeds: Juan is terrified, recognizes his error and asks for death by line 845, fully expecting it. Ludovico has made his point, but continues to drive it home, so that the farmer too continues to repeat his super-*desengaño,* that he is about to be killed. The elaborate symbology defining the function of the monarch in this scene is indeed necessary for Juan Labrador's political education, and it would not be thought wasted on a Spanish audience, either. Once this brief "auto sacramental *a lo profano*"[69] is over, however, if this king were truly discreet, he would send the chastened farmer back to work on the land, and his children with him—if France is as economically hard-pressed as the monarch indicated earlier.[70]

Instead, the King's own zeal, which results in the supercorrection of the farmer—upsetting the *carro,* so to speak—leads to unsound fiscal policy, and is perhaps a symptom of some lingering envy of that *villano's* peaceful if unenlightened existence. The society of *The Villano in His Corner* is an unbalanced one. While the dramatist airs both the positive and pejorative definitions of "villager," "courtier," and "king," all in the world of this play are tainted. In the end, Lope celebrates the yoking of commoner and court as the supreme intranational misalliance, which must end in calamity. Fortune's wheel, in the end, *por no hacer mudanza en su costumbre,* is bound to continue on its course.

Making the historical setting vague—misnaming the Infanta, for example, and reducing the royal weddings from two to one[71]—frees *The Villano in His Corner* from direct affront to living, eminent people with whom Spain was involved in, or had just finished, delicate nuptial negotiations. At the same time, locating the action in France leaves Lope freer to criticize, to the likely applause of a francophobic Spanish public. Availing himself of the oral tradition, social mores, and rampant fiscal woes, Lope portrays in the cowardly farmer, his grasping children, and their economically heedless king, no models for future conduct. The *villano* in his corner, together with all his fellow players, displays not heroism, but behavior to be avoided at all costs.

In this play, an apparently sentimental eulogy of the simple, virtuous country life—characteristic of sixteenth-century pastoral—thinly disguises the wry realization that those tired literary clichés no longer satisfy. The Spanish countryside of the early seventeenth century is as blighted and pretentious as the court. *The Villano* collects and twists literary topoi such as the foundling discovered to be of noble blood, the *alabanza de aldea,* the *serranilla,* the inevitable turning of Fortune's wheel, the red beard, and the fear of *conversos* and of the French. It is a deft exposé of the hollowness of some too-well-worn literary devices. At the same time, this work registers dismay over a nation in economic upheaval, partly due to the peasants' abandonment of the land and of manual labor.

Is Lope, then, the complete pessimist? Does Lope repudiate the countryside for its corrupt materialism, and criticize without supplying an alternative? The next play to be examined, *The King, the Greatest Alcalde* — written at least several years after *The Villano in His Corner* — presents a fresh view of and a different solution to many of the literary and economic issues so gloomily raised in the earlier play. *The King, the Greatest Alcalde* also makes it clear that heroism in the countryside is still possible — within some very specific social limits.

"Nobles campos de Galicia"

Calderón's *Life Is a Dream* and Lope's *The Villano in His Corner* hold the peasant in high enough regard to insist on the indispensability of his participation in national affairs. However, both plays impose strict limits on the spheres in which the "vulgo" or "villano" may exercise his rights: the common man must want and have access to his king; but he ought also to conduct himself peacefully, and through established channels of approach.

In the end, both plays also implicitly uphold the conservative social and political principle of *ser quien se es:* the peasant must observe decorum and confine himself to movement on the lower rungs of the social and civic ladders. An emblem of this conservative cosmology in the first play is the rebel soldier's tower-prison; in the second, Lope formulates with Lisarda's riddle a poetic conceit justifying the maintenance of a strict social hierarchy. What is, she asks her friend,

> a member of the upper class who respects his social
> inferior

> without compulsion,
> and an inferior who aspires to reach the upper
> class?

COSTANZA.   A tune played
> with two chords. . . .
> Although they may be tenor and bass, you see,
> and being as unequal
> as night and day,
> that union in harmony
> makes them in their accents, equals;
> for the tenor in its own place sounds
> with the bass, ever equally,
> because if they sounded off their key,
> they would cause considerable grief.

> (¿ . . . un alto, que un bajo estima
> sin fuerza más poderosa,
> y un bajo que al alto aspira?

COSTANZA.   Una música formada
> de dos voces. . . .
> Aunque alto y bajo estén, mira
> que, aunque son tan desiguales
> como la noche y el día,
> aquella unión y armonía
> los hace en su acento iguales;
> que el alto en un punto suena
> con el bajo siempre igual,
> porque si sonaran mal,
> causaran notable pena.)

> (2.171–74; 176–84)

That is, as long as high and low notes occupy their assigned positions, they will make beautiful music together. Either one's deviation from its natural place on the musical scale wrecks their "sweet harmony." It is dramatically ironic that even as she clambers up the social scale, Lisarda never grasps the wit of her own "enima": she would make a poor musician.

Lope raises the issue of misalliance again in *The King, the Greatest Alcalde* (*El mejor alcalde, el rey*), possibly written in the early 1620s,

and first published in 1635.[72] "Alcalde" may be loosely translated as
"mayor and magistrate," although in addition to this preliminary definition *Diccionario de Autoridades* catalogues an imposing seventeen types
of *alcalde*, among them the *Alcalde de Casa, Corte, y Rastro*, who ranks
highest and whose sentence admits no appeal; the *alcalde ordinario*,
and the village *alcalde* (*pedaneo*) (1:176a–78a).

In this case, King Alfonso VII serves in disguise as his own judicial
representative, an *alcalde* (presumably, of the highest grade) who visits
the farthest reaches of his dominions to uphold the law. The play turns
on the archetypal complication, the pursuit of a country girl by a
nobleman intending seduction. The poor, hardworking young Galician
labrador Sancho loves and is loved by Elvira, daughter of Nuño, who
also works the land. Since Nuño cannot afford a dowry, he urges Sancho
to ask the blessing of their feudal lord, the wealthy, powerful, and
reputedly generous Don Tello. Tello and his sister Feliciana bestow a
liberal dowry on the couple and even decide to attend the wedding
ceremony that very day. But the moment Don Tello sets eyes on Elvira
he is stunned, and soon he becomes obsessed with her beauty. He stops
the ceremony and in the night returns with his henchmen to abduct her.
Knowing that as the weaker party it would be futile to attempt a rescue,
and trusting that Don Tello will quickly come to his senses, Sancho and
Nuño quietly appeal to the aristocrat in the morning. They are, however,
beaten back by his squirely retainers.

Nuño now insists that Sancho go to the king, Alfonso VII, who at
present holds court in León. Sancho, accompanied by the rustic clown
Pelayo, reluctantly assents, although he does not believe that a king
would bother with the problems of a poor farmer. However, the monarch
declares that it is precisely the poor man who needs him the most. He
listens to Sancho's complaint, struck by the young man's sensibility
and bearing. Alfonso draws up for Sancho a letter to take back to Don
Tello ordering Elvira's release, while he regales Pelayo with a purse of
doubloons.

When Don Tello still refuses to free the girl, who has thus far managed to fend off his advances, Sancho returns to the King. Incensed at
the disobedience of his vassal, Alfonso himself hurries to Galicia in his
alcalde-disguise. There he conducts an investigation and confronts the
recalcitrant aristocrat, but too late to prevent the rape of Elvira. The
King commands Don Tello's execution after the culprit has first been
forced to restore Elvira's honor by marrying her. The victim will conse-

quently inherit Don Tello's title together with half of his estate, and be free to marry Sancho. For Tello's apparently orphaned sister Feliciana, the King will arrange a suitable match at court.

Lope concludes the play by firmly anchoring it in its historical context: Sancho turns to the public to explain that *The Greatest Alcalde* is

> a story
> whose truth is verified
> by the fourth part
> of the chronicle of Spain.
> (187)

> (historia
> que afirma por verdadera
> la corónica de España:
> la cuarta parte de la cuenta.)
> (3.2407–10)[73]

The reference is to the *Primera crónica general*, commissioned during the reign of Alphonse X, the Wise.[74] The tale of the confrontation between Alphonse VII ("the Emperor") and the willful nobleman had become legendary. It is the subject of Lorenzo de Sepúlveda's ballad beginning "The Emperor Alphonse / was living in Toledo" ("El emperador Alfonso / En Toledo residía"),[75] which closely follows the *PCG* account. In chronicle and ballad, "Don Fernando" has deprived an unnamed *labrador* not of his bride, but of his *heredad* (property); no *comedia* can do without a romantic complication, and the love story is Lope's most important modification. In the earlier accounts, the nobleman is executed solely for his defiance of and disrespect for the King, who, as Robin Carter points out, is given a "faintly hagiographical" character.[76] Indeed, Alphonse VII (1124–57) was held in unanimously high regard in Spanish oral and written traditions.[77]

While the action of *The King, the Greatest Alcalde* flows from a stock dramatic situation, and is further bound by a proximate fidelity to historical circumstance, this work remains charmingly unique in its finely drawn and well-rounded characters, and contains some of the loveliest and wittiest of Lope's verses. Pelayo is not only a source of humor, but like the best of Golden Age *graciosos*, he plays a key role for understanding the other figures on the stage. This peasant bears the

venerable and "Old Christian" name of several saints and a king of
Asturias descended from the Goths who was popularly credited with
beginning the Reconquest of the Peninsula in the eighth century. Pelayo
takes Elvira's insults for flattery, reveres the pigs in his charge, and
accompanies Sancho to see Don Tello and later the King. He gives
delightful voice to that topos of rustic *desengaño* that court and King are
accessible and human. Anticipating the first journey to León, he expects
to see streets paved with bacon and eggs, and at first believes the King
an angel (146, 152; 2.1230–31, 2.1398–99). Pelayo's foolishness high-
lights to the King—and to the audience of the play—Sancho's contrasting
dignity: Alfonso remarks to himself,

> How curious a pair that land has joined,
> One being so wise, the other such a fool!
> (155)

> (¡Qué dos hombres peregrinos
> aquella tierra juntó!
>   Aquél con tal condición
> y éste con tanta ignorancia.)
>   (2.1479–82)

Pelayo's reverse-apotheosis of the King is a comic variation of Sancho's
new appreciation of a monarch's duty to his subjects.

Pelayo also assists in the delineation of Don Tello's character. At the
beginning of *The Greatest Alcalde,* the clown rehearses for the audience the proper reaction of a spurned suitor. He would like to marry
Elvira, but upon her engagement to Sancho, his change of heart is
instantaneous: "Good heavens, [Sancho's] going to marry Elvira. / This
is where I leave off; my love is suspended" (113) ("Voto al sol que se casa
con Elvira. / Aquí la dejo yo; mi amor se muda" [1.210–11]). The
prompt *desengaño* contrasts with Don Tello's intransigence later; even
his squire Celio once loved Elvira, but got over her when it was clear she
did not correspond (123; 1.513).

When Don Tello arrives at Nuño's home for the wedding, he is
curious about the identities of the peasants attending. The first he calls
"serrana," and it is clear thanks to Pelayo's constant interruptions and
commentary that the *caballero*'s interest is confined to the women. That
the *bufón* again tries to answer for the peasants during the King's

investigation in act 3 emphasizes the fundamental disparity in the two inquiries: Alfonso, who wants to learn the truth about the crime, is businesslike and questions the witnesses without regard to their gender.[78]

Still, in the beginning Don Tello comes across as a decent and generous man; it is these kinds of subtle hints laid by the playwright that indicate a darker side to his character. Our first glimpse of the nobleman shows him discussing the merits of hunting, an activity that conventionally in the *comedia* foreshadows the pursuit of a woman.[79] In *The Villano in His Corner*, King Ludovico's hunting trip led to his encounter with Juan Labrador's way of life and to the flirtation with Lisarda. In *The Abduction of Dinah* (*El robo de Dina*), Lope's *serranilla*-type play based on the biblical episode, Siquen's opening soliloquy praises the virtues of the chase.[80] In the mythological *comedia* by Lope, *The Tale of Perseus, or the Beautiful Andromeda* (*Fábula de Perseo o la bella Andrómeda*), two similar episodes occur; and in *Fuenteovejuna*, the Comendador who terrorizes the village women avails himself of the metaphors of hunting. In all but the last example, the hunters are at least at first, good and blameless men.

Early in *The Greatest Alcalde* Don Tello's sister Feliciana also worries at his lack of interest in marrying. He explains that no one in the region is his social equal, although like Otón in *The Villano in His Corner*, he too has had some experience pursuing *serranas:* enough to know that while some of them are truly beautiful, "they are so disdainful / that their prudery wearies me" (123) ("son tan desdeñosas, / que sus melindres me cansan" [1.519–20]). Despite, then, what were probably originally good intentions, Don Tello's figurative fall when he sets eyes on Elvira will seem wholly within character. And from now on, to him his victims are no longer "labradores," but "villanos."

If Don Tello's unrelenting siege on Elvira exposes the submerged flaw in his character, it also constitutes the ultimate proof of her virtue. Not only is Elvira chaste in reputation, but unlike the women in *The Villano in His Corner*, in demonstrated fact as well. She prefers life with Sancho over wealth and the vanities of the courtly life.[81] Her gentle jesting with her sweetheart at the beginning of *The Greatest Alcalde* shows the earlier play's Lisarda to have been all the more mercenary in her climb up the social ladder. *The Greatest Alcalde*'s opening duet, where lover and beloved seek each other out in the *locus amoenus* of Galicia's paradoxically "noble fields" (107) ("nobles campos" [1.1]), evokes Solomon's epithalamion to his own lovely shepherd-maiden. And the site

of Elvira's tragedy calls forth another fabled outrage in Spanish literature:
Don Tello finally carries her off to a forest,

> where only
> a dense tangle of trees, which
> kept the sun
> from joining it as witness,
> could listen
> to my sorrowful cries.
> (184)

> (donde sólo
> la arboleda espesa,
> que al sol no dejaba
> que testigo fuera,
> escuchar podía
> mis tristes endechas.)
> (3.2317–22)

Thus Elvira relives the Corpes outrage, where the Cid's innocent
daughters— Elvira and Sol—suffered the abuse of their nobler husbands,
later to have their justice under the auspices of the grandfather of this
play's monarch.

It is true that Elvira agrees to an assignation with Sancho after Don
Tello has stopped the ceremony. That night, expecting her betrothed, by
mistake she opens the door to Don Tello's men, who carry her off;
Halkhoree cites this circumstance as the defect in her character and
Sancho's that contributes to their tragedy.[82] In fact, one issue that Lope
appears to skirt—or handle with deliberate ambiguity—is the nuptial
status of the lovers at the time of Don Tello's crime. The culprit's refrain,
which he recites in justification of his extreme behavior, is that the
offense is really not so grave and Sancho has no right to object as the
couple was not yet married (135, 143, 157, 183; 2.886, 1109, 1542–43,
1546–48, 3.2275). "Courtship does not constitute matrimony," as Nuño,
on the point of firing his incompetent swineherd, reminds Pelayo ("El
servir no es casamiento" [1.128]).[83] Sancho and Elvira do consider
themselves wed, nevertheless.[84]

The confusion arises from the differences in canon law of the Middle
Ages, when the play takes place, and that of the seventeenth century,

when the play was written. Until the Council of Trent's Tametsi decree (1563), secret marriages were held valid. Other Golden Age *comedias* also make an issue of secret marriage; for example, in Tirso de Molina's *The Trickster of Seville* (*El burlador de Sevilla*) (by 1625), which is set in the fourteenth century, the peasant girl Aminta is fully and publicly confident of being Don Juan Tenorio's wife even though there has been no ceremony. The Tametsi decree, however, states that for a marriage to be valid, a priest must preside over the wedding, with at least two witnesses in attendance.[85] At the end of *The Greatest Alcalde,* and despite there having been no consummation, the King asserts that it is enough simply that the couple intended to marry (183; 3.2276), even though Alfonso claims to respond to the father's complaint, not Sancho's, and no divorce proceedings appear necessary before Don Tello will be forced to wed Elvira.

In any case, Elvira's (and Sancho's) "flaw" — if it be that — is a comparatively minor one and understandable in light of the circumstances. The two clearly love each other with all their hearts. Sancho responds to the abduction of his bride with great, almost suicidal intensity, yet he always manages, often with Nuño's good counsel, to refrain from rash action against the offender or against himself, which adds to the ignoble effect of Don Tello's uncontrolled frenzy. Also unlike his adversary, Sancho always resorts to peaceful and legal recourse. He may undertake his first embassy to the King reluctantly, but once he has "touched with his own hand" Alfonso's worth, Sancho understands that he can indeed expect justice from his king. Now sensible of his own rights and the King's integrity, the young farmer needs no urging to apply to Alfonso the second time. However, before returning to the court he first exhausts all reasonable alternatives available, seeking the intercession of the local priest, and then the abbot. It is only when these measures fail to move Don Tello that Sancho again approaches the King. The play portrays its hero as a sort of David whose weapon against the giant is the law: Lope makes the biblical allusion on two occasions in a way that associates Tello both with Goliath, and the disordered and ill-fated "[Saul], when he wanted to kill [David]" (153) ("[Saul], cuando a [David] matar quería" [2.1414]).[86] Like Saul, Don Tello is a good man destroyed by passion.

It is also worth noting that throughout the ordeal, Sancho's faith in Elvira never wavers. He may be furious with jealousy of Tello, but he never doubts Elvira's virtue or blames her in any way for inciting the

lord's heinous behavior. Sancho maintains from the beginning a lyrical
dignity and integrity. His opening apostrophe to the "nobles campos" of
Galicia is a highly accomplished rhetorical reconciliation of country and
court, a conceit in fact underlying all of Sancho's attitudes. You noble
fields, he sings, in a series of metaphors which juxtapose both ways of
life without detracting from either,

> [that] nurture the militia
> of flowers of a thousand hues;
> you birds who trill of love,
> you beasts that roam without government,
> have you ever seen such tender love [as mine]
> in bird, beast, or flower?
>
> > (107)

> ([que] dais sustento a la milicia
> de flores de mil colores;
> aves que cantáis amores,
> fieras que andáis sin gobierno,
> ¿habéis visto amor más tierno
> en aves, fieras y flores?)
>
> > (1.5-10)

Sancho explains to Don Tello that he may be mere country folk, but the
refinement of his soul is noble. In word and in person, Sancho constitutes a successful poetic misalliance of the best of two opposing ways of
life. He is a modest, hardworking farmer of distinguished sensibilities,
noble in spirit without greed for the trappings of nobility. He hesitates to
approach his lord for a dowry because, to this gallant lover, the material
is immaterial; Elvira's virtue is dower enough (113; 1.215-16).

Sancho's guiding spirit and companion in worth and tribulation is his
future father-in-law. Nuño is the voice of reason; he understands what
humble people have a right to expect from lord and king. A good father,
he makes certain that Elvira wants the marriage to Sancho before
consenting to it himself (113; 1.184). At only one point, when he steals
an interview with Elvira where she is being held, does he believe or
claim to believe her lost; it is inconceivable that a woman subjected to
such relentless pressure in captivity could resist the determination of her
persecutor:

How well you preserve your honor, that rich dower
Handed down from your ancestors, when you have
So quickly shattered its priceless essence!
Let her who has so disgracefully accounted for herself
Call me father no more,
Because a daughter so wretched—
And I do not overstate my case—
Only has one claim upon a father:
That he spill her blood.

(167)

(¡Bien el honor heredado
de tus pasados guardaste,
pues que tan presto quebraste
su cristal tan estimado!
Quien tan mala cuenta ha dado
de sí, padre no me llame;
porque hija tan infame
[y no es mucho que esto diga],
solamente a un padre obliga
a que su sangre derrame.)
(3.1807-16)

Despite such a ferocious greeting, Elvira does not need to insist much that her virtue remains intact; after all, she is Nuño's daughter, and "From you perforce springs that nobility / Which I proudly repay" (167) ("es fuerza haber heredado / la nobleza que te doy" [3.1824-26]). He accepts her word instantly and they change the subject. Obviously, the talk of spilling her blood was a rhetorical ploy intended to elicit reassurance, to the audience as much as to the father. It was never meant as a serious threat, as it often is in other "honor" plays, beginning with Torres Naharro's prototypical *Comedia Himenea.*[87] This brief exchange underlines her goodness and his concern for her.

In *The Greatest Alcalde,* then, does Lope draw his heroes from an idealized peasant class? Apart from the King, in humanity, dignity, and sheer quality, Sancho, Nuño, and Elvira tower above all the other characters in the play. The natural sophistication that distinguishes them from the other rustics, including Juana and especially Pelayo, is emphasized by the latters' simplicity, sometimes crude humor, and *sayagués* dialect. The three certainly possess more integrity than Tello and the *hidalgos* serving him, although Celio is eventually pricked by conscience. In what may have been Lope's last rustic honor play, the main characters are truly admirable *labradores,* and with typical insight the dramatist has made them human, too. In short, these people could never be classed with the *vulgo* of *Life Is a Dream* or the *villanos* of *The Villano in His Corner.*

However, when Nuño observes that Sancho is "noble and well-born" (114) ("noble y bien nacido" [1.226]), he refers not only to the young man's character. Sancho's parents may have been poor farmers (111; 1.158), but his father never served a lord (119; 1.412–13). If he is able to treat Elvira with "the steadfastness of the laborer" but "the devotion of the courtier" (124) ("firmezas de labrador" but "amores de cortesano" [1.569–70]); if he is "in the passion of the heart a lord" (140) ("en el gusto del alma caballero" [2.1032]); if on occasion he "wields the bright shining sword" (140) ("jueg[a] al limpio acero" [2.1034]), it is because, as he reveals to the King, "I am an hidalgo, / albeit well-ravaged by the whims of fortune" (151) ("yo soy hidalgo, / si bien pobre en mudanzas de la fortuna" [2.1361–62]). He wishes to marry his equal, and indeed she is: Nuño may work the land now, Sancho declares,

> but he can point to the emblazoned shields
> upon the now-faded scutcheons of his door,
> and still retains with them from that proud time
> some lances.
>
> (119)

> (pero . . . aún tiene paveses
> en las ya borradas armas
> de su portal, y con ellas,
> de aquel tiempo algunas lanzas.)
>
> (1.419–22)

Learning that Don Tello will attend the wedding, Nuño is determined to show him "that I am *something,* or I was" (124; italics mine) ("que soy *algo,* o lo fui" [1.578]). According to Cobarruvias, "hidalgo" "means the same as noble, of pure blood and ancient lineage; and to be a son of something ['algo'], which is nobility" ("equivale a noble, castizo, y de antigüedad de linage, y el ser hijo de algo, que es la nobleza" [*Tesoro de*

la lengua castellana, 590b]) The seventeenth-century philologist believes
that the word *hidalgo* proceeds either from "hijo de algo"—son of
something—or "filgod"—son of the Goths:

> [A]fter the loss of Spain [to the Moors], very few nobles descended
> from the previously reigning Goths remained, and those that did
> survive saved themselves by withdrawing to the mountains, and
> afterwards little by little they went about recovering [Spain].
> And those who traced their origin to the Goths were very much
> esteemed.

> ([D]espués de la pérdida de España quedaron poquíssimos nobles
> de los godos que reynavan en ella, y éstos recogiéndose a las
> montañas se salvaron, y fueron después poco a poco recobrándola.
> Y aquellos que trahían origen de los godos eran muy estimados.)
> (591b)

If in the twelfth-century setting of this play Nuño's emblazoned shield is
so timeworn, we are entitled to believe that the lineage of the *hidalgo*-
heroes is ancient and venerable, indeed. That even the peasant swineherd in Nuño's employ is the namesake of an Old Christian hero crowns
the unassailability of this rustic community.

In Elvira's climactic speech to the King in the third act, effectively
summing up the plot to that point, she might be expected to make an
issue of class differences between herself and Don Tello: that the lord
attacked and abused the rights of his defenseless inferiors. Instead, in
her account the culprit's advantage is in strength and numbers alone.
Except for a mention of Sancho's service to Tello, the social disparity is
effaced as she introduces the principal players in the drama by their full
names:

> I am the daughter of Nuño
> *of Aibar* . . .
> In love with me was
> Sancho *of Roelas;* . . .
> Sancho . . . served
> Tello *of Neira.*
>
> (183)

(Hija soy de Nuño
de Aibar . . .
Amor me tenía
Sancho *de Roelas;* . . .
Sancho . . . servía
a Tello *de Neira.*)
(3.2289–90, 2293–94,
2297–98; italics mine)

Sancho, Nuño, and Elvira exhibit such nobility of bearing and sentiment precisely because they *are* of noble blood, a circumstance that modern critics of the work, with the exception of José María Díez Borque,[88] overlook or underplay. Sancho, Nuño, and Elvira are not idealized peasants but idealized *hidalgos: hijos de algo,* descendants of bluebloods, a condition that is unobtrusively reiterated throughout *The Greatest Alcalde.* Lope's creations, hailing from a social class rarely commended in Golden Age fiction, are therefore all the more extraordinary: if the "poor *hidalgo*" is a tautological expression, the productive *hidalgo* amounts to a dramatic oxymoron; it is almost unheard of in fiction for a member of that class actually to make himself useful. Here, although their fortunes have declined, they are not ashamed to earn their livings honestly by working with their hands; indeed, they are proud to do so and have no driving aspiration to recover the wealth and power their ancestors lost.

Michael D. McGaha observes that

> [t]he conflict between love and materialism is an obsessive theme in the work of Lope de Vega, especially in the early period of his career. It seems to have originated in the profound resentment, bordering on madness, that Lope felt when Elena Osorio, his lover for five years, jilted him, letting herself be seduced by another man who was rich and powerful.

> (El conflicto entre amor y materialismo es un tema obsesivo en la obra de Lope, sobre todo en la primera época de su carrera. Parece haber originado en el profundo resentimiento, bordando en locura, que sintió Lope cuando Elena Osorio, su amante durante cinco años, le dejó plantado, dejándose seducir por otro amante rico y poderoso.)[89]

The governing impulse in Juan Labrador's children, and parodied in their servants, was precisely this type of materialism. The truly idealized characters in *The Greatest Alcalde* may be appropriately grateful for Don Tello's wedding gifts, but these things are never their chief concern.[90] Theirs is a genuine love that transcends worldly considerations and that will benefit the realm, as Alphonse VII's great historical success testifies. Ironically but happily, they will be restored to the rank and wealth that must once have been theirs, or their ancestors': Sancho will marry a rich, titled widow, in another faint echo of the *Poem of the Cid.*

Much has been made of the King's delay in arriving ex León to put things right: Halkhoree ("El arte de Lope de Vega," 39) and Carter ("History and Poetry," 193) criticize that after Alfonso's investigation, he lunches while Don Tello finally overcomes the exhausted Elvira. Here, and with the ambiguous treatment of the marital status of the lovers, I think Lope sacrifices Elvira's honor—with every intention of making up for it afterwards—to an artistic good. In order to justify poetically a marriage between Tello and Elvira, the former must actually have carried out the grave offense against her. To justify the additional penalty of the death sentence, Tello must have committed a further, commensurate crime. Like Don Fernando in the historical tradition, by defying the King's written order and usurping kingly prerogatives for himself—Tello reigns hereabouts, he declares (159; 2.1582-83)—the powerful lord has signed his own death warrant. He has offended both the private and the public sectors. Now Lope is free to reinvest his working aristocrats with the prestige and estates to match their merit, with the marriage and the execution. Had Sancho and Elvira been anything beyond figuratively wedded, this neat resolution would have been preempted.

It ought also to be kept in mind that the King has made a hurried journey on short notice from León to Galicia. Upon his arrival in the morning, although he has probably travelled through the night, he declines to rest and insists on undertaking the inquiry immediately (175) ("presto" [3.2066]). He has Sancho's testimony already, but speaks to the other *labradores.* Brito's account may be hearsay (176; 3.2078-80), but Fileno was an eyewitness to the interruption of the wedding, and his report confirms Sancho's complaint:

> Sir, I came to play music
> And I saw that Don Tello ordered

The priest not to come in.
The wedding cancelled,
He carried Elvira away to his house,
Where her father and her kin
Have seen her.

(176)

(Señor, yo vine a tañer,
y vi que mandó don Tello
que no entrara el señor cura.
El matrimonio deshecho,
se llevó a su casa a Elvira,
donde su padre y sus deudos
la han visto.)

(3.2093–99)

As the audience would know, all speak the truth. The attending Count
makes it a point that the King has more than satisfied any doubts that
could have arisen:

With less testimony than this
You could well be assured
That Sancho has not deceived you,
Because the guilelessness of these folk
Is the most convincing proof.

(177)

(Con menos información
pudieras tener por cierto
que no te ha engañado Sancho,
porque la inocencia déstos
es la prueba más bastante.)

(3.2115–19)

King Alfonso has acted as scrupulously correctly as any magistrate in a
Lope play might ever be expected to. It is only now that he agrees to eat
and rest so that in the afternoon he can pay that all-important—legally
and politically—visit to the wayward vassal. The King is not as Carter
implies ("History and Poetry," 197) the only one to call himself the

"greatest alcalde" (165; 3.1776): the words are also Elvira's (185; 3.2339), and at the end of the play, Sancho repeats them (187; 3.2407). And Don Tello admits guiltily, twice (183, 186; 3.2279–80, 2370–73), that he more than deserves his fate.

Lope communicates several messages, explicit and implicit, in *The King, the Greatest Alcalde*. As the title indicates, and as the characters' reiteration of the phrase affirms, a king's personal involvement in matters of justice is of utmost importance. Monarchs of the twelfth century were beginning to consolidate their power at the expense of feudal lords; Alfonso's action in neutralizing Tello is therefore both historically accurate and politically shrewd. At the time of this play's composition in the seventeenth century, such a demonstrated flair for controlling subordinates would be of interest to those in the public concerned with the undue influence of favorites (*privados*) on their own king, Philip IV. Both he and his father had been weak kings falling ever more under the influence of the powerful Gaspar de Guzmán, the count-duke of Olivares.[91] The excessive power of this councillor and the duke of Lerma and Rodrigo Calderón before him had been such a prominent current topic that it gave birth to a subgenre of *comedias de privanza*.[92] *The King, the Greatest Alcalde*, then, dramatically suggests that a sovereign assert himself forcefully over presumptuous subordinates.

Furthermore, in this play as in *The Villano in His Corner*, Lope himself may be seen to continue in the role of *arbitrista:* by idealizing *hidalgos* and putting them to work, he opens dramatically another avenue for the revitalization of the economy. Although at the end Tello's sister Feliciana is sent off to court,[93] we have every reason to believe that these truly honorable aristocrats will remain on the land they love, and devote themselves to its cultivation. The heroes of *The Greatest Alcalde* are, in no sense of the term, *villanos*.

Chapter 3

LOPE'S PEASANT HONOR PLAYS

A Preface to *Peribáñez*

The seventeenth-century Spanish *comedia*, like Shakespeare's drama, usurps some of the prerogatives of epic poetry by its use of verse; by defiance of the classical restrictions on time, place, and action; and on occasion by appropriating subjects that have entered the domain of the "absolute past."[1] Whether it is, like the epic, basically a conservative social artifact remains a subject of controversy.[2]

The *comedias* examined thus far—Calderón's *Life Is a Dream* and Lope de Vega's *The Villano in His Corner* and *The King, the Greatest Alcalde*—like many plays by Shakespeare and Corneille, also place the hero or a major character in conflict with his king. At least in *Life Is a Dream,* the confrontation leads to civil war and a new regime, but one retaining the previous social if not political institutions—the old hierarchy—

wholly intact. The rights of Segismundo, like those of the dispossessed Orestes, Odysseus, and Hamlet (and the Cid) are not protected by a concerned higher authority; therefore he is free, or appropriates the liberty, to act, with only conscience to govern his behavior. "Shakespeare's characters," Hegel writes,

> do not all belong to the princely class and remain partly on historical and no longer on mythical ground, but they are there-fore transferred to the times of the civil wars in which the bonds of law and order are relaxed or broken, and therefore they acquire again the required independence and self-reliance. (*Aesthetics*, 192–93)

Yet the Cid, having the power to make his own law, throws his support provisionally behind his weak king and allows the legal apparatus the opportunity to operate. With its success, both the hero and the King, not to mention the kingdom, emerge enhanced. Hegel goes on to note (193) that in "today's" society our need and indeed the option to act heroically are reduced as we have judges and kings to admit appeal. The rebel soldier in Calderón's play makes the mistake of continuing to proceed under a civil-war mentality after hostilities have ceased: he fails to recognize that the inauguration of the new government signifies that the rules of the game have changed—or rather, that they have become enforceable.

Juan Labrador on the other hand was so quick to flee the kingly presence because he did guess (and envy) its ultimately incontestable power over him. Both *The Villano in His Corner* and *The King, the Greatest Alcalde* are contests of will with royalty, but that higher power in these two plays does exist, is fully confident of itself, and is prepared to insist on submission to its own ascendancy. Nuño knows this; Sancho learns it to his own good fortune; and Don Tello too has to concede it in the end. Tello, like Juan Labrador and the rebel soldier, challenges or impinges on the prerogative of majesty and finally has to pay, in another postepic conclusion that resolutely validates the standing royal authority.

Sancho is a courageous and passionate man who manages at the same time to fulfill the Christian heroic ideal by repudiating violence and appealing to ecclesiastical and worldly hierarchies to resolve his dilemma. He obtains his revenge (or better, his justice) through legal, peaceful channels. In *The Abduction of Dinah* (1615–22),[3] Jacob is willing to allow Siquen to restore the offended family's honor in marrying Dinah; he explains, "for revenge is a barbarity in wise men / when offenses have [other] remedies" ("que la venganza es bárbara en los sabios / cuando tienen remedio los agravios" [44a]). According to Edward Glaser, "In [Jacob's] scale of values, prudence and patience, paired with trust in God, take precedence over the worldly ideal of honor" ("Lope de Vega's *El robo de Dina,*" 333). Glaser points out that Lope departs from the biblical source by making Jacob's sons feel remorse following their revenge. In the play's final scene, realizing their own culpability, they ask and receive forgiveness of a visiting angel (50b). "This detail," Glaser writes, "seemingly reflects Lope's distaste for the treachery and bloodthirstiness of Jacob's sons; the blessing they eventually wrest from the angel is more a reluctant recognition of a *fait accompli* than a reward for a deed pleasing to God" (333).

In the early 1620s, or roughly contemporaneously with his composition of *The Abduction of Dinah,* Lope wrote the *Novellas for Marcia Leonarda* (*Novelas a Marcia Leonarda*), a series of narrative prose fictions on the order of Cervantes's *Exemplary Novels.* "Marcia Leonarda" was the poetic name for Lope's lover, Marta de Nevares, during that later period of his life. The stories are discursive, and the narrator given to commentary on the events he relates. One tale in the collection, *The Prudent Revenge (La prudente venganza),* has commanded particular attention because of a passage in which the narrator comments on violent revenge. After describing a tragic tale of love and adultery that ends in the husband's murders of his wife and her paramour, the narrator remarks to his narratee,

> I have always been of the opinion that the blot on the honor of the offended man cannot be cleansed with the blood of the offender, because what already occurred cannot be undone, and it is folly to believe that by killing the offender the offense is removed: what in fact happens is that the insulted man remains insulted, and the other, dead, satisfying the desire for vengeance, but not the requirements of honor, which in order to be perfect must not be offended. Who doubts that someone will immediately object to this argument? Well, even if the objection is tacit, I answer that the offense must neither be suffered nor punished. Then, what should one do? What a man does when any other type of misfortune befalls him: leave his home, live far away

where he is not known and turn in his affliction to God, keeping in mind that the same thing would have happened to him had he been called to account for any of the injuries he has done others. For to wish that those he has hurt suffer him, but he not suffer anyone in his turn, makes no sense. I say suffer, refrain from violent retribution, because merely for taking away one's honor, which is a vanity of this world, one will be taking [the offender] from God, if [his] soul is lost to Him.

(He sido de parecer siempre que no se lava bien la mancha de la honra del agraviado con la sangre del que le ofendió, porque lo que fue no puede dejar de ser, y es desatino creer que se quita, porque se mate el ofensor, la ofensa del ofendido: lo que hay en esto es que el agraviado se queda con su agravio, y el otro, muerto, satisfaciendo los deseos de la venganza, pero no las calidades de la honra, que para ser perfecta no ha de ser ofendida. ¿Quién duda que está ya la objeción a este argumento dando voces? Pues, aunque tácita, respondo que no se ha de sufrir ni castigar. Pues ¿qué medio se ha de tener? El que un hombre tiene cuando le ha sucedido otro cualquiera género de desdicha: perder la patria, vivir fuera de ella donde no le conozcan y ofrecer a Dios aquella pena, acordándose que le pudiera haber sucedido lo mismo si en alguno de los agravios que ha hecho a otros le hubieran castigado. Que querer que los que agravió le sufran a él y él no sufrir a nadie, no está puesto en razón: digo sufrir, dejar de matar violentamente, pues por sólo quitarle a él la honra, que es una vanidad del mundo, quiere él quitarles a Dios, si se les pierde el alma.)[4]

The *novela*'s opinion in favor of turning the other cheek, which Juan Bautista Avalle-Arce points out is foreshadowed in Lope's 1604 Byzantine-type romance *The Pilgrim in His Own Homeland* (*El peregrino en su patria*),[5] is often characterized as a private sentiment not applying to Lope's public theater, a medium that must cater to less refined tastes. Its nonviolence is suited to quiet reading in the intimacy of an educated, good Catholic's study and would be rejected by the raucous crowd in the *corral* that craves the satisfaction of revenge. Lope's statement seems entirely incompatible with his "honor plays," a number of which end very bloodily, and in Donald R. Larson's words, "on a note of unequivocal rightness."[6]

Larson offers the most succinct definition of the term "honor play," following Aristotle and Francis Fergusson:[7] it is an "'action' whose object is to regain 'honor' that has been lost through an offense of some sort" (*The Honor Plays of Lope de Vega*, 1). Generally involved are two men and one woman; usually she is married to one of the men, who comes to perceive himself offended by her adultery or the possibility of it. The "action" frequently consists in killing the parties who cause the offense. Among the most widely discussed Golden Age "dramas de honor" are Calderón's *Secret Vengeance for a Secret Insult; The Painter of His Own Dishonor;* and *The Physician of His Honor.* In the first two cases the husband kills both his wife and the other man; in *The Physician* the offending intruder, being a prince, is exempt from revenge; therefore the woman alone dies. In all three of these plays, the husband's violent resolution is approved after the fact by the prevailing royal authority; and although in *Secret Vengeance* the wife does finally plan to have an affair, in all three plays at the time of their deaths, the wives are innocent.

Many scholars now detect a dramatic irony in the denouements which condemns as unchristian the murders of Leonor, Serafina, and Mencía; Calderón is no longer held on a moral par with his wife-murderers. By the same token, it is understood that the rulers who approve of revenge to restore honor in these plays are—reminiscent of the tradition of flawed monarchy found in epic poetry—seriously mistaken. This critical reinterpretation of the plays' moral stance has developed since the 1930s, and owes in part to pioneering studies by the British Hispanists E. M. Wilson and Alexander A. Parker.[8] We have, however, withheld from Lope de Vega a similar concession of moral accountability in favor of our admiration for spontaneity, for lyricism, and paradoxically for a democratic heart beating in the most politically absolutist and socially hierarchical of breasts—depending on whether we read Salomon or Díez Borque. The ferocious conclusions of "honor dramas" by Lope tend still, although no longer unanimously,[9] to be taken (as Larson does) at face value, as bearing the playwright's own approval.

Larson's important book studies the honor plays according to the three phases into which Lope's career is customarily divided. The early (pre-1600) *comedias* of this type tend to blame the protagonist for bringing on his own dishonor. Since the "other man" is not therefore a complete villain, he is not killed, and the play ends on a happy note—in true comedy. And as Lope repeatedly involved himself with married women, and his own life (as Alan S. Trueblood has ably shown) so often enters into his art,[10] Larson suggests quite plausibly that the dramatist treats the rival sympathetically because the playwright identifies with the adulterer. In *The Markets of Madrid* (*Las ferias de Madrid*) (1585–88),[11] the "heroic" husband is so insufferable that the play turns into farce and at the end his father-in-law (named "Belardo") kills him with a sword-thrust "through the buttocks" ("por las nalgas"), leaving the lovers free to marry after a respectable period of mourning. Such a resolution may well be, as Larson suggests, the height in Lope's "wish-fulfillment fantasy."[12]

For Larson, the second epoch really begins with *The Comendadores of Córdoba* (*Los comendadores de Córdoba*), written by 1598 according to Morley and Bruerton (44). Here Lope makes no excuse for the pair of offenders, and at the end the husband takes a brutal revenge which is approved by King Fernando.[13] Larson nominates *The Comendadores* as the prototype for the honor plays of Lope's middle period, which lasts until roughly 1620. During this phase in Larson's view the dramatist moves toward romance, producing his masterpieces *Peribáñez and the Comendador of Ocaña* (1605–13) and *Fuenteovejuna* (1611–18). These two works, like *The Villano in His Corner* and *The King, the Greatest Alcalde,* are counted among those physiocratic writings meant to idealize rural life partly for economic reasons. Both *Peribáñez* and *Fuenteovejuna* can, again, be viewed as *serranilla*-type tales, in which innocent peasant women become prey, in Larson's words, to the "monster-like antagonists of the 'pure' forms of romance" (94). These are noblemen, like Don Tello, running amok; in the end they die at the hands of peasants in what Larson describes as "murders [which] are all acts of positive value" (113).

In the later honor plays, however, *To Persist to the Death* (*Porfiar hasta morir*) (1624–28) and *Punishment without Revenge* (*El castigo sin venganza*) (1631), Lope "retreat[s] from romance" (162) and revives sympathy for the adulterous victims of vengeance. Larson finds the middle plays' inclination to romance "fascinating" (161), considering the early ones' charity toward the interloper and the 1624 denunciation of revenge in the *Novellas for Marcia Leonarda,* where authorial sympathy also obviously lies with the lovers.[14] I would add as well that it was during the middle period (1614–16) that Lope took up holy orders and attempted to renounce worldly ties; it is then fascinating that he would support violent retribution while he himself was struggling so hard against his own passions in order to imitate Christ.

One characteristic of the generic "honor drama" is precisely the struggle with conscience, not only or always on the part of the adulterer, but in the husband's mind. According to the so-called honor code, an offense had to be blotted out with an extreme gesture of recompense on the part of the culprit. For example, a rapist or seducer should either marry the girl, or die. When his victim or partner was already married, the only option was the second, and often for the woman as well, whether or not the intended offense had actually been carried out. Not infrequently, then, the avenging husband in these plays feels compelled by social convention, as Francisco Ayala puts it, "atrociously [to] do violence to his own feelings" ("violenta[r] atrozmente sus propios senti-mientos").[15] Some of the most poignant scenes in the honor drama show the husband's inner struggle, as he meditates in soliloquies on the socially prescribed course of action, and protests against this code that drives him to revenge despite his Christian inclinations. Nevertheless, in drama if not necessarily in real life, a man valued his good name on a par with life itself: in his seminal study of Spanish honor, Américo Castro cites Alphonse X's medieval pronouncement,

> According to the wise men who made the ancient laws, two transgressions are equally grave: killing a man and defaming him; for the man, after being defamed, even if he is not at fault, is dead with respect to honor in this world; and moreover, the defamation may be such that he would be better off dead than alive.

> ([S]egund dixeron los sabios que fizieron las leyes antiguas, dos yerros son como yguales, matar al ome e enfamarlo de mal; porque el ome, despues que es enfamado, maguer non aya culpa, muerto es quanto al bien e a la honrra deste mundo; e demás, tal podría ser el enfamamiento que mejor le sería la muerte que la vida.)[16]

C. A. Jones points out (202) that by the seventeenth century in Spain such an extreme view of honor was regarded, at least by many writers, as an anachronism. Nevertheless, Curtis Brown Watson maintains in his discussion of honor in Shakespeare that

> Honor as man's most precious possession, honor as the reward of
> virtue, honor as the ensign of virtue, honor as the testimony of
> the good opinion of others, and dishonor as a thing to be feared
> worse than death itself, are notions which are so all-pervasive in
> the sixteenth century that we hardly think of them as integral
> parts of a systematic philosophy. They do, however, mostly stem
> from Aristotelian definitions of honor in Renaissance textbooks
> on moral philosophy.[17]

And while Corneille's hero (someone like the Cid or Cinna) was a
généreux caught between love and duty,[18] the protagonist in the honor
drama of Spain—a land that was thoroughly Catholic and obsessed with
racial purity—was caught between two equally forceful imperatives, the
social one to maintain an unblemished name, and the Christian mandate
to refrain from violence in private matters regardless of the cost.

Several conditions obtained that could demolish a man's reputation,
or *fama*. A verbal insult, a physical blow, or the illicit behavior of a
female member of one's family could not go unchallenged; on the other
hand, secrecy in the response might be called for, as nobody wanted to
publicize an offense against himself.[19] Because a rumor or suspicion was
in itself sufficient to wreck one's *fama*, a man who came to doubt his
wife, sister, or daughter might at that early point pass the death sentence.
Don Lope de Almeida, the protagonist of Calderón's *Secret Vengeance
for a Secret Insult*, carefully plots his revenge in secret without waiting
for the adultery, and disguises the deaths of his wife and her anticipated
lover as accidental precisely in order to keep the disgrace from reaching
a public dimension. Secrecy, then, is one theatrical imperative in a crisis
of honor.

It is also a dramatic fact that while jealousy between unmarried lovers
in the lighter cape-and-sword plays is all part of the fun, any incidence in
a *comedia* of jealousy in a married couple inevitably signals a fatal lack
of confidence that will end in tragedy, most often including the husband's
murder of his wife, whether or not she has been unfaithful.[20]

A commonplace begging for contradiction (like the naive peasant's
divinization of royalty) in many of these plays was the notion that only
members of the nobility had a sense of honor that could be offended. In
Golden Age theater, the seduction or rape of a peasant woman required
as much reparation as the same offense against any aristocrat. Gustavo
Correa traces the geometry of honor, dealing with the *comedia* in

general and *Peribáñez* in particular.[21] When the question relates to the social hierarchy, "vertical" honor applies; an aristocrat would partake of more vertical honor than a peasant, and the king would surpass them both. "Horizontal" honor, however, refers to a man's self-respect and the regard of his equals; it is this kind that pertains to the peasant as well as to any of his "betters," and it is this kind that is so painfully vulnerable to insult. Pedro Crespo's famous declaration of honor's social independence in Calderón's *The Alcalde of Zalamea* refers to the horizontal variety: "for honor is / the patrimony of the soul, / and the soul belongs to God alone" ("que el honor es / patrimonio del alma, / y el alma solo es de Dios").[22] In this play, as well as in Lope's *Peribáñez, Fuenteovejuna,* and *The Abduction of Dinah,* the offending nobleman believes himself exempt from retribution because peasants can have no sense of honor; in each case he dies at the hands of peasants. Finally, in the honor play the extreme measures taken by the aggrieved party nearly always meet with the approval of a superior authority, most often the monarch, at the work's conclusion: at least apparently, the peasant "hero" and his king end the drama in perfect harmony.

A Look at Casilda's Puns

In the second edition of his novel *The Pilgrim in His Homeland* (*El peregrino en su patria*), published in 1618, Lope de Vega catalogued the titles of the *comedias* he claimed to have written by that date. The list included a play called *The Comendador of Ocaña* (*El Comendador de Ocaña*).[23] This work appeared in print for the first time in the 1614 *Parte IV*;[24] Morley and Bruerton (*Cronología,* 374) judge its composition as most likely between 1605 and 1608, although disagreement on the date continues.[25] In the concluding lines of the play, the peasant Peribáñez turns to the public ("Senado") to proclaim, "[H]ere ends / the celebrated tragicomedy / of the Comendador of Ocaña" ("[C]on esto acaba / la tragicomedia insigne / del Comendador de Ocaña" [3.1044-46]).

After the final lines in the *editio princeps* appear the words added, apparently, by the play's first editor: "End of the tragicomedy of Peribáñez and the Comendador of Ocaña" ("Fin de la tragicomedia de Peribáñez, y el Comendador de Ocaña") (fol. 102r). At the beginning of the *Parte IV* collection it is listed as *Peribáñez y el Comẽdador de Ocaña;* on the first folio of the play (77r.) it is called "LA FAMOSA TRAGICOMEDIA DE PERIBAÑEZ, y el Comendador de Ocaña."[26]

Lope did not take part in the preparation of the *Parte IV* of his own plays; in fact it was not until three years later, with *Parte IX* (1617), that he began to supervise the printing of his *comedias,* this because so many unauthorized and incorrect versions had appeared. The *Peregrino* list indicates that he continued to think of the work as a play about the Comendador of Ocaña, although in the more than 350 years since its first publication, the longest title has either prevailed or been abbreviated in scholarly editions and common usage simply to *Peribáñez.*[27] A modern English translation by Walter Starkie alters the concluding lines to "And thus, dear Senate, ends our tragicomedy, / *Peribáñez and Ocaña's Knight-Commander.* "[28]

The action, like that of *The Greatest Alcalde,* is firmly embedded in Spanish history; it takes place during the final months of the reign of Henry III (1390–1406), who because of chronic illness was sometimes called "the Ailing" ("el Doliente"). At the beginning of the third act Lope appropriates almost verbatim a section from the *Chronicle of Henry III* (*Crónica de Enrique III*)[29] that reviews the eminent citizens assembling for a campaign against the Moors in Andalusia in 1406. Chronicle (261a) and *comedia* (3.37–42) correspond so closely that both begin the inventory of illustrious personages by noting the vacancy in Toledo's seat of spiritual authority due to the death of its archbishop.

This honor drama presents to the audience two young, attractive, determined rivals: the husband, a peasant (Peribáñez), and the intruder, a nobleman (the Comendador Don Fadrique). The play depicts a struggle to the death over the peasant's wife, Casilda. Although the wily *villano* wins this undeclared war for the woman, wealth, and the King's favor, the seventeenth-century spectator attending *The Comendador of Ocaña* would be witness to another struggle, equally compelling and ultimately far more transcendent. The battle for personal growth and Christian *desengaño* —for true heroism in the seventeenth-century Spanish understanding of the word, entailing victory over oneself—will prove to have a different outcome.

The play opens during the wedding celebration of the two peasants, Peribáñez and Casilda. The festivities include a bullfight, and the well-wishing of the happy couple is interrupted by an accident: the young, respected, and locally beloved knight, the Comendador of Ocaña, has fallen with his horse while in pursuit of a rampaging bull. He recovers his senses but loses his heart to Casilda, and spends the rest of the *comedia* attempting to win her, first with gifts and flattery; then with treachery. By early in the second act, Peribáñez is aware of the Comendador's interest in his wife. Since the mere suspicion constitutes a blot on one's honor, Peribáñez decides to kill Don Fadrique, and spends the rest of the play setting a trap. The bait is Casilda.

To a certain extent, both the Comendador and Peribáñez play into each other's hands. Don Fadrique at first wants to pave the way to Casilda's favor by suborning her husband; Peribáñez covets the Comendador's grand tapestries to adorn his cart for a pilgrimage to Toledo. At Casilda's urging Pedro requests them of Fadrique, who is only too happy to oblige. On their own initiative, the Comendador's servants also mobilize in his behalf, reminiscent of the *Tragicomedy of Calisto and Melibea*. The gentleman retainer Leonardo decides to woo Casilda's young cousin and companion Inés, hoping that she will intercede for his master. The lackey Luján takes it upon himself to dress as a reaper and infiltrate the peasant farmer's household. Learning of his lackey's activities, Don Fadrique is delighted; Peribáñez will conveniently be out of town that very night:

> By what a smooth path
> you have brought remedy to my illness!
> For with that jealous *villano*
> out of the way,
> and with your opening me the door
> when the reapers slumber,
> the door to hope in my
> passionate love opens.
> I have had uncommon luck,
> not only that Peribáñez is going away,
> but that he didn't recognize
> you in disguise!
>
> (¡Por qué camino tan llano
> has dado a mi mal remedio!
> Pues no estando de por medio
> aquel zeloso villano,
>   y abriéndome tú la puerta
> al dormir los segadores,

queda en mis locos amores
la de mi esperança abierta.
    ¡Brava ventura he tenido,
no sólo en que se partiesse,
pero de que no te hubiesse
por el disfraz conocido!)

                                    (2.263-74)

In fact, Peribáñez *has* recognized the lackey, having seen Luján
serving the Comendador twice before hiring him himself: when Fadrique
fell, and when Peribáñez asked for the tapestries. No fool, Pedro now
suspects Fadrique's intentions and confirms them shortly afterwards
when he sees a portrait of his wife in Toledo:

PERIBÁÑEZ.	I already know who commissioned it.
	If I am right, will you tell me?
PAINTER.	Yes.
PERIBÁÑEZ.	The Comendador of Ocaña.

(PERIBÁÑEZ.	Ya sé quién la ha retratado.
	Si acierto, ¿diréislo?
PINTOR.	Sí.
PERIBÁÑEZ.	El Comendador de Ocaña.)

                                    (2.661-63)

The peasant wants to buy the portrait for himself, but the painter
refuses:

PAINTER.	I'm afraid that the Comendador
	would get angry, and tomorrow I'm expecting
	a lackey of his here.
PERIBÁÑEZ.	Does that lackey know about it?
PAINTER.	He's coming straightaway
	to pick it up.
PERIBÁÑEZ.	I saw him yesterday,
	and I wanted to get to know him.

(PINTOR.	Temo que el Comendador
	se enoje, y mañana espero

> un lacayo suyo aquí.
> PERIBÁÑEZ.   Pues ¿sábelo esse lacayo?
> PINTOR.   Anda veloz como un rayo
>   por rendirla.
> PERIBÁÑEZ.   Ayer le vi,
>   y le quise conocer.)
>
> (2.677–83)

Peribáñez retains Luján in his employ, after having confirmed who he is and what his intentions are.

Meanwhile, back in Ocaña, the Comendador appears, guided by Luján, in the night at the peasant's house. The reapers Pedro left behind to protect Casilda have decided it would be more prudent not to make a fuss; they feign sleep and allow Don Fadrique to make his appeal to Casilda. She rejects the aristocrat, who remains outside the house, and arouses the reapers for the morning's work. The Comendador, humiliated and further inflamed, slips away. Casilda's cousin Inés, who has by now fallen in love with Leonardo, tries to persuade Casilda to be kinder to the Comendador. By this time, Peribáñez has quietly arrived home and eavesdrops on the conversation: enough to know that Inés hopes to marry Leonardo; that she is attempting to sway his wife; and that Casilda will have none of it. He steps forward and all three pretend that nothing is wrong, although he cryptically declares that Inés will have new shoes for her wedding (2.950).

Peribáñez now understands that Inés and Luján are both working for Casilda's seduction, in behalf of the Comendador. A choleric man, and exceedingly jealous, it may be at this point that the peasant decides to kill the accomplices as well as Fadrique, if the opportunity presents itself. But his priority remains ensnaring the Comendador red-handed.

At the beginning of the third act, Don Fadrique again plays into the cunning peasant's hands. King Enrique "el Tercero" ("el Tercero" can mean "the Go-Between" as well as "the Third") plans his crusade against the infidel in the South; he requests troops of Castile. Here is Fadrique's excuse to remove Peribáñez from the scene: he tells the peasant he would like to make him captain of one hundred men. Pedro accepts eagerly and plays the pompous soldier who leads his rustic troops, described in the original stage directions (fol. 95r.) as "comically armed" ("armados graciosamente"). The peasant asks to be knighted; Fadrique agrees; and Peribáñez now declares himself and the Comendador on equal footing. The new captain takes his troops off to Toledo, providing Fadrique what he believes will be free access to the unguarded Casilda: on the Comendador's previous visit the cowardly reapers certainly gave him no reason to think otherwise. By this time he has resolved to rape her if she refuses him again.

Peribáñez of course knows Fadrique's intent and has been acting the *miles gloriosus* as a diversionary tactic. He leaves Casilda behind to bait the trap, and returns stealthily in the night to Ocaña. Before the Comendador arrives, the peasant enters his own house through the back door "like a burglar" ("cual ladrón / de casa" [3.691–92]) and hides in a sack of flour, waiting possibly for up to an hour.[30] (Normally, a character dusted with flour in a *comedia* is meant to be ridiculous.[31]) Finally, the Comendador arrives, Inés lets him in, and the aristocrat confronts Casilda. As he is about to lay hands on her, Pedro emerges from the sack and runs him through with his captain's sword. Having assured Casilda's safety, the peasant ferrets out and murders the two accomplices, Luján (who has himself taken refuge in the flour sack, and appears "enarinado" [fol. 100r.]), and Inés. Casilda applauds the murder of her cousin. Then the couple dress "as simple farmers" ("todo de labrador" [fol. 102v.]) and make their escape. Leonardo arrives to find Don Fadrique dying. At this point the nobleman recovers his moral faculty and forbids any further violence:

> COMENDADOR.   I don't want
> an uproar or vengeance now.
> My life wanes.
> I can only hope for that of my soul.
> Don't pursue him, or take extreme
>   action,
> because he has been right to kill me.
> Take me where I can make confession
> and let us leave off revenge.
> I pardon Peribáñez.
> LEONARDO.   That a *villano* should kill you,
> and that I shouldn't avenge you?
> This I deplore.
> COMENDADOR.   I vouch for him.
> He is not a *villano,* he is a knight;
> for since I girded on him the sword

	with the gilded edge, he has not used ill his blade.
LEONARDO.	Come, I will knock at the door of Our Lady of Remedy.
COMENDADOR.	My only remedy is God.

(COMENDADOR.	No quiero vozes ni vengdanças ya. Mi vida en peligro está, sola la del alma espero. 　No busques, ni hagas extremos, pues me han muerto con razón. Llévame a dar confessión y las vengdanças dexemos. 　A Peribáñez perdono.
LEONARDO.	¿Que un villano te mató, y que no lo vengo yo? Esto siento.
COMENDADOR.	Yo le abono. 　No es villano, es caballero; que pues le ceñí la espada con la guarnición dorada, no ha empleado mal su azero.
LEONARDO.	Vamos, llamaré a la puerta del Remedio.
COMENDADOR.	Sólo es Dios.)

(3.783–800)

Meanwhile, Peribáñez and Casilda hurry to the court at Toledo. There, Pedro approaches King Enrique, who now calls himself "the Just" ("Justiciero" [3.908]) and emotionally demands the peasant's immediate execution. The Queen intervenes, and all listen to Pedro's version of the Comendador's demise. It so moves the King that he not only pardons Peribáñez, but officially welcomes him into the ranks of the *hidalgos* and makes him permanent captain of his hundred troops. The Queen gives Casilda four more dresses.

Beginning with an important study by E. M. Wilson,[32] scholars have gradually begun to look beyond stereotypes to explore the complexities of this play, with some significant recent advances in the understanding of the relationships between language and actual events.[33] Güntert and Randel analyze the portrait motif; Evans, who especially illuminates the peasant couple's character and Peribáñez's verbal facility, joins Carter in cross-examining the contradictory aspects of the play and putting them into an historical perspective. My own study, which owes a great deal to those mentioned above, will treat as well the literary context of a play dramatizing a peasant's concern for honor, jealousy, and revenge.

The "action" at the heart of any serious work of narrative fiction is, at bottom, the protagonist's journey to self-knowledge. Even the preclassical heroes, Achilles and Odysseus, came to acquire some measure of restraint or release; especially once the "mind" appeared on the intellectual horizon, the hero learned to examine his conscience, pausing in his career toward violence to consider the alternatives and the moral consequences of his actions and, afterwards, accepting them. The moment of hesitation is the banner of true humanity in Aeschylus's Orestes, for example. A man with compelling reasons to murder his own mother, he stops: "What shall I do, Pylades? Be shamed to kill my mother?"[34] After the deed, Orestes must face the Furies, a personification of his conscience, along with a painstaking inquest into the crime, for which he never wins full acquittal.

The consummate pause in Western literature must be Hamlet's. Roland Mushat Frye argues that Hamlet is neither mad, nor weak; his delay in avenging his father would be the one morally correct course for an Elizabethan in the Dane's difficult situation. Hamlet must determine whether the ghost is really his father and whether Claudius is truly guilty; then he must examine the available legal, political, and moral alternatives open to himself under the circumstances: conscience, Hamlet understands, does, or should, make cowards of us all. He is fascinated by Pyhrrus's pause before murdering Priam in the second book of the *Aeneid.* The necessary complication (from the technical standpoint) and the dilemma (from the moral standpoint), in the cases of Orestes, Pyhrrus, and Hamlet, is that after the pause each one proceeds to choose the violent alternative. Arthur McGee has recently shown that for Hamlet, as an unrepentant and despairing Catholic, the choice to avenge his father's assassination may cost him dearly: in contemporary English theater, revenge ghosts (like the one that hounds Hamlet to murder) are invariably from hell.[35] Therefore, not only does Hamlet fail politically — the throne will probably go to the son of his father's enemy, undoing the senior Hamlet's victories—but, guided by diabolical ends personified in that ghost, the Prince fails abysmally on the moral plane. I think Hamlet like Macbeth and Richard III is one of those heroes of finally bad character, whose fate Minturno would still allow to move us.

The audit of conscience is then no guarantee of a finally correct choice, but it is undeniably a sign in tragic literature of a spiritual nobility that separates the thoughtful hero from the less reflective characters who surround him; it is perhaps even that aspect of humane vulnerability sometimes betrayed by the pause which exposes a worthy character to the possibility of tragedy, according to Northrop Frye's definition (*Anatomy*, 38).

Even when the subject is secular, Spain's seventeenth-century theater has unmistakably Catholic underpinnings. Whether tragedy is possible in such circumstances has been an object of debate. Arnold G. Reichenberger writes that tragedy must leave the audience's sense of justice outraged at the end; because a forcefully Christian theater means a belief in salvation—that is, that justice will catch up to us all in the afterlife—tragedy is impossible.[36] For Alexander A. Parker, there are no innocent victims in serious works such as Calderón's *The Physician of His Honor* and *The Devotion to the Cross* (*La devoción de la Cruz*); all characters contribute in some way to the unhappy outcomes of these somber works which might be called tragedies.[37]

E. M. Wilson's view of the tragic ballad, which may juxtapose a local hero's prosperity with his subsequent misfortune,[38] might also apply to a *comedia* such as *The Knight of Olmedo* (*El caballero de Olmedo*). There the protagonist is an admired and respected aristocrat, whose only detectible error is his superfluous reliance in courtship on a *tercera*, a disreputable go-between.

I would also suggest that any *comedia* in which a man of conscience makes a seriously wrong moral choice and never comes to realize it, or pursues his course despite realizing it, would constitute one kind of Spanish tragedy. It is characteristic of many "dramas de honor" that the protagonist feels he has no choice but to respond violently to a perceived offense; often this reluctant conviction is the source of great suffering for him as well as the victims. Arguing along similar lines, A. Irvine Watson considers Calderón's *The Painter of His Own Dishonor* a tragedy.[39] Don Juan Roca makes the mistake of waiting until an advanced age to marry a young woman. He is a decent and generous man who, as Watson puts it, "will become the tragic victim of a cruel social aberration" (218): his wife is kidnapped by a former suitor; the honor code demands their deaths; and despite an anguished struggle with his conscience, at the end he stands with the smoking gun, honor restored, a broken man among the corpses.

Similarly, in Calderón's *The Physician of His Honor,* Don Gutierre agonizes over Prince Enrique's pursuit of his innocent wife, Mencía. Unwilling to lay hands on a man of royal blood, the husband goes for help to Enrique's brother King Pedro. While in the palace, Gutierre believes (mistakenly) that he overhears Enrique attempt to attack the King; therefore Gutierre concludes that he must remove the threat to his own honor and to his King's life. Mencía's presence keeps the doubly threatening Prince in town; therefore he must kill his dear wife. He does allow her shriving time, and afterward joins Don Juan Roca among the most poignant and bereft figures in Spanish drama. The King, understanding all Gutierre's motives, is himself deeply distressed but feels bound to approve the murder to protect himself from what he considers the Prince's continued dangerous proximity. Years after the events described in the play, King Peter will pay with his life when Henry assassinates him in civil war. The text projects the ultimate consequences of the deed onto both husband and king: it also happens to be a fact of life (or art) in these historical honor plays that protagonist and king illuminate aspects of each other's characters; the association is officially sealed at the play's conclusion by the king's approval of whatever solution the protagonist has chosen.

Calderón's *Secret Vengeance for a Secret Insult* is a further example of such disastrous coupling; conversely, we might take the judicious conclusion of *The King, the Greatest Alcalde* to indicate that Sancho and Elvira now deserve, as their king will, to live out their days in success and happiness. In their affliction over Don Tello's crime, it occurred to Sancho and Nuño to petition spiritual and secular authorities for aid. Before his drastic solution, Calderón's Don Gutierre resorted in vain to his distracted and paranoid king for help; even the *vulgo* of *Life Is a Dream* went peacefully to King Basilio before taking up arms against him.

Peribáñez, who perceives early the potential extremity of his own situation, acts in several respects atypically of the husband in an honor play. First of all, he is not torn by ethical considerations: his series of soliloquies is always emotional and strategic, never moral in nature. Secondly, Peribáñez takes care to publicize the offense. During his visit to the painter, Pedro sees the portrait of Casilda and cajoles his reluctant neighbor Antón into inspecting it with him. Without explicitly broaching the unpleasant implication, Pedro communicates to his friend that his marital honor is under siege. In his first major soliloquy, which immediately follows, the peasant reasons that because his disgrace has now become public knowledge (thanks to his own effort!), he will have to kill the Comendador. While he has persistent doubts about Casilda,[40] he never intends to do away with her, although he does risk her safety to catch Fadrique. He makes no serious attempt to avert bloodshed; in fact, Pedro *first* decides on murder and *then* discards several other alternatives. Carter (*"Peribañez,"* 19-21) has exposed the illogic of the peasant's first soliloquy: beginning with a declaration of his own irrationality ("a husband's jealousy / is beyond reasoning" ["zelos de marido / no se han de dar a entender" (2.695-96)]), Pedro convicts and sentences Don Fadrique in one breath:

> if he intends to take my honor,
> I'll take his life:
> for an offense undertaken
> is equivalent to one carried out

> (si en quitarme el honor piensa
> quitaréle yo la vida:
> que la ofensa acometida
> ya tiene fuerça de ofensa.)
>   (2.703-6)

Carter writes, "Peribáñez asks us to accept that a person should be killed (by a private citizen outside judicial processes) for an *intention*, because the intention is as culpable as the deed. . . . Peribáñez feels as if he has been 'killed,' therefore he will physically kill his opponent (19-20)." The peasant next rues his marriage (2.707) and repeats three times the curse on his union with a pretty woman. He realizes that he has purchased inconvenience by assigning so much value to physical beauty (2.725-28).

Having already decided to kill Fadrique, Pedro now backtracks to ponder and discard two other alternatives for coping with the difficulty. Both are certified by the Christian religion, and recommended by Lope himself in the novella *For Marcia Leonarda*. Both involve turning the other cheek. The peasant muses,

> Shutting myself away at home
> will open the shameful door
> to gossip,
> and all my welfare turns bad. . . .
> A curse on the humble man, indeed,
> who seeks out a beautiful wife!
> Moreover, leaving Ocaña
> offers the same drawback,
> and my livelihood prevents
> my dwelling elsewhere.
> What helps me, hinders me . . .
>
> (Retirarme a mi heredad
> es dar puerta vergonçosa
> a quien cuanto escucha glossa,
> y trueca en mal todo el bien. . . .
> ¡Mal haya el humilde, amén,
> que busca mujer hermosa!
>   Pues también salir de Ocaña
> es el mismo inconveniente,
> y mi hazienda no consiente
> que viva por tierra extraña.
> Cuanto me ayuda me daña . . .)
>   (2.731-41)

For reasons of reputation and economic advantage, Peribáñez cannot bring himself seriously to regard nonviolence as a practical alternative. It does not occur to him to talk to the Comendador—as Sancho and Nuño appealed to Don Tello in *The Greatest Alcalde* —or to go to the King for help, as even *The Physician*'s Don Gutierre did. The peasant is left only with what had been his first impulse, killing the Comendador. It must be at this point, then, that Peribáñez takes the moral fall, which matches that of his nemesis. Upon his arrival in Ocaña he hears Inés coaxing his wife, but instead of discussing the problem openly with Casilda, and removing the corrupting cousin from his household, he spins for them a dark allegory:

Something bad happened to me;
so that, I swear, it was a miracle
for me to arrive home alive. . . .
I fell down a high slope
onto some rocks.

(Sucedióme una desgracia;
que, a la fe, que fue milagro
llegar con vida a mi casa. . . .
Caí de unas cuestas altas
sobre unas piedras.)
                    (2.966–68, 970–71)

He attributes his safe recovery to his devotion to San Roque, known as
the " 'miracle-worker' ":

For if I hadn't commended myself
to the saint in whose service
I fell from the bay mare,
I would be dead now

(Que si no me encomendara
al santo en cuyo servicio
caí de la yegua baya,
a estas horas estoy muerto.)
                    (2.972–75)

Ironically, Pedro eschews poverty and opts for murder, believing himself
under the protection of the saint who "became known for his love of
poverty and his gift of healing."[41]

Later, when Fadrique's long-anticipated attack on Casilda is finally
about to commence, the peasant does fleetingly hesitate and consider
what under the circumstances would be the logical thing to do, the one
which he had in fact promised his foe earlier (3.201–4): that he would
make complaint in the event of some impropriety. Pedro now says to
himself, "It would be a good idea to go up and talk to him" ("Bien será
llegar y hablalle" [3.760]), not because it would be the *moral* or the
Christian thing to do—it is not conscience which makes a coward of
Peribáñez—but his *social disadvantage:* that "I am a poor farmer" ("soy

pobre labrador" [759]). This is the first time that Peribáñez stops to
ponder nonviolent discourse as a real alternative, indeed, his fourth
alternative. Having the physical advantage over his unsuspecting target,
Peribáñez turns over in his mind a peaceful solution. It would give the
Comendador a chance to defend a weak case: after all, the King (prodded)
will overcome his own rage to accord Peribáñez precisely that opportunity later. The King's first impulse at sight of the peasant is a violent
"Kill him, guards, kill him" ("matalde, guardas, matalde" [3.937]). The
Queen intercedes, to "the Just" Enrique's chastened "I didn't remember
/ that both sides should be heard, / *and especially when one's excuse
appears so flimsy*" ("no me acordaba / que las partes se han de oír, / *y
más cuando son tan flacas* [3.944-46; italics mine]).

Perhaps it is no coincidence then that the two seats of religious
authority in this play are conspicuously vacant. Toledo's archbishop has
died; and once the crazed bull has gotten loose in the *comedia*'s first
scenes, Ocaña's village priest flees to the roof, literally rising above and
out of the lives of the peasants. Afterwards he is nowhere to be found.

And so it is with the peasant protagonist: having his victim at a
complete disadvantage, Peribáñez, himself untenanted by any Christian
scruple, pauses a moment only for the practical, social reason: "But I'm a
poor farmer . . . / it would be a good idea to go up and talk to him . . . /
but better to kill him" ("Mas soy pobre labrador . . . / bien será llegar y
hablalle . . . / pero mejor es matalle" [3.759-61]). The peasant then
carries out the execution he had intended all along, surprising his
victim, probably from behind.[42] As he does so, he begs the Comendador's
pardon, "for honor carries / the most weight here" ("que la honra es
encomienda / de mayor autoridad" [3.763-64]), a rehearsal of Pedro
Crespo's famous phrase. Only by some nimble contortions of the imagination is Pedro's murder of Don Fadrique the heroic, Christian, or even
the honorable thing to do—much less the subsequent slaughter of the
two accomplices to the crime that was never committed. And the
Comendador's truly graceful, heroic, and honorable acceptance of responsibility when dying supplies the ironic context that makes the peasant's
behavior all the more appalling.

All of the mitigating (for the Comendador) and incriminating (for
Peribáñez) circumstances are left out of Pedro's speech to King Enrique,
whose first impulse would have been as bloody as Pedro's final recourse.[43]
Since gaudier dress and language would be unbecoming to his cause, for
their court appearance the peasant and his wife humble themselves by

dressing with uncharacteristic modesty and by—in figurative language at least—observing the social hierarchy that the peasant's sword and dagger had so audaciously torn asunder only hours before: as the "pastor" he had to rescue his "corderilla simple" ("simple lamb") from the "lobo." Peribáñez pretends that he had been carrying "the dagger and sword" ("la daga y la espada") only to serve the King, "not for such a sad deed" ("no para tan triste hazaña" [3.1004]). He forgets to mention—although the audience would have sat through a play-full of evidence—that he had thoroughly premeditated and organized the entire death scene.

Indeed, if the peasant has admired the painter's re-creation of the image of Casilda in Toledo, he speaks as a fellow artist, a sort of playwright and director combined: a man with the imagination, discretion,[44] and luck to write and direct two separate scripts. One, which lures the impassioned Comendador to the farmer's home and murders him, might be called "The Mousetrap," or the "Tragicomedy of the Comendador of Ocaña." It is the text we read and the seventeenth-century Spanish public saw acted out on the stage. The second script is a revision of the "Mousetrap," now named after its peasant hero, and a much simpler story; it is the version presented to King Enrique. In "Peribáñez," the lecherous Fadrique foists on the idealized peasant couple unsolicited gifts, and tries to rape Casilda on *two* occasions; on the second, however, the unsuspecting Pedro arrives home in the nick of time to find his door broken in, and his wife in the Comendador's clutches. Here, there is no choice but to kill Fadrique, and the villain must have gotten in all by himself because, according to this script, he is the only victim of Pedro's sword. The lives and harrowing deaths of two other defenseless characters, who in the original text beg in vain for mercy, are omitted from the peasant's "corrected" account. It is this version of the events that Pedro tells the royal couple, and his rhetorical re-dressing of what was actually a far more complicated situation dazzles the King and Queen. Although the audience would have seen brutal events on the seventeenth-century stage graphically invalidating Peribáñez's account, it is the peasant's bowdlerized tale that moves us in the twentieth century to misremember the rest and regard this work as Peribáñez's play: as if Iago had finally, craftily, won the starring role.

While Peribáñez is subtly perfidious, probably the most patently malicious character in the play is Luján, who hails from Pedro's own social class. Fadrique's lackey advises suitably rustic gifts to incur the favor of the peasants, disguises himself as a reaper, and penetrates

Casilda's very bedroom in his pragmatic zeal on the Comendador's behalf. But he is a poor match for Peribáñez, who sees through the disguise; Luján fatally informs the painter of his master's passion for Casilda and convinces Fadrique incorrectly that the reapers sleep while the nobleman pays court. In fact, the Comendador's first clandestine visit to Casilda is so ineptly disguised that the reapers later compose songs about the encounter. These they sing in the hearing of Peribáñez on his return—to his consolation. Not only has Casilda been faithful; perhaps the peasant realizes that his enemy's importunings having been so public will support his own case later. He has forced Antón to take note of the painting, so that nobody in Ocaña could be unaware of Don Fadrique's suit by the end of the second act, thanks in large part to Peribáñez himself.

None of Don Fadrique's actions is wise or in keeping with the sterling reputation he had earned before his fall. In Casilda's own words, he was "the flower of Spain" ("la flor de España"):

> Oh, gallant knight!
> Oh, valiant warrior!
> Are you the same one who sowed fear
> with that naked blade
> in the Moors of Granada?
> Are you the one who killed so many?
> A rope did in
> him whom a sword could not!
> With a rope you are mortally injured;
> but it did so by *thieving*
> the glory and good name
> of such a strong captain.

> (¡Ah, gallardo caballero!
> ¡Ah, valiente lidiador!
> ¿Sois vos quien daba temor
> con esse desnudo azero
>   a los moros de Granada?
> ¿Sois vos quien tantos mató?
> ¡Una soga derribó
> a quien no pudo su espada!
>   Con soga os hiere la muerte;

mas será por ser *ladrón*
de la gloria y opinión
de tanto capitán fuerte.)

(1.291–303)[45]

The Comendador, then, is a brave and generous man whose *brío* by an accident becomes lackey to his passion for a peasant woman. Luján as the embodiment of his master's *cupiditas* on a figurative level deserves annihilation. On a more literal level, the lackey's crude and unsuccessful attempts at "discreción" throughout the play are the foil for Peribáñez's far more shrewd and subtle devices. On the moral level, Luján would merit his fate if aiding and abetting the attempted seduction of a married woman warranted the death penalty. But whether he acts in the name of honor or of revenge, Peribáñez's murder of Luján has nothing to do with self-defense, or the defense of a loved one. In metaphorical terms, since the lackey is the instrument of the Comendador's illicit desires, it may represent poetic justice. In legal terms, as Carter points out (20), the homicide is hardly justifiable; in Christian terms, it is an abomination.

But if Luján's fate seems extreme under the circumstances, that of Inés is truly incommensurate with her "crime." The young cousin who keeps Casilda company obviously hails from a less prosperous household: lacking Casilda's finery, she regrets the "poor garments" ("galas . . . pobres" [1.667–68]) she will wear next to her cousin's finery for the pilgrimage to Toledo. This relative poverty must sting, considering the fact that Peribáñez keeps Casilda's closet filled with lovely dresses. Inés, then, is in a particularly vulnerable position, and the reapers' "trébole" song casts a sympathetic light on her dilemma: Inés is

the maiden . . . ,
kept shut away behind walls
who is easily deceived
in her first love

(la donzella . . . ,
entre paredes guardada,
que, fácilmente engañada,
sigue su primero amor.)

(2.415–18)

Lope has in effect composed a *canción de tipo tradicional,* a second, purer variation on this play's *serranilla.* It tells the tragic story of the young, naive maiden deceived by the worldly wise courtier, a nobleman who cunningly appeals to her deepest longings. In order to obtain her help for the Comendador, Leonardo has resorted not to seduction, but to the "honorable" production of a legal document promising marriage. That with this dangling in front of her the young girl lets Fadrique into the house is surely a betrayal, but to claim that such a moral lapse calls for her death is to accuse Lope of advocating a vicious barbarity.[46] Having assassinated the Comendador and executed his lackey, Peribáñez proceeds to chase down and slaughter the weakest and most defenseless character in the play. To maintain that this act proves the courage and honor of the peasant protagonist is surely a perverse and callous reading. It makes the first line of the play, spoken by Inés, all the more ironic: "May you enjoy long life together" ("Largos años os gocéis"), she wishes the happy couple—or rather the mutually suspicious couple, whose own opening conversation is a portentous (and unavailing) reciprocal admonition against feeling jealousy, or causing it.

Casilda's reaction to the murder matches her husband's lack of conscience: "The punishment has been very just" ("Muy justo ha sido el castigo" [3.812]), she declares to Pedro, commending the gratuitous attack on her own flesh and blood, whom she had earlier claimed to love so well. She has turned a deaf ear to Inés's plea for help, since "blood relation counts for nothing when honor is involved" ("no hay sangre donde hay honor" [3.810]). Peribáñez does not mention his murder of Inés in the court scene at the end of the play because it would hardly accord with the view of himself as the innocent victim that he wants to present to the King.

If the peasant is a playwright, he is also a sort of crafty Odysseus, a consummate role-player who sets up his victims for the kill and does not stop with the one who is directly responsible for his affront. I think Larson is indeed correct that *The Comendadores of Córdoba* may be a prototype for Lope's later honor plays. However, Alix Zuckerman-Ingber and Melveena McKendrick have taken the early work for a satirical critique, not an approval, of the husband's solution.[47] The guilty parties and the murderous husband are all made to look persistently absurd. Discovering his wife, her cousin, and their two silly lovers all in the same bed, the pompous and punctilious Veinticuatro not only does in the four of them, but all the household servants as well, and for good measure, the pet monkey and parrot. Furthermore, Lope sets that play during "one of the low points of [the approving King] Fernando's career."[48] The play hardly validates such preposterous behavior, and Peribáñez's mayhem is merely a more sophisticated version of it.

Early in the Comendador of Ocaña's tragicomedy, Peribáñez designates himself and his wife "king" and "queen" (1.76–85). Their picture of seeming domestic bliss is paralleled in the third act by the appearance of the loving monarchs; and at the end, Evans notes ("*Peribáñez,*" 144), Casilda receives the "real queen's cast-off clothes." The only point at which Casilda's interest in grand apparel momentarily wanes is at the play's center, where she is trying to discourage Fadrique with redherring claims of desire only for the simple life ("I love Peribáñez more, / with his rough cape" ["más quiero yo a Peribáñez / con su capa la pardilla" (2.545–46]). At any rate, in their materialism and concern to outshine their equals, Evans observes, the peasant bride and groom "are like kings and queens: haughty, whimsical, patronising and violent" (144).

When in the third act Casilda learns of her cousin's part in the conspiracy to let in the Comendador, she excoriates Inés, "turned from *prima* [first; cousin] into *tercera* [third; go-between]" ("vuelta de prima, tercera" [749]). The characterization is most arresting, because it is the second time Casilda has made the same pun. In the first act, her witticism prefaces the recitation of that tale of treachery well known in the historical and oral traditions. In Toledo, Casilda sets eyes on King Enrique III and exclaims, "What a fine *tercero*!" ("¡Qué buen tercero!" [1.971]). Her play on words only makes sense in the light of Peribáñez's gloss, where he describes the manner in which the reigning king acquired his sceptre:

> PERIBÁÑEZ.   Es hijo del rey don Juan
> el Primero, y assí, es nieto
> del Segundo don Enrique,
> el que mató al rey don Pedro,
> que fue Guzmán por la madre,
> y valiente caballero:
> aunque más lo fue el hermano;
> pero, cayéndose en el suelo,
> valióse de la fortuna,
> y de los braços assiendo

a Enrique le dio la daga,
que agora se ha vuelto cetro.
Ines.   ¿Quién es aquél tan erguido
que habla con él?
(1.972–84)

Because this passage is difficult and has been generally misunderstood, in a moment I will render it into readable English. It will be recalled that King Peter of Castile is known variously in Spain's oral and written traditions as Peter "the Just" or Peter "the Cruel," a confusion also reflected in Golden Age theater. During his reign he fought a civil war against his bastard half-brother Henry of Trastámara, the son of Alphonse XI and Doña Leonor de Guzmán. It is this civil war that is foreshadowed in Calderón's *The Physician of His Honor.* Henry finally assassinated Peter and became King Henry II. The fatal confrontation is described in chronicles and ballads: Henry tricks Peter into entering the tent of a supporter at the Montiel battlefield, and attacks him by surprise. The two brothers struggle until a third party (*tercero*) intervenes. According to Mariana's account in the *Historia general de España,* it is a traitor called "Beltrán."[49] In the ballad it is an anonymous page, who with the fateful and proverbial words, "I neither break the king nor make the king" ("No quito rey / ni pongo rey de mi mano"),[50] helps Henry, in fact deciding the course of history. Henry II was succeeded by his son John I, and he by his own son Henry "el Tercero," the king of our play. Notoriously unstable and sickly, he became king at a very early age, and died in his late twenties.

In Peribáñez's version of the confrontation, King Peter is made out to be the better man, defeated by Henry's good luck and the aid of a third party: not the page of the ballad, but, in flagrant anachronism, our Enrique "el Tercero." Having glossed Peribáñez's gloss, I will now translate it:

PERIBÁÑEZ.   He [Enrique III] is the son of King John
the First, and thus, is the grandson
of the Second Henry,
the one who killed King Peter,
and who was a Guzmán on his mother's side,
and a brave knight;
although his brother [Peter] was more so;

but, [Peter] falling on the ground, he
[Enrique III] took advantage of the opportunity,
and grabbing his [Peter's] arms
he [Enrique III] gave Henry II the dagger,
which has now become a scepter.

INES.   Who is that distinguished man
who speaks with him?

The bloody dagger has now become the scepter of Enrique "el Tercero."

Mariana writes that Henry III's judgment was clouded and his features distorted and ugly because of the illness.[51] Yet Costanza finds the young king extremely handsome (1.969); perhaps it is the aura of majesty that blinds her as it does so many other theatrical peasants.[52] In any case, she like all the other characters in this play is too intoxicated by image to perceive clearly the essence of matters. And judging from the strong suggestiveness of hair color described by Herrero García and Américo Castro, it cannot be Lope's careless touch that Costanza laments not having gotten close enough to the King to tell whether Enrique "el Tercero" is "blonde- or red-bearded" ("si es barbirrubio o taheño" [1.999]).

The playwright has therefore established an interesting set of correspondences. Peribáñez and his king are both inclined to execute without a hearing. Both at least in Lope's version have been involved in trapping unsuspecting victims of higher rank on their own turf. The social ascent of the peasant Peribáñez and the political ascent of Enrique III owe to their brutal deeds. And the victims of the treachery, the better men, are the Comendador and King Peter, both essentially stabbed in the back. Frances Exum shows that Lope's plays did tend to make out Peter to be a hero, although in certain works he had his flaws.[53]

King Enrique appears in the first and last acts of the play. It is August 1406. The monarch wants to raise troops and money to fight the Moors in Granada. In effect, he too considers himself an artist, explaining that he wants to create, on the nearby plain, the image of another Toledo:

I intend to free Andalusia,
if our army can be prepared,
before harsh winter covers the fields
with its ice, making the ground difficult to tread.
Juan de Velasco, you shall proceed to prepare,
since there is enough room on the plain,

the great review of troops that I propose,
so that the fame of the assembly will inspire awe
along the golden shores of the Tagus, and ascending
to the wall in diamond steps,
there will be seen the pavilions and tents
of another Toledo by the green pathways.
Let the audacious Moor in Granada tremble
at the red flags and pendants.
May his joy turn to sorrowful lament.

(Libre pienso dexar la Andalucía,
si el exército nuestro se previene,
antes que el duro invierno con su yelo
cubra los campos, enternezca el suelo.
    Iréis, Juan de Velasco, previniendo,
pues que la Vega da lugar bastante,
el alarde famoso que pretendo,
porque la fama del concurso espante
por esse Tajo aurífero, y subiendo
al muro por escalas de diamante,
mire de pabellones y de tiendas
otro Toledo por las verdes sendas.
    Tiemble en Granada el atrevido moro
de las rojas banderas y pendones.
Convierta su alegría en triste lloro.)

                                         (3.827–41)

Enrique's resplendently bellicose rhetoric anticipates that of King
Sebastián in Calderón's *Secret Vengeance for a Secret Insult*. There, the
Portuguese king looks forward to the conquest of Africa. Historically, his
crusade ended in ignominious failure and his own death, circumstances
we now construe as reflecting on the denouement of that *comedia*. Nor
did Henry "el Tercero" ever fulfill his own grand vision. In fact, he never
left Toledo, dying there in December 1406, soon after the events described
in this play.

King Enrique first appears near the end of act 1, standing at the
entrance to the cathedral at Toledo. The wording and substance of his
remarks, which may seem incidental to the main action of the play,
summon up two issues of overriding concern in the lives of the other

characters. Awed at the splendor of the city and its cathedral, Enrique remarks on the power first of image, and then of "el interés." Referring to the city, he calls himself "the most passionate devotee / of her rare beauty" ("de su rara hermosura / el mayor apassionado" [1.915–16]).

A central issue in the *tragicomedia* is of course the effects of appearance and adornment, and the destructive consequences of admiration for the object instead of what that object represents. Güntert ("Relección del *Peribáñez*) and Randel ("The Portrait") mark well the Comendador's confusion of earthly beauty with the spiritual glory which it ought to suggest, or sign with signified. That leads the Comendador to adore Casilda, and her portrait as well. But it is not just Fadrique's values that go askew, as Randel and Evans ("*Peribáñez*") show; Peribáñez and his wife, obsessed with appearances, covet ostentation and material goods. Randel writes,

> The bull, the *galas* [fine clothes], the cart, the portrait all lure Peribáñez to the brink of folly as much as they do Don Fadrique. Many times Peribáñez himself comes perilously close to indulging in very similar excesses: when he wants to take on the bull, when he becomes too much concerned with adorning his person and his cart with *galas*, when he is tempted to be extravagant about San Roque's image, when he starts to see his wife as an angel, and when he lets a representation of her take precedence over herself. (137)

However, Pedro concludes the play not with *desengaño*, but by misrepresenting the murders of three individuals caught defenseless: hardly a moral or spiritual victory. It seems that obsession with image and the material afflicts every citizen of the play.

Near the end of the third act, the young King appears again, this time in private conversation with the Queen. He asks about his infant son Don Juan (who will eventually become the weak and ineffectual King John II [1406–1453]). King Enrique sees in his son a mirror or portrait of his ancestry: "May God protect him; for he is a divine mirror / where now, rather than those present, / those past see themselves portrayed" ("Guárdele Dios; que es un divino espejo, / donde se ven agora retratados, / mejor que los presentes, los passados" [852–54]). Peribáñez has already traced that less-than-illustrious family tree in the first act. "Metaphorically," according to *Diccionario de Autoridades*, "árbol [tree] refers to genealogical succession, in which the ancestor is called the *tronco* [trunk], and the descendants, branches" ("Metaphóricamente se llama la sucessión genealógica en que el ascendiente es llamado tronco, y los descendientes ramas" [1:373b]). In conversation with his familiars, then, we have heard the King's surpassing admiration for his ancestry — *el tronco* — and for the city of Toledo, crown of Castile (1.922), and, like Rome, founded on a mount (1.929).

If the excessive preoccupation with image afflicts every subject in the realm, Don Fadrique's famous sonnet in the second act, then, may not suggest only or even principally his own flaws, but those of the whole community. Peter N. Dunn and others have studied this sonnet, which sings first of Xerxes, and then of an Athenian youth.[54] Xerxes was the Persian king dreaming of greater empire, whose huge army was defeated by a much smaller force at Thermopylae. The sonnet implicates most directly the character to whom the entire community and nation turn for guidance, the young king who we have seen worships his family tree and a city on a mount:

> They tell of a *king* who adored a *tree,*
> and that a *lad* stayed close by a *marble statue,*
> to which, never parting night and day,
> he confessed his love and complaints.

> (Cuentan de un *rey* que a un *árbol* adoraba,
> y que un *mancebo* a un *mármol* assistía,
> a quien, sin dividirse noche y día,
> sus amores y quexas le contaba.)
>   (2.794–97; italics mine)

The second quatrain is peculiar because grammatically, it fuses the king and the youth into one character:

> But he who loved a *trunk* and a *stone*
> had more hope of happiness,
> because, after all, he could draw near,
> and without anyone seeing, embrace it.

> (Pero el que un *tronco* y una *piedra* amaba
> más esperança de su bien tenía,

pues, en fin, acercársele podría,
y a hurto de la gente le abraçaba.)
$$(798-801)^{55}$$

Many of the play's characters also attempt to exploit the power of *el interés;* and even the King speaks in the same language. Enrique needs from Toledo troops and money to fight in Andalusia; therefore he will parade in the procession for the city's patron saint

> as testimony of my faith
> with the sovereign Image;
> for I would like to oblige her
> to intercede for me
> in this great undertaking.

> (para exemplo de mi fe,
> con la Imagen soberana;
> que la querría obligar
> a que rogasse por mí
> en esta jornada.)
> (1.938-42)

In the context of the other characters' intense concern with image and interest in this play, the King's rhetoric takes on a mercenary tone. He wants to show his devotion not so much out of love, but to extract from the icon a personal favor: an appeal to *el interés* echoed by Peribáñez later as he describes his own metaphorical fall and rescue by the image of San Roque. But as in the Comendador's sonnet, as the youth who never left the marble statue, King Enrique will never depart from Toledo, and his heavenly petition will be denied. By association, his fate must somehow extend to the peasant whom in the end he rewards for murder.

While in no sense sinister, then, the King cannot at the same time claim our admiration for the quick temper that threatens to cut off justice, or for the inordinately ambitious and far from disinterested devotion to image that his character suggests in the play. By association, he too has taken a figurative fall—or perhaps the fall occurred in his family two generations before. King Henry's father was the son of Henry the Bastard; and incidentally, his mother descended from (the enemy)

King Peter:[56] therefore King Enrique fuses into one the warring dynasties, as Lope fuses the two idolaters in the sonnet.

If all the characters in this *comedia* participate morally in the Comendador's fall, who is left for the audience to admire? Who is the hero? If by "hero" we mean the character who through his experiences achieves *desengaño* and conquers his defect, if the "hero" is the character whom in the end the spectator is meant to emulate, can it be the peasant Peribáñez? At the beginning of the play he is already jealous of his wife; she returns his suspicions then and during his first solo trip to Toledo. We soon learn of his angry temper: Casilda keeps quiet about the Comendador's advances in order not to provoke Peribáñez. Antón shudders to think of the consequences of Pedro's wrath.

If by "hero" we mean the man who examines his conscience but still makes the wrong choice—like Pyhrrus, Hamlet, or Don Juan Roca—the hero cannot be Peribáñez, whose soliloquies reveal no conscience, only an acute consciousness of his social options, and whose actions reveal a shrewd head for strategy. It is true that the *villano*'s final speech to the King is a model of humility, but it is also a tissue of lies, calculated to transform his "delitos" into "valor." His humility, in short, is feigned in the service of his designs to get away with murder—his "discreción." Peribáñez has known since early in the play that the Comendador was interested in Casilda, and planned with great intelligence since the second act to trap and kill Don Fadrique. The peasant hired Luján knowing full well that he was the Comendador's lackey, and knew also in advance that he would kill Inés. Peribáñez hid for up to an hour in a flour sack waiting for Fadrique to approach his wife. He had plenty of opportunities to deal peacefully with the Comendador, but rejected all in order to satisfy his "locos zelos." Peribáñez himself has made certain that the entire community has been aware of the offense so that he might claim justification for the murder. Arming his troops "graciosamente" and appearing to take so seriously and pompously his new rank as captain is Pedro's diversionary tactic. He will lure Don Fadrique into his trap and expose his own jealously coveted wife to possible rape, all in the interest of satisfying a lust for revenge. Pedro constantly tests and doubts Casilda. Both keep crucial secrets from each other. Peribáñez's supreme *discreción* and secrecy certainly lead to the success of his revenge. If he changes at all, it is to gain in cunning. Pedro learns not to covet appearances, but to manipulate them for further ends. His vision finally transcends *lo material*, but in a purely negative sense: the peasant's love of his wife's corporeal beauty leads not to his contemplation of divine truth, but to his perversion, to his prostitution of it for an infernal end. The curses he repeatedly confers on his wedding and himself culminate in his utter spiritual bankruptcy. Or rather, if he transcends *lo material,* risking all he owns and holds dear, it is in the service not of a higher spiritual good, but of a most diabolical evil. Peribáñez's fall is an infinitely profound one. That he triumphs in his treachery is simply a further perversion, a Christian outrage, the ultimate profanity, and made possible by his "tercero," the deteriorating King.

While peasant and king are metaphorically linked in this play and in the end the monarch ratifies the peasant's behavior, the more striking and adversarial doubling is that of Peribáñez and the Comendador. Luján assures the painter in act 2 that out of passion for Casilda his master is "changed into a savage" ("convertido en selvaje" [2.1044]); by that point his master is Peribáñez as well as Fadrique. Evans believes that in marrying, Peribáñez had to suppress the individualistic, virile side of his nature and content himself with a peaceful, domestic existence. The Comendador, a brave and famous warrior—and a single man— represents in Evans's words Pedro's "repressed heroic self" (145): tension is bound to result between the comfortable farmer who craves the hero's life, and the hero who craves the farmer's wife. Indeed, Pedro eventually operates as if he were a prince in that pre-law society described by Hegel (see chapter 1)—like Orestes, or Odysseus, for example—in which a man is forced to play the vigilante because no institutions will answer a complaint, instead of as a peasant in a fairly settled society with plenty of alternatives, including ready access to a king.

If Evans is correct that the conflict between his domestic responsibilities and his ambition partly explains Pedro's desire to be knighted, then I would further suggest that with the knighting ceremony, the peasant has now put himself in a perfect position to integrate these two normally incompatible roles, of husband and hero; and it is a most lethal merger. Peribáñez becomes a *villano* with a license to kill. And in Spanish oral tradition, *villanos* on a rampage are a most horrifying spectacle. Cobarruvias comments on the curse "May *villanos* slay you, Alphonse" ("Villanos te maten, Alfonso"):

> These words became proverbial, having been pronounced by the Cid Rodrigo Díaz to King Alphonse, in the oath that he took at Santa Gadea de Burgos, along with other curses that should

befall [the King] should he break the oath [that he had not killed
his brother King Sancho in order to gain the crown]. *Villanos*
generally kill by beating or stoning without mercy; and beyond
dying, it is a great misfortune for a worthy and well-born man to
die at the hands of such wretched people.

([E]stas palabras quedaron en proverbio, por las que dixo el Cid
Rui Díaz al rey don Alonso, en la jura que le tomó en Santa
Gadea de Burgos, con otras maldiciones que le cayessen y
sucediessen quebrantándola. Los villanos matan de ordinario a
palos o a pedradas sin ninguna piedad; y ultra de la muerte, es
gran desdicha morir un hombre de prendas y hidalgo a manos de
tan ruin gente.) (*Tesoro de la lengua castellena*, 1008b–9a)

Bartolo, one peasant who is truly distressed and concerned in the first
act at Fadrique's fall, lays a similar oath on the bull whose rope tripped
the nobleman's horse:

> Oh, curse you, young bull!
> . . . .
> May your enemy always defeat you
> when you are jealous,
> and bellowing through the forests,
> may you find the streams dried up.
> May you die at the hands of the *vulgo*,
> run through in the bullring;
> may you not be killed by a knight
> with a lance or a golden knife.
> May a lowlife lackey, from behind,
> with a moldy blade
> cut you down and make you
> stain the dust with blood.
>
> (¡Oh, mal hayas, el novillo!
> . . . .
> Siempre te vença el contrario
> cuando estuvieres zeloso,
> y por los bosques bramando,
> halles secos los arroyos.

Mueras en manos del vulgo,
a pura garrocha, en coso;
no te mate caballero
con lanza o cuchillo de oro.
Mal lacayo por detrás,
con el azero mohoso,
te haga sentar por fuerça,
y manchar en sangre el polvo.)
                    (1.230, 234-45)

On the other hand, Pedro's response to Fadrique's accident is much less sentimental and more practical:

If the Comendador
dies here,
I'll have to leave Ocaña.
A curse on the [wedding] party!

(Si aquí
el Comendador muriesse,
    no vivo más en Ocaña.
¡Maldita la fiesta sea!)
                    (1.286-89)

Simply put, Peribáñez is one of those *villanos* who lack the sensibility of compassion, that and the innate quality of nobility in spirit which qualified Sancho for true nobility in *The Greatest Alcalde.* Pedro's coating with flour during the murder scene would emphasize to the audience that he should not merit their respect as a true hero; he is simply a cagier version of the unscrupulous and similarly dusted Luján.

But what of Don Fadrique, then? This man goes from hero, to fool for love, to a man with criminal intent. Unlike Don Tello in *The Greatest Alcalde,* however, the Comendador never spews out general abuse of the peasant class; his is a very particular malady. He would have settled for the portrait if he could not have Casilda; it is Peribáñez himself who goads Fadrique into action and gives him hope by hiring Luján.[57] This lovesick man grows desperate from the resulting humiliation of his first rejection; however, Pedro's ambush brings him back to his senses. Mortally wounded but once again morally whole, his true character emerges.

C. M. Bowra observes that often the measure and the full realization
of a genuine hero—Achilles, for example, or Roland—can only be taken
as he faces death.[58] And a degree of the tragic hero's melancholy
grandeur issues precisely from the element of self-destructiveness that
leads to his downfall. One thinks in tragedy of Telemonian Ajax, Oedipus,
and Othello. In epic at least, according to Thomas M. Greene, "the most
important recognition scenes . . . are not between two people but between
the hero and his mortality."[59] Like Telemonian Ajax in the play by
Sophocles, Lope's Fadrique is the victim both of himself and his opponent;
his final recovery of his moral sense, and the "manner of his death,"[60]
redeem him. The dying man realizes Christian heroism when his conscience prevails. Fadrique's recognition of and remorse for his error is
the most highly developed and poignant palinode uttered by Lope's
erring Comendadores. If any character indisputably changes for the
better in this play, it is Don Fadrique, the Comendador, who, compre-
hending his trespass, not only rejects revenge, but forgives the man who
has just wounded him mortally. By contrast, the peasant "hero" of this
comedia, begging the nobleman's pardon, stabs him in the back.

In Lope's "tragicomedia," Don Fadrique's Iago is a peasant named
Peribáñez who spends the play plotting and luring a great, if imperfect,
man to his death. It is, then, the Comendador's story, the tragedy of his
moral fall, but the celebration of his ultimate moral resurrection. In the
"Tragicomedia insigne del Comendador de Ocaña," all fall together, but
in the end, Don Fadrique stands alone and Castile loses one of its
noblest Christian soldiers.

It is worth noting that for all the disdain the peasants in this play
harbor for the *hidalgo* class—expressed especially in the anti-Semitic
remarks against the company of "hidalgos cansados" (3.368)—in the end
Peribáñez is happy to abandon his own class to become one of them. As
of his marriage, the peasant has already lost interest in the land, in any
case. He immediately throws down his plough to squire Casilda to
Toledo; they extend their stay so long that Pedro's brotherhood suffers;[61]
upon his return to Ocaña the peasant instantly agrees to go back to
Toledo that very day with the image of San Roque, even though it is
harvest time and he will have to leave his new wife alone; next he gladly
accepts the captain's commission. Pedro is very busy in this play, doing
everything but his own occupation. And in the end, as in *The Villano in
His Corner,* this rich peasant's desertion of the land is sanctioned by
royal decree.

The *Tragicomedia insigne del Comendador de Ocaña* can, then, be considered consistent with the early honor plays, and with the later *The King, the Greatest Alcalde, The Abduction of Dinah,* and the *Novellas for Marcia Leonarda,* in its criticism of violent revenge for an affront to honor. Sancho de Roelas and the Comendador Don Fadrique gain or regain their Christian heroic status by overcoming the impulse to violence. The foreboding first scene of the *Tragicomedia,* which pits Peribáñez's jealousy against his wife's, airs their materialism, and eliminates the town priest, would serve as a red flag to alert the contemporary spectators to expect less than perfect harmony from this marriage and this bucolic community. And at the end of the play, Pedro continues to be the volatile, materialistic, and spiritually barren man who first married Casilda, a woman whose temperament suits him well. In keeping with the other works examined so far, this play generally (although by no means exclusively) assigns the baser conduct to socially inferior characters, and reserves the truly noble, finally admirable and imitable redeeming actions, to a true noble.

A Tale of Two Cities

I swear, this is more tragedy than celebration.
(A fe, que es más tragedia y no fiesta).[62]

The entire population of a town on the Iberian Peninsula during the Roman conquest is a main character and arguably the hero of Cervantes's early and near-epic four-act *Siege of Numantia* (*El cerco de Numancia*) (c. 1580). Beleaguered by the Roman general Scipio, the starving people of Numancia commit suicide rather than surrender; the action culminates in a small boy's defiant leap from a tower. The collective entity, *el pueblo,* subsequently often became a significant presence in the Spanish *comedia,*[63] and as Francisco López Estrada points out,[64] not in the classical capacity as chorus (that became the province of the *bufón*), but as an active and sometimes major character.

In the case of *The Tragicomedy of the Comendador of Ocaña* (or *Peribáñez*), the community acquits itself with something less than distinction. Although in the third act Blas, one in the group of one hundred peasants commanded by Peribáñez, trumpets the cowardice of the *hidalgos* (3.388–90), and Belardo crows (3.391–92) that the *hidalgos* fled in undignified panic before the rampaging *novillo* at Pedro's wedding, it was in fact Blas who scrambled comically away from the bull, "for no Italian [acrobat] / was ever seen to trip so lightly / across a tightrope" ("que ningún italiano / se ha vido andar tan liviano / por la maroma jamás" [1.175–77]); it was Tomás bereft of his breeches; and the clown-priest, Casilda's uncle, who disappeared in flight to the roof.

In the opening scene of the second act of the same play, Pedro's brotherhood meets to discuss the inexcusable and embarrassing disrepair into which they have allowed the image of their patron saint (San Roque) to fall. It is the more disheartening that although the meeting was duly publicized, so few villagers bother to attend, and the most illustrious of them—Peribáñez—arrives late. And the reapers to whom in his absence Pedro entrusts his wife's safety are so valiant that they feign sleep rather than have to ask the Comendador his business (surely not to save Peribáñez's reputation, since they sing in public about the nocturnal visit afterwards). They leave it to Casilda to find a politic way out of a potentially deadly and certainly discomfiting situation.

However, the second peasant "honor play" in Lope's middle period, and perhaps the most famous of his *comedias* among non-Hispanists, boasts a truly active and finally united collective protagonist. *Fuenteovejuna* actually tells an historical tale of two cities under siege, the larger community of Ciudad Real ("Royal City") being the foil for the humble village of Fuenteovejuna ("Sheepwell"). Indeed, although the main focus is on the way in which the inhabitants of the village deal with the abuses of its Comendador, Lope devotes an unusually large proportion (nearly 29 percent)[65] of lines to the play's "segunda acción," which parallels—excepting the all-important resolution—the main plot line. That second action is the historical circumstance of Ciudad Real's unwilling subjection to the Comendador's superior, the Maestre of Calatrava,[66] and the city's manner of throwing off his yoke. Both communities are pawns in the late-fifteenth-century civil war between the Catholic Monarchs, Ferdinand and Isabella, and the supporters (including the Comendador and the Maestre) of Juana la Beltraneja. Lope draws a large part of his inspiration from the *Chronica de las Ordenes y Cavallerias de Santiago, Calatrava y Alcantara* (Toledo, 1572).[67]

Crucial to the two parallel actions is the figure of the Comendador, Fernán Gómez. In the opening scenes of the play he persuades the adolescent and impressionable Maestre to side with la Beltraneja in civil war against the Catholic Monarchs; they will first take Ciudad Real. The Comendador then retires to his own fiefdom of Fuenteovejuna, where he abuses its meek inhabitants. At whim he seduces and rapes the women, and now has his eye on the beautiful and chaste maiden, Laurencia. The *labrador* Frondoso loves her; she reciprocates after he rescues her at crossbow-point from the Comendador's disordered advances. Subsequently, Fernán Gómez intrudes on their wedding to arrest Frondoso and carry off Laurencia. By that time his and the Maestre's forces have been expelled from Ciudad Real by Fernando and Isabel: the royal city had sent two aldermen (*regidores*) to the King and Queen requesting their aid; the monarchs responded instantly and successfully to rid Ciudad Real of the oppressor-insurgents.

In the third act, the citizens of Fuenteovejuna also consider an appeal for help to the royal couple, but are driven by the Comendador's excesses to a frenzied attack on him in his own home. Laurencia and then Frondoso have escaped; they and the whole town arise in a mob and literally tear Fernán Gómez limb from limb. Afterwards they abuse even the remnants of the corpse, carrying the head about on a pike as they compose *coplas* in praise of King Fernando and Queen Isabel.

Meanwhile, the young Maestre makes his appearance at court, begs the pardon of the King and Queen for his rebellion, and is accepted back into the royal fold; the monarchs reason that he is too young to have known any better, and had been misled by bad counselling. At this point, one of the Comendador's henchmen, who has escaped the wrath of the popular uprising, arrives at court and asks the royal couple to bring the citizens of Fuenteovejuna to justice. Fernando and Isabel send a judge to the village to investigate Fernán Gómez's death, but even under torture, man, woman, and child will only respond that "Fuenteovejuna did it" ("Fuenteovejuna lo hizo"). In frustration, the judge reports to the monarchs that he can get nothing on paper, so that they will either have to pardon the whole town, or execute it. The citizens themselves turn up at court and recount the offenses that led to their violence.

In the end, declaring that "although the crime [of rebellion] was serious" ("aunque fue grave el delito" [3.2444]), since the investigation has officially failed, Fernando decides that "it will have to be pardoned" ("por fuerza ha de perdonarse" [3.2445]). The King then takes the town under his own protection.

Geoffrey Ribbans and Robin Carter have pointed out that the town's

uprising is never applauded by royal authority or held blameless.[68] Lope
represents the rebellion as a grave misdeed; in fact, the stage King reacts
more severely than did the historical one. In this *comedia*, the monarch's
thorough investigation, like King Alfonso's in *The Greatest Alcalde*,
contrasts markedly with royal procedure—or lack of it—in *Peribáñez*,
where only one side of the story is heard, and that mendacious account
is uncritically accepted. In *Fuenteovejuna*, Fernando and Isabel first
listen to Flores's biased report; afterwards they hear the townspeople's
story, along with the report of their own energetic but stymied judge.

I agree with Carter (*"Fuenteovejuna* and Tyranny," 324) that one of
the problems Lope poses in this play is, precisely, the difficulty of
judging and the equivocal character of apparent knowledge. The first
act is woven with near-pastoral interludes in which the peasants first
discuss the deceptions of rhetoric: how flattery and calumny can equally
distort the truth. Next, Mengo and Frondoso debate the nature of love,
appointing Laurencia and Pascuala as judges. The two girls listen but
abdicate, declaring themselves unequipped to render an opinion. The
conversation carries on in the manner of a Socratic dialogue, and in fact
these "philosophical" scenes possess a dialectical character that might
be said to apply to the *comedia* as a whole. The first and third acts
coincide in the judging theme; even in the second act the Comendador
informs the alcalde Esteban that the latter will have to judge his own
son-in-law's "crime" of defending Laurencia, imposing upon him an
untenable judicial office that can have nothing to do with justice. And
the second act begins with a discourse on the inadequacy of book-
learning for arriving at true knowledge. In *Fuenteovejuna*, Lope constantly
exposes two opposing points of view without unequivocally affirming
either, allowing the polemic to show that there are few simple answers
to the questions of love, honor, loyalty, and violence which trouble the
villagers.[69]

Similarly, between the exemplary and unmitigatedly evil character of
this play's Comendador and the idealized goodness of the Catholic
monarchs lies the true character of the citizens of Fuenteovejuna. Fernán
Gómez can in no way be classed with Don Fadrique, the Comendador of
Ocaña; no scruple or lovestruck tenderness redeems the character of
this man who is often cursed by his peasant vassals and called a "demonio."
If any Comendador in Lope's honor plays does fulfill Larson's designation as a monster from romance, it is Fernán Gómez, who treats his
vassals as senseless possessions, as "meat" ("carne"). His abuse of the

populace is the most extreme version of Don Tello's behavior in *The Greatest Alcalde*. Like Tello's crime in that play, which itself recalls the Corpes atrocity in the *Poem of the Cid*, Fernán Gómez's transgressions are not just private affairs. This Comendador offends the monarchy by urging the impressionable Maestre to rebellion, and offends the Faith by exploiting forces meant for the Reconquest in his civil war. His affront, then, in its universal character, classes him with the Infantes of Carrión, among the worst of Spanish villains.

If anything could excuse the eventual violence of the villagers of Fuenteovejuna, it is the complete malevolence of their Comendador. But Ribbans and Carter note that these peasants, who are generally regarded in criticism as an idyllic community under the thumb of a fiend,[70] are not themselves entirely blameless. Fernán Gómez treats the women of the town like whores ("rameras") partly because many of them act that way: with Flores he reviews his easy conquests of Pascuala, Olalla, and Inés (2.1059–84), and Laurencia declares to him that she is not like Sebastiana and Martín del Pozo's wife, who

> were already,
> from having been with other men,
> on the road to pleasing you,
> because many other young fellows
> enjoyed their favors.
>
> (ya tenían,
> de haber andado con otros,
> el camino de agradaros,
> porque también muchos mozos
> merecieron sus favores.)
> (1.805–9)

Laurencia is at first herself an emblem of self-interested love as she and Pascuala (presumably there are two "Pascualas" in Fuenteovejuna) abandon their "dear" friend Jacinta to the Comendador, "for if he takes liberties with you, / with me he will be cruel" ("que cuando contigo es libre, / conmigo será cruel" [2.1195–96]).[71] We can guess the "liberties" Jacinta subsequently endures at the hands of the Comendador's troops.

The villagers do respond legally and correctly to the Comendador's insults for the longest time, often protesting peacefully. Like Peribáñez,

Frondoso has a clear shot at his unarmed noble nemesis when Fernán Gómez puts down his crossbow to approach Laurencia, but unlike Peribáñez (and like David with King Saul), Frondoso refrains from violence. The idea of a meeting of concerned citizens at the beginning of act 3 would doubtless have been approved by Juan de Mariana, whom Lope admired.[72]

We might also consider this assembly the collective equivalent of an honor soliloquy, in which the community examines its options for dealing with the offending Comendador. And just as Peribáñez reviews the alternatives but, ruled by passion, makes the wrong choice, so also do the people of Fuenteovejuna. Juan Rojo offers the first explicit suggestion: because the King and Queen have prevailed in Castile and are now en route to nearby Córdoba, "let *two aldermen* go to the city / and throwing themselves at [the monarchs'] feet, ask for help" ("vayan *dos regidores* a la villa / y echándose a sus pies, pidan remedio" [3.1678–79; italics mine]). They have petitioned the Comendador without results; now appeal to the King! This solution is of course Sancho's in *The Greatest Alcalde,* who at first had worried—and was proved wrong— that royalty would not bother with the troubles of a humble man.

In fact in each of the plays by Lope that we have studied, the monarch has shown himself completely accessible to commoners. *Fuenteovejuna,* like all of Lope's *comedias,* is a love story, but also like so many of them it is in part a political and civic one, having to do with the proper response of social inferiors to abuses by their superiors. Rozas explains that Ciudad Real was founded as "Villa Real" by Alphonse X "the Wise" in the thirteenth century in the midst of Calatrava's feudal territory as a strategic royal stronghold against the nobility. By 1420 it had grown enough to be called "Royal City," Rozas writes, "signifying very noble and very loyal" ("título de muy noble y muy leal" [*"Fuenteovejuna,"* 179]). On several occasions it was deeded over to noblemen, but in each case the citizens succeeded in returning to royal patronage. In general, during Lope's time as well as earlier, communities preferred to belong to the crown rather than to a feudal lord.

Ciudad Real, in Rozas's words, "could serve as an example for the towns under the Comendadores of Calatrava, especially in cases where the Comendador was a tyrant" ("podía ser ejemplo para los pueblos sometidos a los Comendadores calatravos, especialmente en los casos en que el Comendador fuese un tirano" [178]). That city is then exemplary in history; and in the play it is the illustration of the correct solution to the abuses of the aristocracy. In the *Chronica,* "those of the city" ("los de la ciudad") appeal to the King; Lope deliberately changes "those of the city" to "two aldermen" and then draws the parallel in the speech of Juan Rojas for Fuenteovejuna: we could, the peasant suggests, send to the monarchs two aldermen — the exact response which, as the audience would know, has in this play already succeeded for Ciudad Real.

Moreover, Juan Rojas has just pointed out that Fuenteovejuna's own petition could now conveniently be heard by the King and Queen. Consequently, Barrildo's persuasive negative is groundless:

> While King Fernando is overcoming
> so many enemies, some other solution
> will be better, because he'll be too busy,
> in the midst of so much war, to help us.

> (En tanto que [aquel Rey] Fernando humilla
> a tantos enemigos, otro medio
>   será mejor, pues no podrá, ocupado,
> hacernos bien con tanta guerra en medio.)
>   (3.1680-83)

The choice dictated by right reason (and ratified in so many other Golden Age *comedias*) has just been overruled, and as other less feasible recourses are pondered, the meeting, like the offended husband in an honor soliloquy, grows ever more restive. It is too late to abandon the village; finally, the Alderman himself suggests open rebellion (3.1697-98), and the idea begins to gather support, except for Mengo's Erasmian objection that those most likely to suffer in armed conflict will be the "simples labradores" (3.1705) for whom he speaks. Juan Rojas is in the space of thirty lines converted; all his moderation flies out the window. His cry "Let us take our revenge!" ("¡A la venganza vamos!" [3.1711]) is Laurencia's cue to appear disheveled, hurling insults and inciting the rumbling crowd to physical and not just oral violence. The orderly meeting dissolves in an uproar into an attack on their noble master, in Mengo's words, "without order" ("sin orden" [3.1805]).

Juan de Mariana, the most ardent advocate of the people's right to resist tyranny, could never have approved the mob action that ensues. "The massacre," Carter writes, "is not the result of an orderly reasoning process, but of the opposite: the complete breakdown of reason and order" ("*Fuenteovejuna* and Tyranny," 326). He continues,

> I suggest that the pattern we are meant to see is one of disorder and tyranny among the villagers bringing the Comendador's evil home to roost, their mass behaviour being a reflection of, as well as the result of, the Comendador's behaviour. . . . The process of cause and effect has come full circle, destroying the cause—but not the effects—of the disorder, and the motif of "Fuenteovejuna lo hizo" in the torture scene emphasizes the fact that the villagers' act was a crime, that all of them did take part, and that the whole village is indeed guilty. (328)

Judging from the time and attention King Fernando devotes to the investigation afterwards, he certainly could have spared enough of both to help the villagers had they gone to him before turning violent. Their group action is also group guilt, and they purge their guilt in that torture scene. In the end, forgiven but not celebrated, Fuenteovejuna becomes another *ciudad real*, a royal city taken under the monarchs' wing. And as Calderón distinguishes by rank in *Life Is a Dream* between the final deserts of the erring nobles and those of the *vulgo*, the Maestre here is not asked to pay for his rebellion in anything beyond the coin of humiliation—and the loss of Fuenteovejuna as a fiefdom.[73]

Still, despite their obvious flaws, more than any other peasant community in Lope's plays about humble people—certainly more than Juan Labrador's *co-villanos*, and Peribáñez's neighbors—many citizens of Fuenteovejuna have their modest dignity. Laurencia's speech is often rustic without being crude, and her admiring description of country life (1.215-48) is a genuine and pure *beata illa*, unadulterated by Juan Labrador's fatuous self-congratulation, or Casilda's sensuous materialism. Laurencia is also the only peasant in a secular Golden Age play that I know of who is allowed to pronounce a sonnet (3.508-22).[74] Frondoso, like Sancho in *The Greatest Alcalde*, would be happy to do without a dowry. C. Alan Soons calls these peasants "bookish,"[75] and López Estrada situates them "between rustic and pastoral characters" ("criaturas entre rústicas y pastoriles"),[76] both in their mixture of *culto* and country names (Laurencia, Frondoso; Juan Rojo, Barrildo, etc.); and in their rustic discourse about platonic philosophic topics.

Indeed, if in his major plays Lope does ever approach the idealization of Spanish peasants, of conferring the pastoral magic on pseudohistorical commoners, it is in *Fuenteovejuna*. Lope's religious *comedias* such as those glorifying Saint Isidro, *labrador de Madrid*,[77] and the *Comedia de Bamba*, must be considered a genre apart, although in *The Youth of Saint Isidro*, Lope's hero finds himself in that standard, potentially catastrophic position of the husband who has been told (here, by the allegorical Lie [Mentira], sent by Envy [Envidia]), that his wife is unfaithful. While his soliloquy begins like that of the typically distraught husband, his solution most critics would proclaim extraordinary in Lope:

> All right, I will go and scold her,
> because I can't excuse it:
> if she doesn't want to straighten herself out,
> I'll take her to the village.

> (Ahora bien, iré a reñirla,
> que no lo puedo excusar:
> si no se quiere enmendar,
> traeréla luego a la villa).[78]

That is, Isidro will first try peaceful discourse; if María persists in her disgraceful conduct he will leave her. It may not be a very dramatic remedy, but it is consistent with those tacitly or explicitly proffered Christian alternatives in Lope's early honor plays, as well as in *The Abduction of Dinah*, the novella *For Marcia Leonarda*, *The Greatest Alcalde*, and *Peribáñez*.

Peter N. Dunn has suggested to me with respect to Calderón at least (and I think it would apply to Lope as well) that

> it was clearly possible for him — as for many others — to believe in the dignity of man (made in the image of God, etc.) with one part of his mind, and also to see the common "mob" as irrational, incapable of making judgments, a danger to the *res publica* with another part. "Man" as a philosophical and religious concept and *vulgo* as a social and political one are certainly not coterminous. . . . You can find parallels in Shakespeare, . . . especially in the way the Roman populace is swayed first one way, then the other by Brutus and Mark Antony in *Julius Caesar*.[79]

Likewise, Lope's pastoral or mythological works with idealized shepherds descending from the poetic innamorati of Theocritus, Virgil, and
Ovid (plays such as *Belardo, el furioso* and *La Arcadia; Adonis y Venus,*
etc.), also belong to a class separate from the Spanish rustics like Blas,
Barrildo, and Peribáñez, whose own lineage might be traced back to
Roman comedy, the comic shepherds in liturgical drama, and the unscrupulous picaro. It is possible that *Fuenteovejuna*'s dialectic terminates in
the fusion of these two distinct dramatic *troncos* —the ideal and the
vulgar—cut with the humanity of Sancho Panza, into one skittish and
volatile but graceful, lovable, and redeemable humble community.

I think it also possible that Spanish writers, including the most
aristocratic among them, could be comparatively receptive to the lowly
points of view, partly thanks to the special respect in which they held
Spanish popular verse during the Renaissance. For Lope at least, as the
most eager appropriator of the traditional-type poetry, that respect—or
better, that affection—for simplicity, also infuses his *comedia*'s treatment of some humbler characters. Speaking of Lope's most celebrated
comedias, if a regard for the peasant is scarcely indulged in *The Villano
in His Corner,* and is categorically rejected in *Peribáñez,* it is most fully
realized, and yet still plainly qualified, in *Fuenteovejuna.*

Chapter 4

PEASANT HONOR IN CALDERÓN

The Invincible Luis Pérez

"Galician, did you go to mass today?" "Yes, God be praised."
"Did you see God?" "I didn't pay that much attention."

"Galician, do you want to go to mass?" "I have no shoes." "Do
you want to go to the tavern?" "I have four dollars here."

"Galician, turn Moslem." "I don't want to." "I'll give you two
dollars." "I don't want to." "I'll give you two-fifty." "Hand it over:
I'll throw my wife and kids into the bargain."

I'd rather be a bastard than a Galician.

(Gallego, ¿fuiste oi a misa? —Sí, si a Dios plugo, i seia loado.
—¿Viste a Dios? —No miré en tanto.

Gallego, ¿quiés ir a misa? —No teño zapatos. —¿quiés ir a la taverna? —Aquí teño cuatro cuartos.

Gallego, vuélvete moro: —No qeiro. —Y te daré dos reales. —No qeiro. —Darte he dos y medio. —Ora daca, fillos e muller y todo.

Antes puto que gallego.)[1]

That Calderón could, at least in the abstract, consider a humble man worthy of respect is evident from his well-known *auto sacramental The Great Theater of the World* (*El gran teatro del mundo*).[2] An allegorical play-within-a-play directed by God ("El Autor"), its cast includes the King, the Rich Man, the Unborn Child, Beauty, Discretion, the Labrador, and the Poor Man. The most interesting character and indeed the one of major focus is the Poor Man; the others are tested by their treatment of him and by their reaction to approaching death. Only Discretion and the Poor Man—who comport themselves with a seemly humility—gain immediate admittance to paradise; the Unborn Child goes to limbo,[3] the Rich Man directly to hell; and the others are assigned purgatory. The King at first acts as arrogantly and irresponsibly as any other character; a remarkably frank treatment, considering that the premier performance of each *auto sacramental* in Madrid customarily played to the king himself.[4]

In this religious drama, a measure of the Poor Man's heroics consisted, after an initial protest, in resigned acceptance of his lot in this world and a glad anticipation of passage into the next world. The Rich Man on the other hand failed to put to good use his "libre albedrío" (free will), and death caught him obstinate and unprepared. While an *auto sacramental* is primarily intended to celebrate the Eucharist—here God throws a cast party patterned after the Last Supper—in this particular play the audience also learns a reassuring (for the humbler citizens) and conservative social lesson: that regardless of caste or economic condition, we all achieve equality in death. Since it can take us at any moment, worldly goods and privilege ought not to be envied: they can only hinder our acceptance of divine will. The social disposition of *The Great Theater of the World* is consistent with Dunn's distinctions: abstractly, ideally, evangelically, "Man" is better for simplicity, and Calderón's Poor Man could also be taken for Everyman.

Sánchez Escribano and Porqueras Mayo have examined the attitudes toward the common man conveyed in Golden Age dramatic theory.[5] The varying treatments are complex and often self-contradictory, especially Lope's in *The New Art of Writing Plays*. There he scorns or pretends to scorn the *vulgo*, but realizes it is they he must please in order to sell his plays. One suspects that he shares their lack of patience with the classical precepts, while at the same time he wants to make clear his reluctance to be identified with the rabble. Again, it would seem that two contrary forces govern his equivocal rhetoric: that which respects the abstract, noble, reasonable "Everyman," the ideal public; and that plagued by the real and rowdy mob; the biblical versus the Roman conceptions of the people. *Fuenteovejuna* I think successfully realizes both visions of the *pueblo* and the *vulgo;* in the end the less worthy side of this collective protagonist must be punished and purged. Presumably by the final scene they will have gotten the savagery out of their systems and will now become civilized—the more humble, the more civilized— citizens in the unified Spain of the idealized Catholic kings.

Certainly *Life Is a Dream,* written during the same period as *The Great Theater of the World* (c. 1635), does not flatter its *vulgo,* which is portrayed as a visceral and balky Polish throng, in the end herded reluctantly toward civilization. Among Calderón's secular *comedias,* in fact, only two accord central roles to plebeians. And both *Luis Pérez, the Galician* and *The Alcalde of Zalamea* can be shown to concord with *Life Is a Dream* in their skeptical portrayal of lower-class sensibilities. Both plays contain implicit criticism of the king who allows the peasants in his realm to break the law, and who is too busy or distracted with dreams of empire to call the outlaws to account.

According to Shergold and Varey, Part 1 of *Luis Pérez* was performed by 1629.[6] The promised continuation was apparently never produced; consequently the text we have is only half of Luis Pérez's story, and it is admittedly impossible to claim with confidence a thorough understand- ing of the dramatist's attitude to his creature. Still, since common protagonists are so very uncommon in Calderón, a look at this aristo- cratic playwright's early rendition of a plebeian subject, and the schol- arly reaction to it, will serve as a useful preface to our consideration of *The Alcalde*'s extraordinary Pedro Crespo.

As it stands, ending on a farcical note wholly incompatible with poetic justice, *Luis Pérez* could be classified alongside those early comic honor plays of Lope, *The Markets of Madrid* (*Las ferias de Madrid*) and *The Comendadores of Córdoba*. Although *Luis Pérez* is not by Larson's definition an honor play, its wealthy commoner-protagonist worships the gods of honor and friendship. In their names he gaily perpetrates the equivalent of a comic-book series of violent and warped-heroic crimes on the comparatively impotent officials and citizens of Galicia, Portugal, and Andalusia.

As the play begins, the wealthy *villano* Luis Pérez is chasing his servant Pedro across the stage with a dagger. The *bufón* has had the bad taste to act as *tercero* for the Jew Juan Bautista, who wants to court Luis Pérez's sister Isabel. The plot's pace never slackens. Two supplicants soon arrive separately at Luis Pérez's doorstep, characters fleeing the law who ask the rich peasant's help. A man of honor, Luis Pérez cannot but take the parts of Manuel Méndez, wanted for murder, and then Don Alonso, an illegal duelist, even though to defend them our hero must set upon the officers of the law in their pursuit, killing at least one and injuring another.

From this point on, Luis Pérez is on the wrong side of the law, and his story is a string of serious crimes committed under the lofty banners of "honor" and "friendship." He does not mind earning the reputation of "a scoundrel, an insolent fellow / . . . a vile man, / who . . . makes his living by murdering and robbing" ("un bellaco, un insolente / . . . hombre vil, / que . . . vive de hacer muertes / y delitos"),[7] of "a villainous man / and a homicide" ("facineroso / y homicida" [304a]); but when Juan Bautista lies, reporting to the law that Luis Pérez killed a man in an unfair fight—dishonorably—it is a blemish on his good name ("mi honor" [307a]) that the peasant cannot abide. Without warning, he runs through his slanderer with a sword. Juan Bautista is fatally wounded, but enough breath remains for him to concede graciously, "My death is justified, / for all that I said was a lie / intended to get his sister" ("muero con justa causa, / pues cuanto he dicho fingí / por conseguir a su hermana" [309a]).

Luis Pérez now supports himself "honorably" by waylaying travelers and politely asking for a handout. Once they learn what famous murderer begs this boon, they willingly part with their money; therefore Luis claims that his practice cannot be called "robbery." The *villano* blames his criminal profession on bad luck, "the cruel dictate / of my star and my destiny" ("el rigor crüel / de mi estrella y mi destino" [304b]), which would be a good joke to seventeenth-century Spaniards indoctrinated in the theology of Catholic free will—as would Luis's excesses committed in the interest of maintaining his mottled reputation, and out of comradeship with his fellow criminals.

In *Luis Pérez* Calderón seems deliberately to evoke two Cervantine prose narratives. At one point the protagonist calls himself the "curioso impertinente," the man of ill-advised curiosity, which is the title of one of the interpolated stories in Part 1, chapters 33 through 35, of *Don Quixote*. It tells the tale of *"los dos amigos,"* two men renowned for their unshakable friendship, which they take to such an absurd extreme that both finally die in disgrace. Luis Pérez's view of himself as "a very honorable thief" ("ladrón muy de bien" [303b]) would also qualify him for initiation into Monipodio's den of farcical cutthroats brought to life in Cervantes's exemplary novel *Rinconete and Cortadillo*. There a society of lowlife hoodlums profess their respect for religion, honor, and friendship. Luis Pérez's manifold transgressions for "amigo" and "amistad" particularly summon up Monipodio's fastidious admonition to a pimp quarreling with his prostitute-lover: " 'Friends should never anger their friends, nor joke at the expense of their friends, and especially when they see that their friends are getting angry' " (" 'Nunca los amigos han de dar enojo a los amigos ni hacer burla de los amigos, y más cuando ven que se enojan los amigos' ").8

By the end of the *comedia*, Luis Pérez has gathered an assortment of loyal followers ("friends") who include several ladies and a gentleman, as well as his other compatriots. These all finally converge to free the Galician criminal from the ineffectual hands of justice and the jaws of death, so that Luis Pérez might continue his adventures in Part 2. At the end Pedro the clown proposes that this colorful criminal should next become a monk, and it is no wonder that Calderón never caught his breath to write the continuation.

If as it stands *Luis Pérez* bears any discernible moral intent, it might be a criticism of the gross abuse of free will; that would put the protagonist in the same league as Tirso's Don Juan Tenorio. In any case, I wonder whether our playwright might not have been aghast at his modern editor's admiration for this ludicrously hypocritical, violent and destructive character. According to Valbuena Briones, Luis Pérez is the victim of "la adversa fortuna";9 Calderón paints "the pleasing portrait of the protagonist" ("la genial pintura del personaje protagonista"): "The author has created a real crowd-pleaser with the intention of entertaining the spectator without transmitting any moral lesson whatsoever" ("El autor ha creado una obra de gran público con el entendimiento de entretener al espectador sin esbozar lección moral alguna"). Luis Pérez is a man with a "robust" ("recio") sense of honor:

His arbitrariness and zeal on behalf of his friends, his ingenuous malice—demonstrated in the way he robs travelers—his gallantry and generosity, bestow on him chivalric touches of a preromantic type, along the lines of a Cyrano de Bergerac. . . . The course of events leads toward a tragic denouement, but friends and enemies of the valiant character, in a final apotheosis, free the Galician.

(Su arbitrariedad y celo por los amigos, su ingenua malicia—se explaya en la manera de robar a los caminantes—, su gallardía y generosidad, le otorgan características caballerescas de signo prerromántico en la línea de Cyrano de Bergerac. . . . El curso de los acontecimientos conduce hacia un *dénouement* trágico, pero amigos y enemigos del valiente personaje, en una apoteosis final, dan la libertad al gallego. [280a])

Although seldom attracting scholarly inquiry, the play, especially in the nineteenth century, found a large audience in translation, having been rendered into English, French, and German.[10] It would appear that the true apotheosis of this character occurred centuries after his artistic birth, in a sort of "Romantic Lie," one reminiscent of José Zorrilla's, which in 1844 disinters Tirso's *Burlador* and sends him to heaven;[11] or of Miguel de Unamuno's, which makes a Christ-figure out of Don Quixote.[12] Valbuena Briones here enshrines a Romantic rebel of his own design, not the silly thug that Calderón originally created in Luis Pérez. Parker has shown that the exceptional interest in the figure of the bandit in the Golden Age *comedia* is not a result of esteem for the social rebel as might be the case elsewhere: Spanish drama begets no Robin Hoods. On the contrary, characters such as Enrico in *Damned for Despair* (*El condenado por desconfiado*), Eusebio in *The Devotion to the Cross*, and Young Lope in *The Three Justices in One* (*Las tres justicias en una*)—not to mention the female *bandoleras*—are all fascinating because spectacular sin makes for spectacular conversion, that is, *desengaño*. "In these plays" and other similar ones, Parker writes,

heroism is not directed towards worldly glory, neither is it anarchical nor destructive: because it is strongly influenced by the Christian sense of life, it is a heroism directed towards heaven. The action of these plays is violent, but their psychology is not extravagant. Below the surface violence there is a profound humanism, a deep sense of social values and a lofty moral feeling combined with a great compassion for sinners, recognising even in them the immense spiritual value of the human soul. This distinctive humanism is, in my opinion, the most valuable legacy that Spanish culture has transmitted to us.[13]

The plebeian Luis Pérez is not a man of the passion that admits such affecting conversion, but an unreflective hooligan who transgresses on impulse. Spanish oral tradition deprecatory to the *gallego* testifies to the low esteem that a character like Luis Pérez, a common man if not a humble one, would earn among Calderón's audience. Of the saying "I would rather be a bastard than a Galician," Gonzalo Correas comments, "taunt against Galicians, because the lower-class ones tend to blanket their land with discredit; the aristocrats from there are [however] very good" ("Matraca contra gallegos, porque la gente baja suele encubrir su tierra por haber ganado descrédito; la gente granada de allá en [*sic*] muy buena" [54]). It will be recalled that the heroes of Lope's *The Greatest Alcalde* are Galician *hidalgos.*

Nor would the implied royal context of this play merit the public's applause. During the later years of Philip II's reign (1556–98), J. H. Elliott writes,[14] the King became more and more interested in emulating the imperial successes of his father Charles V (1516–56). Not satisfied merely with the territories brought under the Spanish scepter by New World explorers, Philip wanted to pacify his troublesome northern possession, Flanders, along with various unruly regions closer to home. In 1580 he succeeded through some questionable legal and military maneuvers in claiming the crown of Portugal. In 1588 he sent off the Invincible Armada to conquer England with the further hope of securing the domination of Flanders; in 1591–92 he deployed troops to Aragon to subdue the unrest fomented in part by his suppression of Aragonese *fueros,* or traditional liberties.[15]

These three historical moments crucially figure directly or indirectly in at least four of Calderón's *comedias.* The death of King Sebastian of Portugal in 1578, which was to leave the door open to Philip's accession two years later, looms over *Secret Vengeance for a Secret Insult.* The Castilian king's vigorous efforts, both legitimate and suspect, to secure the Lusitanian crown have momentous impact for an understanding of

The Alcalde of Zalamea; and the suppression of the Aragonese *fueros,* viewed by Mariana among many others as tyrannical,[16] is tacitly condemned in *The Three Justices in One.*[17] Furthermore, King Philip II's standing among his people had been damaged by the fate of his firstborn son, Charles, who died under suspicious circumstances while imprisoned. The Charles affair also reached the Spanish stage, being depicted critically in Lope's *The Great Duke of Muscovy (El Gran Duque de Moscovia),* Diego Jiménez de Enciso's *El príncipe Don Carlos,* and possibly even constituting an inspiration for Calderón's own *Life Is a Dream.*[18]

Luis Pérez, the Galician is set in 1588 during the embarkation of the ill-fated Spanish Armada.[19] "If any one year," according to Elliott, "marks the division between the triumphant Spain of the first two Hapsburgs and the defeatist, disillusioned Spain of their successors, that year is 1588."[20] In their subsequent efforts to account for Spain's economic and political failures, Pedro de Rivadeneira and Juan de Mariana both assigned blame to immorality among the Spaniards. In a letter to one of Philip II's favorites written shortly after the defeat of the Armada, Rivadeneira advises among other remedial measures, that the King set a better personal standard than he has in the past:

> that more care be taken in eliminating sins and public scandals, especially if some concern eminent personages who have the obligation to set an example: because with the wickedness that [this scandalous behavior] imparts, they infect or corrupt the republic, and since His Majesty is head and master of [the republic], and is able so simply and with but one act of his will to emend and correct his excesses, it seems that Our Lord will be able to call him to account for it if he doesn't.

> (que se ponga mayor cuidado en quitar pecados y escándalos públicos, especialmente si hubiese algunos de personas grandes que tienen obligación de dar ejemplo: porque con lo malo que dan inficionan o corrompen la república, y pues Su Majestad es cabeza y señor de ella, y puede con tanta facilidad y con sola una demostración de su voluntad enmendar y corregir los excesos, parece que nuestro Señor le podrá pedir cuenta de lo que en esto no hiciere.)[21]

Rivadeneira hoped that his advice would reach the King, and this letter appears diplomatically to impute the loss to royal moral deficiencies. Mariana's criticism, published after Philip II's death, is more explicit. Portugal was defeated and its king (Sebastian) lost in Africa, he writes in *On the King* (*Del rey*), because of offenses against God by the Portuguese. However, so that Spaniards might not gloat over the faults of their neighbors, a few years later the Armada was lost,

> a defeat and an insult from which we will not recover in many years, but which is no more than revenge for the grave crimes which are committed in our nation, and if my heart does not deceive me, revenge for the ill-concealed lewd behavior of a certain prince, who, forgetting about his dignity and his already advanced age, it was well-known that at that very time he surrendered himself unrestrainedly to lust, a fact that obliged all the towns and cities to make public vows and supplications, to placate the saints in such bad times, who, provoked by the insanity of but one man, wanted to expiate so many crimes with a general punishment and ignored the prayers of the people.

> (derrota y afrenta que no podemos subsanar en muchos años, pero que no es mas que la venganza de los graves crímenes que en nuestra nación se cometen, y si no me engaña el corazon, la de las mal encubiertas liviandades de cierto príncipe, que olvidándose de su dignidad y de su edad ya avanzada era fama que por aquel mismo tiempo se entregaba desenfrenadamente á la lujuria, hecho que obligaba á todos los pueblos y ciudades á hacer votos y rogativas públicas, para aplacar en tanto riesgo á los santos, que irritados por la locura de un solo hombre, querían expiar tantos crímenes con un castigo general y despreciaron las oraciones de los pueblos.) (557b)[22]

Calderón must have had some reason for setting his tale of the Galician outlaw at the low point in Philip II's reign, indeed, at one of the most decisive and humiliating turning points in Spanish history. Since we lack the continuation—if there was one—it is risky to attempt to judge the import of this puzzling play. It is possible that Calderón made his protagonist such a blackguard so that his conversion, like the retrospective recantation of the picaro, would be all the more satisfying and edifying to his Counter-Reformation audience. A *comedia* by Cervantes, *The Fortunate Thug* (*El rufián dichoso*), tells the story of that type of brutal character, whose reform occurs between the first and second acts. In *Damned for Despair*, attributed to Tirso de Molina, the ostensibly incorrigible outlaw Enrico repents at the last moment; and in Calderón's own *Devotion to the Cross*, a similar character, Eusebio, is miraculously brought back to life so that he may confess and achieve absolution. These plays are all, then, formally speaking, comedy, of a kind meant to divert the audience cathartically before bringing it back into the moral fold. Of delinquency in Golden Age comedy, Wardropper writes that the public at the *corral* may be gratified witnessing the departure from society's ethical standards of conduct,

> but from all truancy there must be a return to normal life. And in this return to normality the audience finds a second source of gratification. It is comforted when it sees the truants resume their proper places in a divinely ordained social hierarchy, in a world right-side-up. . . . As the Spanish theoreticians put it, comedy cleanses the soul of its passions.[23]

It is also possible that as in so many other Golden Age *comedias*, the dramatist means for the audience to draw a parallel between the character of the protagonist and the events in the historical context, perhaps in this case between Luis Pérez and the implied stage king himself. It has become clear that Calderón like Mariana and like other dramatists[24] did not hold Philip II in the highest regard, and the play's several allusions to the Spanish Armada could only remind the audience of this monarch's, and by association, Luis Pérez's, sensational failure.

In any case, neither Luis Pérez nor any other character in his play, excepting the minor villain Juan Bautista with his dying confession, achieves any sort of self-knowledge. If historically the reputation of this plebeian protagonist has for readers and spectators of subsequent centuries been rehabilitated by Romantic (or "pre-Romantic") scholarly sensibilities, for Calderón's contemporaries this criminal's lack of conscience (it is always "destiny" and not his own doing that gets him into trouble) and his comic idolatry of honor and friendship would exclude him from any moral awareness, which is ultimately the only real kind of heroism in Golden Age drama. I would speculate that *Luis Pérez, the Galician* was planned to be a comedy, with an accounting at the end—so that if the audience did delight in this amoral character's escapades, they would also applaud, finally, his comeuppance, or as with the picaro, his reform.

Pedro Crespo's Hidden Agenda[25]

About Rivadeneira's and Mariana's supernatural-retribution explanations for Spain's ills, Elliott writes,

> There would be no more victories . . . until morals were reformed. The age revealed its corruption in sexual immorality and religious hypocrisy; in the idleness and insubordination of youth; in luxurious living, rich clothing and excessive indulgence in food and drink; and in the addiction to the theatre and to games of chance.[26]

Calderón's second play with a peasant protagonist, *The Alcalde of Zalamea,* is, next to *Life Is a Dream,* the most widely known and often-produced of his *comedias.* Hispanists regard *The Alcalde* as an anomaly in the generally aristocratic opus of this dramatist because of the respect and dignity it confers on its humble hero. Indeed, it is this play's apparent high regard for the honor of the wealthy rustic Pedro Crespo that has caused critics to rank Calderón with Lope as a democratic sympathizer *avant la lettre.* Salomon (*Recherches,* xvi) finds in *The Alcalde* a "veritable apotheosis of the peasant theme" ("véritable apothéose du thème paysan").

Dated between 1636 and 1642,[27] the play takes place in August 1580 as Philip II hurries through Extremadura to Lisbon to claim the Portuguese crown; the King appears in Zalamea in the final scenes. The rich peasant farmer Pedro Crespo has two children, the beautiful and modest Isabel; and Juan, whom Pedro, loving father though he is, describes as "a loafer, a spoiled boy" ("un holgazán, un perdido").[28] Juan apparently lacks a vocation and spends a good deal of time and money gambling. Early in the play, when he asks his father to cover his gambling debts, he receives into the bargain a gentle lecture, not on the evils of gambling per se, but on the inconvenience of wagering more than he can cover. "Never," Pedro admonishes,

do either of these two things:
offer what you don't
know if you can produce, or risk
more than what you have at hand;
so that if by chance
you lose, you won't also lose your good name.

(Dos cosas no has de hacer nunca:
no ofrecer lo que no sabes
que has de cumplir, ni jugar
más de lo que está delante;
porque si por accidente
falta, tu opinión no falte.)

                                        (1.453–58)

Pedro Crespo repeatedly stresses to Juan the importance of keeping up appearances if he wants to succeed in life. Later, when the boy is about to join the military, his father counsels him to seem humble:

In this world, how many people,
having some personal defect,
have concealed it by being humble!
And how many, who have had
no defect, have been blamed for one
simply because they're not well-liked!

(¡Cuántos, teniendo en el mundo
algún defecto consigo,
le han borrado por humildes!
Y ¡a cuántos, que no han tenido
defecto, se le han hallado
por estar ellos mal vistos!)

                                        (2.704–9)

The elder Crespo is an extremely proud man, but takes care to veil his actions with humble words. With this calculated humility he soon wins the favor of General Don Lope de Figueroa and, later, the respect of the King himself. But Pedro also thinks he knows how to gain the esteem of his equals, advising Juan,

Be very courteous,
be generous to many;
for a tip of the hat, and money
are what will make friends,
and all the gold that
the Indies yield up
and all that is lost at sea, is not worth as much
as being well-liked.

(Sé cortés sobre manera,
sé liberal y esparcido;
que el sombrero y el dinero
son los que hacen los amigos;
y no vale tanto el oro
que el sol engendra en el indio
suelo y que consume el mar
como ser uno bienquisto.)

                                        (2.710–17)

The importance of honor as reputation sinks in; three times during the play in the name of honor Juan Crespo gets into scrapes, from which his father must rescue him. Simultaneously, Pedro Crespo watches carefully and learns from these encounters, so that by the last and gravest of his son's escapades, Pedro not only is able to protect Juan, but retains for himself for life the office of Alcalde of Zalamea.

On each of the three occasions, a captain in Felipe II's imperial army is also involved. The company is to be billeted in Zalamea; because Crespo lacks noble blood and refuses to purchase a title, he must put up his share of soldiers. Juan Crespo does not mind at all; he is impressed with what must be the exciting life of the military. But his father, expecting trouble, sends the lovely Isabel and her cousin to hide in the attic. That action piques the curiosity of Captain Don Alvaro de Ataide, who is to lodge at Crespo's. He now determines somehow to get a look at this peasant girl whose beauty is so worth hiding.

The opportunity arises when the lowly soldier Rebolledo, who like Juan Crespo has a fondness for gambling, approaches the Captain for money. Don Alvaro makes up a little play-within-the-play: he will help Rebolledo if Rebolledo will pretend to fight with him and escape to the attic; then the Captain, in hot pursuit, will get his chance to see Isabel without arousing Pedro Crespo's suspicions. The "invención" works, except that the boy Juan Crespo is present, divines the deception, and gets into a row with the soldiers, muttering to himself, "I'm ashamed / that they think they're putting one over on me / and I will not stand for that" ("Corrido en el alma estoy / de que piensen que me engañan, / y no ha de ser" [1.737–39]). Claiming jurisdiction over his son, Pedro Crespo comes to aid Juan in the fray.

At this point, General Don Lope de Figueroa arrives at the house to settle the dispute. Although the elder Crespo assures the General that it was nothing, to himself he remarks that the lad nearly caused quite a brawl (1.783–84). Don Lope investigates, questioning Rebolledo. The soldier, fearing a whipping in punishment, immediately "sings": it was, he reveals, all a scheme of the Captain's. Don Alvaro and the soldiers are sent in disgrace outside the village, and the General himself will stay at Crespo's. He is above suspicion with respect to Isabel, he explains, because of advanced age and a sore leg that troubles him so.

From this first of Juan Crespo's scuffles, Pedro takes note of several facts that will serve him well later. Firstly, he sees that his son is easily provoked and hard to control. The peasant sees that Don Lope is an impartial arbiter and a zealous prosecutor. Pedro Crespo also observes the Captain's disdain for peasants; finally, he notes that Rebolledo is easily cowed by the threat of physical pain.

The second crisis occurs in the second act. Now consumed by passion for Isabel, the Captain dreams up another scheme. He sends musicians to sing outside Isabel's window, instructing them not to betray his part in the serenading. It is evening and Pedro, Juan, and Isabel sit with the General, who by this point has become quite fond of the family. At the commencement of the music all are incensed, but pretending not to hear it, they say good night. Pedro and Don Lope separately sneak outside with swords to accost the musicians. The culprits flee, so that the two friends unknowingly fight each other; only when Juan joins them also intending to teach the soldiers a lesson, is the mistake discovered. Don Lope again claims jurisdiction, scolding Pedro that this has been a military matter and not the peasant's business. The Captain is then seen with his men and pretends to be arresting the troublemaking soldiers.

During this second incident, Pedro again beholds General Don Lope's jealous concern for military jurisdiction. Furthermore, this time Captain Don Alvaro has escaped direct blame although his guiding part in the disturbance is pretty evident: this time he has planned more thoroughly his assault on Isabel's resistance. Therefore Crespo can see that a good maneuver to hide wrongdoing is, when caught in compromising circumstances, to have considered all contingencies in advance in such a way that one might claim the zeal of the prosecutor, rather than having to admit the guilt of the perpetrator. This evasive strategy will be useful to Pedro in the third act, when he wants to divert King Felipe's attention from Juan's gravest offense and from Crespo's own murder of a prisoner in his custody.

Again Pedro Crespo notes his son's volatility. Juan Crespo is a real problem, an emotional and idle youth. It is then a great relief to Pedro—and a delight to Juan—when, late in the second act, Don Lope, the General, recruits the boy into the army. Now Juan, who has been a real handful, will be in Don Lope's hands, and legally in his jurisdiction.

But the Captain has not given up in his pursuit of Isabel. At the end of the second act, after Juan has gone off to join the soldiers, Don Alvaro, Rebolledo, and the others kidnap Isabel. In pursuit, *Pedro Crespo falls.* He is bound to a tree. The final words of the act are spoken by Pedro's son: riding to join his military troupe, with his horse *Juan Crespo falls.* Then, hearing the cries of a man and a woman—Pedro and Isabel—he chivalrously chooses to follow the woman's voice.

At the beginning of the third act, the night has passed. Wandering alone in the wild, Isabel comes upon her father, still tied to a tree. She knows that the honor code calls for her father to kill her; she wants to die but not without first telling her tragic story. She leaves Crespo bound while narrating the previous night's calamity and Juan's third and most serious *pendencia.* The night before, as the soldiers turned their backs, the Captain raped Isabel. Drawn by her cries, Juan came upon the two; imagining his sister's willing part in the dishonor, he tried to kill her. The Captain, "who, now coming / to my aid, against [Juan's] blade / takes out his own white knife" ("que el tardo socorro mira / en mi favor, contra el [acero] suyo / saca la blanca cuchilla" [3.219-22]). Captain Don Alvaro, who had *rescued* Isabel from her brother's honor-inspired rage,[29] was himself wounded *and fell.* Closing in for the kill, Juan was chased off by the Captain's men.

Meanwhile, Isabel relates, she escaped. Still bound to the tree, Pedro Crespo, who had been lamenting (first) the loss of his honor, and (second) the loss of Isabel, now, suddenly, tables these considerations. His daughter, expecting death, unties him, but his foremost concern is not now honor, nor Isabel, but what will happen to Juan:

Isabel, let us hurry:
let us return home;
for this boy is in danger,
and we will have
to use all our wits
to find him
and get him to safety.

(Isabel, vamos aprisa:
demos la vuelta a mi casa;
que este muchacho peligra,
y hemos menester hacer
diligencias exquisitas
por saber dél y ponerle
en salvo.)

(3.290-95)

The recruit Juan Crespo has attempted to murder his captain, Don
Alvaro; the Captain must be prevented from lodging a complaint because
it would be a military matter, and Don Lope would have indisputable
jurisdiction. The General, who has in the past confrontations shown
scrupulous interest in arriving at the truth and vigorous enforcement of
his decisions, has a reputation for "knowing how / to render just judgment on the best of his friends, / without wasting time on legal niceties"
("sabe[r] hacer / justicia del más amigo, / sin fulminar el proceso"
[1.56-58]). Consequently, Pedro Crespo is worried that this time Juan
has gone too far. Apprehensive for his son's security—which Don Alvaro's
survival threatens—he tells Isabel, "my concern / won't be put to rest
until / I kill [the Captain]" ("el ansia mía / no ha de parar hasta darle [al
Capitán] / la muerte" [3.306-8]).

However, these musings are interrupted by the news that Pedro
Crespo has been elected the village *alcalde*, the mayor and judge of
Zalamea. The Escribano (court clerk) informs him that two great matters await his attention: first, the imminent arrival of King Felipe II, on
his way to claim the crown of Portugal. But the second matter is far more
alarming:

for today they've brought into town
in secret for hurried medical attention

that Captain, who yesterday
had his company here.
He doesn't say who wounded him;
but if this information is discovered,
there will be a great legal case.

(que ahora han traído a la villa
de secreto unos soldados
a curarse con gran prisa
a aquel Capitán, que ayer
tuvo aquí su compañía.
El no dice quién le hirió;
pero si esto se averigua,
será gran causa.)
                    (3.320–27; italics mine)

It bears repeating that, pricked by conscience, Don Alvaro was injured
saving Isabel from her own brother—at which point the Captain fell.
   Pedro Crespo pauses to examine his conscience, or at least his changed
circumstances, before he answers the Clerk. To himself he exclaims,

       Heavens!
When I imagine getting revenge,
the staff of justice
becomes the proprietor of my honor!
How can I transgress,
if at this very hour
they have made me a judge
so that others do not transgress?
But matters such as these
should not be too hastily considered.

       (¡Cielos!
¡Cuando vengarse imagina,
me hace dueño de mi honor
la vara de la justicia!
¿Cómo podré dilinquir
yo, si en esta hora misma
me ponen a mí por juez

> para que otros no delincan?
> *Pero cosas como aquestas*
> *no se ven con tanta prisa.*)
> > > > (3.328–36; italics mine)

He does not discard the idea of revenge or of killing the Captain to keep him quiet; it will simply require more wit to carry it off, now that the peasant has become the town's mayor and judge. Pedro Crespo turns to Isabel and declares, "Daughter, / now your father is alcalde: / he will guarantee you justice" ("Hija, / ya tenéis al padre alcalde: / él os guardará justicia" [3.347–48]).

The phrasing of his reassurance to his daughter would alert the Spanish audience to Crespo's true intent, since it evokes the well-known Spanish expression, "He whose father is alcalde, goes to trial in safety" ("Quien tiene al padre alcalde, seguro va a juicio").[30] Indeed, for the spectators, Crespo's new office would endow him with a specific set of qualifications useful for saving Juan from prosecution. Salomon points out that alcaldes in Spanish oral tradition, including proverbs and numerous *comedias,* are notorious for corruption, strong family ties, and swift, bloody misapplication of justice (*Recherches,* 112).

One way of simultaneously keeping Don Alvaro quiet and repairing Isabel's honor would be for the Captain to marry her. The marriage would presumably prevent him from lodging a complaint against his new brother-in-law. When the Captain, who has made clear his disdain for peasants, arrogantly rejects that proposal, his "impartial" judge declares, "I swear to God / that you'll pay me for this" ("Pues juro a Dios / que me lo habéis de pagar" [3.548–49]). Don Alvaro, beginning to fear the wrath of this formidable alcalde, announces that he will complain to the King. In order to get the Captain to give up his sword, Crespo assures him that he will have that chance for appeal, pledging that "he [the King] will hear / us both" ("nos oirá / a los dos" [3.568–69]).

Crespo, of course, has no intention of keeping his promise. The Captain is never allowed the opportunity to tell his side of the story, and the circumstances of his injury which are so incriminating to Juan. When Felipe II arrives, the peasant presents him with Don Alvaro's corpse. He cheekily answers objections to the violation of due process: "That," he announces,

> falling under the dead man's jurisdiction,
> is for him to complain about,

and until he himself protests
it doesn't concern anyone else.

> ([E]sa es querella del muerto,
> que toca a su autoridad,
> y hasta que él mismo se queje
> no les toca a los demás.)
>
> (3.932–35)

In the meantime, the peasant has put into action all that he has learned during the course of the play and his son's imbroglios. Once Don Alvaro's intent to bring the matter before the King has become apparent—and he has been disarmed—the alcalde proceeds swiftly. Announcing to the Captain, "By God, I'm going to hang you" ("[O]s he de ahorcar, juro a Dios" [3.589]), Crespo sets in motion his own "invención" that will disguise the murder as justice, circumventing the scrupulous Don Lope and gambling that the King will not take the time to investigate.

The immediate problem is to silence the witnesses to Juan Crespo's attacks on Isabel and the Captain. Pedro already knows about Rebolledo's terror of physical pain. As the soldier is brought to him, Crespo remarks in his hearing, "This is the picaro who sings; / with one slit across the throat / he'll never perform again" ("Este el pícaro es que canta; / con un paso de garganta / no ha de hacer otro en su vida" [3.595–97]). The peasant threatens Rebolledo and his camp follower and fellow witness La Chispa with torture and death until they tell him what he wants to hear:

> CHISPA.   Yes, we'll tell
>   even more than we know;
>   for it would be better than dying.
> CRESPO.   That will save the two of you
>   from torture.

> (CHISPA.   Sí diremos
>   aún más de lo que sabemos;
>   que peor será morir.
> CRESPO.   Eso excusará a los dos
>   del tormento.)
>
> (3.623–27)

Since Crespo is seconded throughout his illegal procedures by the court Clerk, these scenes recall another alcalde-saying: "May God free you from new alcaldes and old court clerks" ("Dios te libre de alcalde nuevo y de escribano viejo").[31]

Meanwhile, Juan Crespo knows he has really gotten himself into a jam this time. Believing both his life and his honor in danger (3.646–48), he hurries home to his father for help. His appearance now very nearly exposes the lie of Pedro Crespo's "investigation": while a disinterested judge would be happy to have in custody the man suspected of a grave crime, Crespo is furious. Angrily the father scolds the son,

> it's a mistake
> that you dare to come . . .
> before me today like this,
> having just wounded
> a captain in the wilderness.

> (es error
> que os atreváis a venir . . .
> delante así de mí hoy,
> acabando ahora de herir
> en el monte un capitán.)
>   (3.665–66, 668–70)

When Juan tries to explain, Crespo interrupts, calling over the other peasants:

> CRESPO.   That's enough, Juan.
>   Hey, take him prisoner,
>   too.
> JUAN.   Your own son, sir,
>   you treat so harshly?

> (CRESPO.   Ea, basta, Juan. —
>   Hola, llevadle también
>   preso.
> JUAN.   ¿A tu hijo, señor,
>   tratas con tanto rigor?)
>   (3.673–76)

Crespo replies loudly, "And even my father, too / I would treat so strictly" ("Y aun a mi padre también / con tal rigor le tratara" [3.676-77]), but adds to himself,

> This will assure the safety
> of his life, and they're going to think
> that it's the most wonderful justice
> in the world.

> (Aquesto es asegurar
> su vida, y han de pensar
> que es la justicia más rara
> del mundo.
>
> [3.679-82])

Soon afterwards Crespo adds in another aside, "I will get him off" ("Yo le hallaré la disculpa.") (3.693)

Thus Pedro Crespo's hidden agenda is made evident to the audience, if not to the public in the play. The peasant's priority is not the application of justice, as he declares in public utterances, but the safety of his son, as he declares in asides. Pedro is prepared to use the camouflage of his new rank to save the boy *from* justice—for attacking a senior officer (who was, let us remember, at that point *defending* Isabel).

Calderón depicts similarly conflicting interests in his religious drama *The Prodigious Magician* (*El mágico prodigioso*) (1637), set in third-century A.D. Antioch. There, the Governor arrests his own son and a rival, who have been fighting over the chaste Justina:

GOVERNOR.	Enough, Laelius, enough! Are you—my son!—so quick to draw your sword? Do you abuse my good will to the point of causing a disturbance in Antioch?
LAELIUS.	Sir, let me explain that . . .
GOVERNOR.	Take them away. No exception, no privilege of blood, shall make their punishments unequal for their crimes are equal.

(GOBERNADOR.   Baste, Lelio, baste.
                    ¿Tú inquieto, siendo mi hijo?
                    ¿Tú de mi favor te vales
                    para alterar a Antioquía?
LELIO.   Señor, advierte . . .
GOBERNADOR.   Llevaldes;
                    que no ha de haber excepción
                    ni privilegios de sangre
                    para no igualar castigos,
                    pues son las culpas iguales).[32]

A few lines later, the Governor proclaims with pride that he does not want it said that he would "pass sentence as an interested party, as a biased judge" (175) ("no digan / que sentencio como parte, / siendo apasionado juez" [1750-52]). Although he represents a government that persecutes Christians, at this point the Governor appears committed to impartiality. In the third act, however, as he wages a campaign of harassment against the Christians, among them Justina, he confides to an underling: contrary to appearances, he has kept his son imprisoned not out of fairness, but, as a loving father, to keep Laelius out of trouble (245; 2781-88). And by killing Justina, he will remove the cause of the quarrel.

In the third act of *The Alcalde of Zalamea,* Pedro Crespo proceeds to distract attention from his son's case by drawing attention to that of his daughter, even though Isabel would rather let the matter drop than face the shame that publicity will bring (3.701-5). But honor is no longer Crespo's concern: to silence Juan's victim is, and if the Mayor can get revenge into the bargain, so much the better.

Pedro Crespo's actions now are guided by past experience. He knows that Juan will raise a fuss; by arresting the erratic youth he preserves him from military justice and keeps him out from under foot. Pedro Crespo also knows that General Don Lope will eventually make vigorous inquiries; he must, then, hurry to eliminate the only other witness besides Isabel to the attack on the Captain, Don Alvaro himself. As the General and the Alcalde soon face off over custody of the Captain, the King materializes.

Pedro Crespo learned in the first act from Don Alvaro how to "invent" a means to a desired end; he learned from Don Alvaro in the second act how to get away with it: by claiming to be on the side of the prosecutors. In this climactic ex machina scene, Pedro diverts attention from Juan's crime against the Captain by emphasizing the Captain's crime against poor Isabel, so that his boy's excesses receive only passing note and are soon forgotten. By now he has removed all contrary witnesses with threats of torture and death, so that his forensical claim to the King of impartiality in Isabel's case handily overrules Don Lope's challenge:

DON LOPE.	This is the alcalde, and the father of Isabel.
CRESPO.	It doesn't matter in such a case, because if a stranger came to file a complaint wouldn't I have to carry out justice? Yes; well what's the difference if I do for my daughter the same that I would do for anyone else? Apart from that, since I have arrested a son of mine, it is clear that I wouldn't favor my daughter, since it's the same blood relationship. . . . See if the case isn't correctly prosecuted, see if there is anyone who says that I have proceeded in it wrongly, *if I have coerced any witness,* if anything is written beyond what I have said, and then kill me.
KING.	The case is well supported.

(DON LOPE. Este es el alcalde, y es
          su padre [de Isabel].

CRESPO.   No importa en tal
           caso, porque si un extraño
           se viniera a querellar
           ¿no había de hacer justicia?
           Sí; ¿pues qué más se me da
           hacer por mi hija lo mismo
           que hiciera por los demás?
           Fuera de que, como he preso
           un hijo mío, es verdad
           que no escuchara a mi hija,
           pues era la sangre igual. . . .
           Mírese si está bien hecha
           la causa, miren si hay
           quien diga que yo haya hecho
           en ella alguna maldad,
           si he inducido algún testigo,
           si está escrito algo de más
           de lo que yo he dicho, y entonces
           me den muerte.
REY.   Bien está
           sustanciado.)

                          (3.874–94; italics mine)

Because Crespo has covered his bets by removing the unfavorable witnesses, his argument is quite safe. He may have wrecked his daughter's reputation, but with a virtuoso performance, employing tactics learned from the Captain himself, he has saved his son from justice, and gotten his revenge to boot. If we were to describe the action of this play in infinitive phrases along the lines of Francis Fergusson's and Donald Larson's formulae, it would certainly not rank among those works where the primary motivating force is to recover one's honor. *The Alcalde of Zalamea* is distinguished by three actions, corresponding with its three acts. The first two are Don Alvaro's initiatives: in act 1, to see Isabel; in act 2, to have Isabel. The motivating force of act 3 is Pedro Crespo's: to save Juan from prosecution. To that end he willingly sacrifices his daughter's—and by extension, his own—reputation, gambling that this empire-minded king will not take the time to examine the *causa* more closely.

Pedro Crespo wins. Remarking "It is well-supported," King Felipe II orders the prisoner (the Captain, that is, not Juan Crespo, who has been conveniently overlooked) handed over to the proper venue for punishment, as Pedro Crespo has no legal power to carry out the death sentence. The point is moot; Crespo has already done away with the Captain. He asks (poker-faced, no doubt) "What does it matter to have misstepped in such a minor way / when I have gotten the main issue right?" (¿[Q]ué importa errar lo menos, / quien ha acertado lo más?" [3.922–23]). He has had Don Alvaro garrotted because, he avows, his executioner lacks experience at decapitation, the form of capital punishment reserved for the nobility. Felipe accepts this sophistry, makes Crespo alcalde for life, and hurries off to Lisbon.

Pedro Crespo may all along have been a shrewd calculator, and he may have spoiled Juan and taught him to care too much for honor, but I see the father as originally a potentially good (or at least neutral) man who made the wrong choice at the crucial moment. The three characters who fell in short succession—Pedro, Juan, and the Captain—became enmeshed in a vicious and bitter trap of pride and self-interest; the sacrificial victim of all their pride was Isabel. Crespo is certainly a memorable character; not for any rustic virtue or simplicity, not for any imitable heroism, but for a very believable emotional life, which Calderón subtly exposes through asides. Several scenes in this play are composed almost entirely of asides, self-directed dialogue betraying the isolation of these characters from their fellows, and motives they dare not declare in the open.

Throughout acts 1 and 2, Pedro's zealous determination to maintain his own honor intact remains foremost. His first words in the first act are to himself, asides muttered against the "hidalgote" Don Mendo who wants to court Isabel. Someday, Pedro Crespo says to himself, I am going to get that man where it hurts ("alguna vez he de darle / de manera que le duela" [1.420–21]).[33] The sentiment is echoed by Juan Crespo, also in an aside (1.422). Soon, at the conclusion of that first confrontation with the Captain, Pedro swears that he would have killed Don Alvaro if the General Don Lope had not stopped him:

> Yes, by God,
> and even if he were the general,
> in threatening my reputation,
> I would kill him. . . .
> Whoever would dare to touch

one atom of my honor,
by heaven . . . ,
I would hang him.

(Sí, vive Dios,
y aunque fuera el general,
en tocando a mi opinión,
le matara. . . .
A quien se atreviera
a un átomo de mi honor,
viven los cielos . . . ,
que . . . le ahorcara yo.)
(1.858–61, 865–68)

In the context of this lethal rhetoric claiming the right to violent retalia-
tion for the slightest hint of a potential offense, the assertion that follows
and that has become proverbial among *Calderonistas* as an expression
of the peasant's Christian dignity, amounts at best to supreme indelicacy;
at worst to blasphemous contortion of Christian tenets. "[H]onor," Crespo
expounds in justification of his savage speech, "is patrimony of the soul,
/ and the soul belongs to God alone" ("el honor / es patrimonio del alma,
/ y el alma sólo es de Dios" [1.874–76]). After Isabel is carried off,
Pedro's first laments are not for his lost daughter, but for his lost honor
and the lack of a sword to avenge it (2.839–40, 851–52).

We know then, thanks to these remarks and to Crespo's parting
advice to his son, that the peasant prides himself most of all on his
unblemished reputation and the high regard of his neighbors, "for a tip
of the hat and money are what will make you friends." He declares
proudly to the Captain in the third act that Isabel would make a good
match:

I think it would certainly be sufficient
proof of this, sir,
my being rich, and there being no one who gossips about
me; my being modest,
and there being no one who speaks ill of me . . .

(Bien pienso que bastará,
señor, para abono desto,

el ser rico, y no haber quien
me murmure; ser modesto,
y no haber quien me baldone . . .)

(3.438-42)

But Crespo deceives himself: his neighbors do not admire him so much
as he would like to believe. At the beginning of the play the sergeant has
heard rumors that the peasant

> is the vainest
> man in the world, and that
> he is more pompous and presumptuous
> than an infante from Leon.

> (es el más vano
> hombre del mundo, y que tiene
> más pompa y más presunción
> que un infante de León.)
>
> (1.168-71)

Don Mendo calls him "villano malicioso" (1.409).

Juan Crespo learns from his father to covet reputation; it is his pride
in honor that in each case—the scene in the attic, the row over the
musicians, and the sexual relations of the Captain with his sister—causes
trouble. After Don Alvaro is wounded saving Isabel from her brother's
wrath, the boy comes home and tries to kill her again:

Isabel.	Brother!
	What are you trying to do?
Juan.	Avenge thus
	the danger in which today you have put
	my life and my honor.
Isabel.	Listen—
Juan.	I'm going to kill you,
	by heaven!

(Isabel.	¡Hermano!
	¿Qué intentas?
Juan.	Vengar así

> la ocasión en que hoy has puesto
> mi vida y mi honor.
> ISABEL.   Advierte —
> JUAN.   Tengo de darte la muerte,
> ¡viven los cielos!)
>
>   (3.656–61)

In any case, Pedro Crespo is an egotistical man and loving father whose main preoccupation during the first two acts, passed on to his son, is honor.

Then he falls. At this point, his abiding concern, that which will govern his actions to the end of the play *in despite of his honor,* is to save his beloved son, the "holgazán," the "perdido." Soon after, Crespo becomes Alcalde. One of Calderón's most important modifications of *The Alcalde of Zalamea* from the source play of the same title emphasizes the dilemma of the peasant's possible conflict of interests. In the original version, the pathos of duty versus revenge was diffused by Pedro Crespo's assumption of office in the first scene of the *comedia*.[34] Calderón's postponement of the peasant's election until the third act, after the Captain's rape of Isabel and Juan's attack on them both, considerably heightens the dramatic effectiveness and ambiguity of the problem.

However, the delay serves a second purpose. Albert E. Sloman notes that putting off the election allows Calderón to retain the striking denouement — the sudden unveiling of the garrotted Captain and its approval by the King — without "writing a play about an alcalde" (*Dramatic Craftsmanship,* 226). For the first two-thirds of the work, the dramatist emphasizes along with the protagonist's scrupulous concern for honor and his indulgence of his son, Crespo's cleverness and success in life. For two complete acts, Pedro Crespo is to the audience the epitome of the rich peasant, presenting an image quite apart from that of the typical alcalde and corresponding in most respects with the theatrical stereotype of an intelligent, prosperous, and proud man.[35]

By the end of the second act, the audience knows Pedro Crespo to be a rich and canny farmer with deeply paternal concerns — qualities most of which, Sloman notes (229), are lacking in the alcalde of the source play. Finally, Calderón adds to his characterization of Pedro Crespo the role of the village alcalde. Impressed with the protagonist's position and conduct in the first two acts of the play, the audience already knows that Pedro Crespo is not stupid. The peasant does, however, fit the stereotype of the alcalde in his pride and strong family ties. Crespo also ratifies his suitability for his second calling in his precipitate and violent version of "justice." The two-act delay in making Pedro Crespo mayor clashes with and grafts to the image of the rich peasant the sanguinary alcalde, yielding the highly potent hybrid of an intelligent mayor. Upon his election, Crespo becomes a man with the motive, determination, and opportunity to mangle justice secretly, disguising his revenge and cover-up with "diligencias" so "exquisitas" that even his king does not recognize the atrocity. The potentially hostile witnesses have been effectively silenced by a clever peasant in the guise of a simple alcalde.

Although the moral flaws in the world of the play lie in Pedro Crespo and the Captain, it may be argued that King Felipe should have attended to justice in his own land before rushing off to claim Portugal. If it is true that Calderón's *The Alcalde* was written in the 1640s, the recent loss of Portugal (1640) might influence the audience's view of the monarch's haste. In his discussion of justice in *On the King*, Mariana writes,

> it is necessary to deliberate carefully in choosing judges of great integrity and gravity, who will listen willingly to whoever approaches them and who are besides mild in their judgments, active and zealous in determining the truth and in giving complete satisfaction to the innocent party.

> (es preciso andar con mucho tino en elegir magistrados muy integros y de mucha gravedad, que oigan con agrado á cuantos se les acerquen y sean además blandos en sus juicios, activos y celosos en averiguar la verdad y en dar cumplida satisfaccion al inocente [555a].)

Rivadeneira warns that "just as it is the people's sin which gives them a bad prince, thus it is the fault of the prince when the judges are bad" ("como es pecado del pueblo cuando el príncipe es malo, asi es culpa del príncipe cuando los jueces son malos").[36] The dimensions of Pedro Crespo's success are a sobering admonition about the destructive potential of a corrupt judiciary. "Feigned justice," Rivadeneira observes, "is not justice, but evil twice over" ("La justicia fingida no es justicia, sino doblada maldad").[37]

Consequently, *The Alcalde of Zalamea* can be seen as a condemnation of the abuse of power on all social levels. The play is not necessarily

a glorification of the common man, and in this light is consistent with
Calderón's patrician treatment of the *vulgo*. When Pedro Crespo becomes
mayor, he is degraded, stripped of the respect and integrity that he
would claim before his elevation to the new office. Salomon sees in the
comedia's tendency to idealize country life evidence of the trend toward
deprecation of the court and praise of the country (*menosprecio de corte
y alabanza de aldea*) that developed during the Renaissance (*Recherches,*
167–68). In the following century, Calderón contaminates the idyllic
peasant existence with the Captain's intrusion and Pedro Crespo's ferocious *invención*. Like Juan Labrador's hermetic cowardice and Peribáñez's
revenge, the Alcalde's corruption may be a sign of the Baroque period's
propensity to reverse the trend, to expose the complexity of the simple.

   And once again, the solution approved by the King will yield unfortunate economic consequences. This prosperous farmer's heirs will not
follow in his footsteps by working the land as their father did. In the end,
Isabel, despoiled by the Captain and her own father of any chance at a
normal life in the world, must now join a convent. The farmer's only son,
the unheroic, unpromising issue of his father, goes off to the military, to
assist in the dubiously legal and historically injudicious annexation of
Portugal, leaving barren the land so fruitfully tilled by his father.

Chapter 5

CONCLUSION

Semifinal Considerations

Calderón's *Luis Pérez. the Galician* and *The Alcalde of Zalamea* reaffirm the social conservatism pervading *Life Is a Dream.* Granted, it is worthy of note that *Luis Pérez* and *The Alcalde* concede major importance to characters of low social standing, and Pedro Crespo is portrayed as a man of some stature. Yet the two plays withhold from their protagonists the integrity that distinguishes Calderón's more aristocratic characters, like Segismundo, or even Don Gutierre in *The Physician of His Honor.* Luis Pérez and Pedro Crespo share a certain vigor, but this lively sense of purpose becomes a defect because it is not tempered with humanity. It is true that the Galician acts in behalf of the ideals of honor and friendship, but he twists these beyond recognition to suit his violent inclinations. Pedro Crespo's view of honor evolves from its jealous maintenance into a hollow homage meant to disguise an outrage against it. Both protagonists' unreflective egotism is of a piece with that of Lope's Peribáñez and Juan Labrador. It is incompatible with the conscience and restraint that develops in the noble characters, Segismundo, Sancho de Roelas, and Don Fadrique, the Comendador of Ocaña.

The major *comedias* singled out as exceptional by Salomon (*The Greatest Alcalde, Peribáñez, Fuenteovejuna,* and *The Alcalde of Zalamea*) are truly unique in the European dramatic tradition, but not necessarily in the way that Salomon means. None of these works can be said unequivocally to exalt the peasant. Nor do any of these plays, excepting *Fuenteovejuna* and *The Greatest Alcalde* but including *The Villano in His Corner,* applaud their stage kings' final dispositions of the peasants with respect to their agricultural callings. On the contrary, King Ludovico of France, King Enrique "el Tercero," and King Felipe II blunder ex machina, removing their nations' most productive citizens from the land, along with, in the last two cases, accidentally approving murder.

I repeat that these plays *are* significant, however, and unique compared at least to the English and French dramatic practices, in the same way that the Spanish picaresque genre is outstanding in contemporary European prose: that is, for concentrating so attentively on the predicaments of common people. This special interest might be due in part to the particular vigor of Spain's oral traditions—the ballads, proverbs, and folklore—and the unusual esteem in which the popular forms were held by learned poets. The poetic affection for *lo popular* and *lo natural,* as Menéndez Pidal points out,[1] had its most patent effect on Lope de Vega; evidence for it in Calderón is more debatable.

Notwithstanding his sympathy for the humbler citizens, however, Lope's attitudes toward honor and *el pueblo* may be fairly consistent after all. Heroism still depends on spiritual growth, and there is no evidence of the arrival at any transcendental truth—*desengaño*—in Lope's Juan Labrador or Peribáñez. Despite their expiatory ordeal under torture, neither do the villagers of Fuenteovejuna at any point express regret over their brutality or their affront to the social order. In Lope, as in Calderón, true heroism is reserved for nobles like Sancho de Roelas and Fadrique, the Comendador of Ocaña. Lope's plays, like those of Calderón, can be said to support the conservative social principle of *ser quien se es* (conforming to one's station in life) and censure the flagrant violation of that tenet by Juan Labrador's children and Peribáñez. The theorist Martín González de Cellorigo writes in 1600 that social and economic inequality are necessary for a healthy republic: precisely one of Spain's current ills, the lack of a productive middle class, is the reluctance of certain citizens to keep to their proper place.

> [I]f inequality has its drawbacks, carefully considering this business, many more will be found in equality and in equal distribution of goods. . . . [M]any people have risen to the ranks of the rich that weren't badly off in the middle classes: and others who have joined the ranks of the caballeros were better off socially speaking in trades, in professions, and in the middle class to which their ancestors belonged.

> ([S]i desygualdad tiene inconuinientes, bien examinado este negocio, muchos mayores se hallaran en la ygualdad y comunidad de los bienes. . . . [S]e han passado muchos al numero de los ricos que no estuvieran mal en el de los medianos: y otros que se han puesto en el de los caualleros, que estuvieran mejor, en los tratos, en las ocupaciones en los officios, y en la mediania, que siguieron sus passados.")[2]

The above sentiment, Elliott explains, "was a commonplace of the times, repeated by *arbitristas* and royal ministers and echoed by playwrights. Once again, inevitably, it pointed to return—return to an age when society was in balance."[3]

By that token, Lope's plays depicting real or apparent misalliance must be reexamined. *The Villano in His Corner*, ending as it does with the betrothal of the peasant Lisarda to the courtier Otón, can be interpreted clearly to condemn that crossing of social lines. What, then, of a play like Lope's splendid *The Gardener's Dog* (*El perro del hortelano*)? Here the Countess Diana loves her secretary, Teodoro, whose background is uncertain. In the end Teodoro's rascally servant Tristán reveals—or fabricates—Teodoro's illustrious lineage, "information" that allows Diana and Teodoro to wed. As in *The Villano in His Corner*, characters conclude in this play apostrophizing Fortune to stop her wheel's turning, while they perch on the precarious secret of Teodoro's possible fraud. The play ends as its meta-playwright's fiction-within-the-fiction is on the point of exploding.[4]

In view of early honor plays like *The Comendadores of Córdoba*, and later works such as *The Abduction of Dinah* and *The Youth of Saint Isidro,* along with the prose narratives *The Pilgrim in His Homeland* and *The Prudent Revenge,* the preceding studies of honor and revenge in *The Greatest Alcalde, Peribáñez,* and *Fuenteovejuna* should have shown that Lope's condemnation of violence for honor may be the rule and not the exception. In this light, Larson's perceived abortive movement toward romance in the middle plays, *Peribáñez* and *Fuenteovejuna,* does not exist. Based on these most important *comedias,* it is reasonable, then, to call for a reassessment of the moral position of the husbands in all of Lope's honor dramas, therein, reassessing the plays as a whole.

Furthermore, keeping in mind *Luis Pérez* and *The Alcalde of Zalamea* as well, the preceding studies should have shown that both Lope and Calderón can be read as more humane (if less democratic) than has been conceded in the past. The Epilogue will outline some possible explanations for our willingness to attribute socially radical ideas to these two conservative Catholic playwrights. Because I have considered primarily only major works with important peasant characters, the less well known *comedias* of these and other playwrights—for example, *The Labrador of the Tormes* (*El Labrador del Tormes,* of uncertain authorship) and Tirso de Molina's *The Galician Mari-Hernández* (*La gallega Mari-Hernández*)— must await future analysis.

Epilogue: Critical Trends

A thorough deconstruction of Carlos Blanco's essay[5] would note his ideological position, and his evident projection of the "two Spains" upon Alemán ("closed," "dogmatic") and Cervantes ("open," "free") so that the "quarrel" between them may be read as a kind of historical allegory. It would not be difficult to find other commentators during the Franco era who by implication clothe Alemán in the uniform of "authoritarian Spain," but reserve the greater triumph for Cervantes. I think it is fair to observe, without disparaging anyone, that political exile creates cultural dramas with their protagonists and antagonists, which impose their structure on the historical imagination.[6]

The first point worth stressing about the plays treated in the preceding chapters, and which bears repeating with respect to all Golden Age *comedias*, is each one's distinctness from the next. Eighteenth- and nineteenth-century scholars like Ignacio de Luzán and Marcelino Menéndez y Pelayo[7] would have agreed with today's students who complain about the lack of variety in characterization. In 1957 Alexander A. Parker came to a backhanded defense of the *comedia* by asserting that characterization in this genre is for the most part subordinated to the interests of action and theme.[8]

Such generalizing judgments have contributed to our tendency to view characters as "types" more than as individuals. Consequently, we look for what plays have in common rather than for what distinguishes them: our reading strives to classify rather than comprehend. Thus, for example, Salomon (*Recherches*) treats *The Alcalde of Zalamea, Peribáñez, Fuenteovejuna,* and *The Villano in His Corner* in the same critical breath, all upholding peasant dignity; and John V. Bryans establishes the subgenre of "the *comedia* of the *villano* who avenges an offense" ("la comedia del villano que venga su agravio").[9] In this category, Bryans includes Lope's *Peribáñez, The Greatest Alcalde* and *Fuenteovejuna; The Labrador of the Tormes;* and Calderón's *The Alcalde of Zalamea.* "The hero" of each one,

> an honorable *labrador* and of certain importance in a rustic community, sees his honor threatened by a nobleman who lacks noble ideals. The *labrador* resists the efforts of the nobleman and finally the nobleman dies as a direct or indirect result of his resistance. This death always implies a break in the traditional norms of society. Finally, the King intervenes to change the social status of the hero, in two cases making him noble (*The Labrador of the Tormes* and *The King, the Greatest Alcalde*) and in one case confirming already acquired nobility (*Peribáñez*).

> (El héroe, un labrador honrado y de cierta importancia en una comunidad rústica, ve su honor amenazado por un noble que falta a los ideales de la nobleza. El labrador resiste a los esfuerzos del noble y finalmente el noble muere como resultado directo o indirecto de esta resistencia. Esta muerte siempre implica una ruptura con las normas tradicionales de la sociedad. Finalmente el Rey interviene para cambiar el estado social del héroe, en dos

casos haciéndole noble [*El Labrador del Tormes* y *El mejor alcalde, el rey*] y en un caso confirmando la nobleza ya adquirida [*Peribáñez*].)

The above description, which contains several defensible assertions, is nevertheless inaccurate, and oversimplifies each *comedia*'s unique dilemma. For example, Nuño, the valiant protagonist of *The Labrador of the Tormes*, is not a peasant. He reveals at the end of the play that he was born a member of the high aristocracy.[10] Sancho de Roelas, hero of *The Greatest Alcalde*, is also not a peasant. He was born an *hidalgo*, and the King's action at the end of the play merely enhances that nobility. These two characters are neither rustics nor *villanos*.

Furthermore, it can be argued that the principal commoners of *The Tragicomedy of the Comendador of Ocaña* and *The Alcalde of Zalamea* do not revere honor; rather they exploit it. Peribáñez and Pedro Crespo noisily celebrate it as a smokescreen to camouflage dishonorable behavior. The two peasants are indisputably clever, but the plays could be directed to show that one is ruled by a voracious appetite for revenge and the other by paternal love, to the exclusion of all other considerations, moral or humane. Both are in the end rewarded for murder by kings with grave character flaws: Enrique "el Tercero" too sick and volatile to see to justice; Felipe II in such a hurry to bestow the coup d'état on Portugal that he is blind to Pedro Crespo's improper coup de grâce on the Captain. Of the historical monarchs we have encountered, only Alfonso VII in *The Greatest Alcalde*, along with Fernando and Isabel in *Fuenteovejuna*, can be said to act with deliberation, and the Catholic Monarchs by no means applaud the violence of Fuenteovejuna.

Bryans's statement is therefore erroneous in principle as well as in fact. It would lead the novice reader to preconceive notions of peasant heroism. It would divert that reader from registering the defects in Peribáñez or Pedro Crespo, single-minded rustics who never pause to examine conscience, but only to get a better angle on their prey. It is the kind of statement found in the introduction to almost any modern edition or translation of the works in question.

Along the same lines, each aristocratic "villain" should be discriminated from the next by degree of initial dignity, later culpability, and final remorse. *Fuenteovejuna*'s Fernán Gómez, the blackest of malefactors, cannot occupy the same category as Don Fadrique, the Comendador of

Ocaña, whose recovery of his moral sense and forgiveness of his murderer make him the true hero of his *Tragicomedia*.

Each of the above characters, antagonist as well as protagonist, is unique in gradations of the development of conscience, or lack of it; likewise we would do serious injustice to *The Greatest Alcalde*'s Elvira and *The Alcalde of Zalamea*'s Isabel by putting them in the same class as Lisarda and Casilda, the crass and materialistic "heroines" of *The Villano in His Corner* and *Peribáñez*. The four female principals have only their beauty in common; each is a finely drawn, many-sided individual. ("Casilda" is, incidentally, also the name of the fickle adulterous wife in *The Labrador of the Tormes.*)

In short, we may disregard the very particular shades of the characters so that they will fit neatly into preestablished categories, or subgenres. I suspect that many of the members of the original audiences were just as undistinguishing; witness Lope's numerous complaints in his prologues against the theatergoers too crude or distracted to pay proper attention to the plays' true import. For example, in the 1619 Prologue to *Parte XII*, "The Theater" ("Teatro") speaks to "Friend Reader" ("Letor amigo"):

> I am consoled that the rabble won't abuse me as they usually do; for in your room, where you will read [the *comedias*], you won't allow anyone to disturb you with noise, or incorrectly to explain what you will know how to understand, free of the disruptions of the gentleman who arrives late, of the actor who misinterprets his part, and of the disagreeably ugly and poorly dressed woman.

> (Quedo consolado, que no me pudrirá el vulgo como suele; pues en tu aposento, donde las has de leer, nadie consentirás que te haga ruido, ni que te diga mal de lo que tú sabrás conocer, libre de los accidentes del señor que viene tarde, del representante que se yerra, y de la mujer desagradable por fea y mal vestida.)[11]

The continuing complaint throughout the seventeenth century against the perceived immorality of the plays and their actors, especially by the Jesuits (including Rivadeneira and Mariana), and the impassioned defenses by religious as well as secular writers, are testimony that even by their contemporaries these plays were not always taken in the spirit in which they were written.[12] Lope was finally reconciled to the publication of the scripts precisely so that his ideal audience could *read* them in peace and better extract the polished fruits. In his highly favorable 1682 "Aprobación" to *Parte V* of Calderón's *Comedias,* Fray Manuel Guerra y Ribera nevertheless worries about their effects on the less discerning sector of the public ("necios"), who can easily be led astray by their failure to understand that "saints' plays set an example, historical plays undeceive [*son . . . de desengaño*], love stories divert innocently, without risk" ("las comedias de santo son de ejemplo, las historiales de desengaño, las amatorias de inocente diversión sin peligro").[13] In fact, here Guerra has spelled out the guiding principle in the correct reception of the dramas that was to be lost on succeeding generations: that while saints' plays show behavior for imitation, the historical plays (*Peribáñez, The Greatest Alcalde, Fuenteovejuna,* and *The Alcalde of Zalamea* are historical plays) would induce a certain *undeception* in their audience, not purely *imitation.* We might arrive at *dis*approval of Pedro Crespo's actions, not take them as models for our own conduct. Later generations of theatergoers, who historically have become ever more middle class, have insisted on identifying with Pedro Crespo instead of learning, as the aristocratic and highly moral Calderón may well have intended, to censure him and his defiant, unchristian conduct.

We ought to keep in mind the likelihood that many educated theatergoers and readers of seventeenth-century Spain were more qualified than we twentieth-century students to comprehend the subtleties, ironies, and contemporary allusions of these plays. As the preceding studies should have shown, there is room for interpretations of the peasant plays that do not find their protagonists worthy of tragic heroic status. We can rightly ask whether a thoughtful Christian would have viewed favorably the murders perpetrated by Peribáñez, Pedro Crespo, or Luis Pérez, just as some of us now believe that this ideal public was not expected to approve the wife-murders in Calderón's honor plays.

What is it, then, in the intervening 350 years, that has caused scholars to see in plays like *The Villano in His Corner, Peribáñez, Fuenteovejuna,* and *The Alcalde of Zalamea,* manifestos for democracy? What led the respected Hispanist Duncan W. Moir to claim for Spain's seventeenth-century theater a pioneering democratic spirit, showing the rest of Europe "that even the peasant may be a truly tragic hero or heroine"? Moir is by no means alone in this assertion. Francisco Ruiz Ramón writes of Lope's plays in his *Historia del teatro español,* that relying on his honorable conscience, the *villano* becomes, for the first time in the history of European theater, a hero, of equal dramatic prestige as the character of noble blood and illustrious birth, the only hero previously admitted in the theater. . . . The radically original and unprecedented aspect is—I repeat—the theatrical image of the common man in Lope. In this sense, Lope, as a dramatist, is much more innovative and revolutionary than Shakespeare or Corneille. Peribáñez and the town of Fuenteovejuna are the true *new* heroes of the Renaissance stage.

(Estribado en su conciencia honrosa el villano se convierte, por primera vez en la historia del teatro europeo, en héroe, con igual categoría dramática que el personaje de noble sangre e ilustre nacimiento, único héroe hasta entonces admitido en el teatro. . . . [L]o radicalmente original e inédito es—repito—la imagen teatral del hombre del pueblo en Lope. En este sentido, Lope, como dramaturgo, es mucho más revolucionario e innovador que Shakespeare o Corneille. Peribáñez y el pueblo de Fuenteovejuna son los verdaderos *nuevos* héroes del teatro renacentista).[14]

Why do we in the twentieth century embrace the heroism of the common man when, as the introductory chapter of this study shows, it is debatable whether the seventeenth-century playgoer would have been equipped to see the plays in that radical light? A truly complete answer would require volumes; that I leave to some future Hispanist. The following pages are meant only to outline some possible reasons for our eagerness to attribute democratic sentiments to Golden Age Spanish playwrights, and to their public.

A partial explanation already offered is our schooling to overlook details and irony in characterization. Often figures such as Peribáñez or Pedro Crespo say one thing but do just the opposite. Because we so seldom see the plays in performance, we tend to take the stories from the points of view of those kings who arrive at the end and receive a censored version—from the peasant "heroes"—of what has taken place. A director I think could very easily present these pieces in a way that would stress to the audience the hypocrisy of the peasant protagonists, and the preceding character studies have offered solid justification for believing that the original productions could have been contrived to emphasize the disparity between the commoners' words and their actions. Because of the sordid reputation of alcaldes in the oral tradition, the very title "*Alcalde* of Zalamea" would prepare the contemporary public to regard Pedro Crespo's climactic behavior with suspicion.[15]

While Shakespeare continues to be a perennial favorite for Anglo-American audiences, Hispanists traditionally lament the comparative lack of interest in mounting modern productions of Spanish classical theater. As the second chapter's discussion of *Life Is a Dream* demonstrated, there seems in Spain and abroad to be little faith in the current public's taste for these vehicles of highly conservative social and sometimes religious values; modifications in the texts are practically de rigueur in the occasional modern production. That taste, which is shared if in a refined sense by the directors and scholars who sometimes guide them, and by the modern conditions which shape the way we think, is a natural consequence of 350 years of social and political change.

While Spanish Neoclassical theorists such as Luzán and the early nineteenth century's Leandro Fernández de Moratín had little use for the extravagances of Spanish Golden Age drama, many *comedias* enjoyed nearly immediate success in adaptations and translations outside Spain, as Alexandre Cioranescu, Martin Franzbach, and Henry W. Sullivan have shown.[16] The eighteenth-century favorites tended to be Calderón's *Life Is a Dream* and *The Alcalde of Zalamea.*[17] In the twenty years preceding the French Revolution, France's growing middle class imputed to Pedro Crespo qualities it considered as ideal. By 1770, Franzbach writes,

> France now possessed a rich and independent bourgeoisie that began to do away with the last privileges of the nobility. . . . The sudden fortune of *The Alcalde of Zalamea* must be understood in this historical frame. The work acquired an important political significance on the very eve of the French Revolution.
>
> (Francia poseía ya una burguesía rica e independiente que comenzaba a liquidar los últimos privilegios de la nobleza. . . . La repentina fortuna del *Alcalde de Zalamea* ha de comprenderse en este marco histórico. La obra consiguió un importante significado político la misma víspera de la Revolución Francesa. [114–15])

Before the revolution, Franzbach continues, Pedro Crespo was played as a monarchist; afterwards, as a republican. In a 1795 version, Captain Don Alvaro does wed Isabel at the end: "Pedro Crespo becomes a symbol of *liberté*. The marriage between the daughter of the *labrador* and the Captain is a proof of *egalité* and the General reconciles with the *labrador* in *fraternité*" ("Pedro Crespo es convertido en símbolo de la *liberté*. El matrimonio entre la hija del labrador y el capitán es una prueba de la *egalité* y el general se reconcilia con el labrador en *fraternité*" [116]).

In fact, each successive period seems to see in *The Alcalde of Zalamea* a mirror for its own values. Similarly, in the twentieth century, Cervantes's *La Numancia* has been mounted frequently (after 1939, especially outside Spain) as a political play criticizing fascism and Franco's regime,[18] and in the late 1960s Miguel Narros presented it with great success as a condemnation of the American involvement in Vietnam.[19]

Perhaps drama, as a genre that is so public and whose success or failure is so tied to the immediate reaction of its receptor, is the most susceptible to change in favor of its audience's feelings, the genre most bound to prevailing values. The receptor acts as immediate censor; therefore the changes in a text to suit its public, or the particular aspects of the work seized upon by that public, or the plays whose production the public would support, become good measures of the changes in that public itself. Today in Madrid, according to Ignacio Amestoy, a production of *Fuenteovejuna* (speaking of it as a subversive work) would be viewed by theatergoers, who already have their socialist-democratic government, like Picasso's *Guernica:* as a museum piece arousing no special sentiment.[20] A "revolutionary" play might be more enthusiastically received in restive areas of Spain where independence from the central government is a pressing issue — in Catalonia, for example, or the Basque country.

The critical fortunes of Calderón's *The Alcalde of Zalamea* and wife-murder plays, and Lope's *Fuenteovejuna* provide a useful index of the evolution in historical sensibilities leading up to current attitudes toward the works and their authors. Calderón was the first Golden Age playwright to win a fairly wide audience in northern Europe. Sullivan points out that numerous eighteenth-century writers, including Voltaire and later Goethe, used Calderón's dramas in arguments both for and against Neoclassical values (*Calderón in the German Lands,* 123). By the early nineteenth century German Romantics led by the Schlegel

brothers, William and Frederick, had declared Calderón superior even
to Shakespeare, and named him the greatest poet of Christianity since
Dante. Lope's dramaturgy was considered by comparison superficial,
improvised rather than carefully crafted, misled by the demands of the
public; Calderón on the other hand was the "most Christian, and for
that reason the most Romantic"; "as it were, the last echo of medieval
Catholicism."[21]

Count Adolf Friedrich von Schack (1815–94) wrote a *History of
Literature and Dramatic Art in Spain* (*Historia de la literatura y del arte
dramática en España*), first published in German in 1845–46. There he
looks relatively carefully at a large number of plays by both Lope and
Calderón. Schack appreciates Calderón's "valiant Pedro Crespo, who
represents to perfection the Spanish peasant, with his most noble traits,
faithful to his King and to his duty, and of an unbending constancy" ("el
valiente Pedro Crespo, que representa á la perfección al campesino
español, con sus rasgos más nobles, fiel á su Rey y á su deber, y de una
firmeza inflexible").[22] Schack influenced the Spaniards' view of their
own theatrical tradition. Even Menéndez y Pelayo, who, writing in
1881, disputed the Romantic apotheosis of Calderón, applauded the
"admirable Pedro Crespo," in a play that he viewed as a product of the
seventeenth century's "friar's democracy" ("democracia frailuna"); in
that era, he declares, men enjoyed "Christian equality sui generis"
("igualdad cristiana *sui generis*" [59]).

Here, I think, the critic sacrifices the Roman for the biblical conception of the people, a conception that would better apply to a work like
The Great Theater of the World. The only defect of *The Alcalde*,
according to Menéndez y Pelayo, echoing Schack, is the scene in the
forest at the beginning of the third act. Isabel's lengthy narration of her
disgrace is in terrible taste, in language affected and redundant (219,
227). But of Pedro Crespo, Menéndez y Pelayo approves unconditionally:
combined in him are

> in the strangest and most marvelous way passion for revenge
> and a sense of justice: a singular and unique amalgam, which
> gives this character a vigor mixing passion and nobility, which
> is emphasized still more by his status as *labrador* and *vil-
> lano* which the author has given his character, synthesis and
> sum of all that was great and poetic in the old Spanish munici-
> pality.

(del modo más extraño y maravilloso la pasión de la venganza y
el sentimiento de la justicia: amalgama singular y única, que da
a este carácter un vigor mezclado de pasión y de nobleza, que
todavía se acentúa más por el carácter de labrador y de villano
que el autor ha dado a su héroe, síntesis y cifra de cuanto había
de grandioso y poético en el antiguo municipio español. [220])

During the late nineteenth and early twentieth centuries, Spanish
writers grew more and more alarmed at a political condition called
"caciquismo," which they held responsible for many of Spain's ills,
especially following the disaster of the war with the United States in
1898. The *cacique* was a powerful local boss in rural areas, often
ruthless and corrupt, who usually operated in behalf of a greater authority.
Caciquismo had entered fiction in novels such as Benito Pérez Galdós's
Doña Perfecta and Emilia Pardo Bazán's naturalistic *The Country Estate
of Ulloa* (*Los pazos de Ulloa*). In 1901 the philosopher-historian Joaquín
Costa addressed Madrid's literary society at the Ateneo to throw still
more forcefully the blame for Spain's political and cultural backwardness
on this condition. Costa's discourse, *Oligarchy and "Caciquismo" as the
Current Form of Government of Spain, Urgency for and Manner of
Changing It* (*Oligarquía y caciquismo como la forma actual de gobierno
de España, urgencia y modo de cambiarla*), appeared in print in several
editions between 1901 and 1904. Among its first audience were a
number of Spain's most important writers, including Pardo Bazán and
Miguel de Unamuno. Some wrote responses to the paper that were also
published; in any case Costa's address had a great effect, direct or
indirect, on the so-called literary "Generation of '98," including Unamuno,
Pío Baroja, Ramón del Valle-Inclán, and Ramiro de Maeztu,[23] and the
novela de cacique came into its own. These works, according to José
Carlos Mainer, often ended on a pessimistic note, with the *cacique*'s
defeat of the hero. They

> corresponded to a fixed typology whose obsessive moralizing
> might have become somewhat ambiguous: only the case of
> offended honor—which followed the accredited model of *The
> Alcalde of Zalamea* —motivated rebellion and only the confron-
> tation of an individual hero—or of a victim—could conclude
> with the ominous victory of a figure who combined the traits of
> the patriarch and of the rival.

(respondían a una tipología fija cuya obsesiva moralización podía llegar a ser algo ambigua: sólo el caso de honra—que seguía el acreditado molde de *El alcalde de Zalamea* —motivaba la rebeldía y sólo el enfrentamiento de un héroe—o de una víctima—individual podía concluir con el nefasto dominio de una figura que entremezclaba los rasgos del patriarca y del rival.)[24]

Clearly, Pedro Crespo was classed among those heroic resisters to the abuses of the *caciques,* whereas the text read another way casts *him* as a wealthy, powerful, and corrupt rural boss: if anything, Pedro Crespo embodies the abuses of the *caciques.*

The popularity of the play continued throughout the early twentieth century precisely because the character of its protagonist was believed to support the values of the upright individual, to uphold respect and personal integrity in the face of a greater, malevolent power. Dru Dougherty has shown that in the 1920s, of all Golden Age plays revived and adapted to the modern stage in Madrid, by far the most often chosen was *The Alcalde of Zalamea.*[25] Indeed, the popular actor Rafael Calvo was one vehicle for the success of Calderón's *comedia,* since the heroic role of Pedro Crespo was a favorite of his. Calvo enjoyed playing in alternating performances—sometimes on the same day—Zorrilla's Romantic hero Don Juan Tenorio, and Calderón's champion of the underdog, Pedro Crespo.[26]

In the context of the bourgeois exaltation of this character in the eighteenth century, his Romantic idealization in the nineteenth, and his continued politically and artistically induced lionization early in this century, there is little wonder that scholars should continue to affirm now that this peasant merits the designation of hero. To Georg Lukács, Pedro Crespo is a prime example of a "world-historical individual."[27] Dunn, inclined to a similar position, writes,

> In Crespo Calderón portrays the courage of a man who, having incurred the public stigma of dishonour, accepts it, renounces vengeance, and consequently risks the further public disgrace of being thought a coward. . . . The two categorical imperatives of conventional morality—revenge and secrecy—are both overruled by the demands of law. . . . When Crespo has the office of magistrate put upon him, he is given a dignity, and honourable rank under the Crown, and this new honour is bound up with the exercise of justice.[28]

In *A Literary History of Spain: The Golden Age: Drama,* which he coauthored with Moir, Edward M. Wilson states that "Crespo's vengeance on the Captain defied legal niceties but was humanly justified, as Philip the Prudent saw. The play combines the rich humanity we associate with Lope at his best with the superb technique of Calderón" (112). Ciriaco Morón Arroyo considers *Life Is a Dream* along with *The Alcalde of Zalamea* as "potencialmente revolucionaria," going so far as to maintain that "in Calderón's *comedias* there takes place a dialectical movement toward the rupture of established social barriers, toward the affirmation of the true equality of all men" ("en las comedias calderonianas se da un movimiento dialéctico hacia la rotura de las barreras estamentales, hacia la afirmación de la igualdad sustancial de todos los hombres").[29]

In the midnineteenth century, Count von Schack had made a concerted effort (*Historia de la literatura y del arte dramático en España*) to fathom and excuse the violence of the honor dramas, which had shocked so many of his predecessors and which would continue to disturb subsequent writers; how many late-nineteenth-century Spanish plays melodramatize the cuckold's jealousy and obsession with Calderonian-type honor?[30] Ramón del Valle-Inclán still satirized these exaggerated fixations in *Don Friolera's Horns* (*Los cuernos de Don Friolera*) in the 1920s. At any rate, Schack exhorts us to study Calderón's honor plays with special care because the values they espouse are so different from our own. Paradoxically, Schack's readings detect no irony undermining the violence of the husbands and the kings who approve their extreme measures. Honor and bloody revenge sanctioned by the king was the custom of the day, in Schack's opinion: Calderón's best heroes carry out the worst vengeances because that was the way things happened. *The Physician of His Honor,* for example, "is a tragedy horrible, repugnant, and offensive to our ideas" ("es una tragedia horrible, repugnante y ofensiva a nuestras ideas" [4:359]), but a product of its fanatical times. The King's blessing certifies the correctness of Don Gutierre's truculence:

> The kings in Calderón . . . seem to belong to another, better world than that of the rest of mortal men; the laws and customs that govern others do not govern [the kings], and even their weaknesses and flaws are mitigated by embellishment. The poet's veneration of absolute power was so great that even the laws of honor had to be sacrificed in deference to it.

(Los reyes de Calderón... parecen pertenecer á otro mundo
mejor que los demás mortales; no les obligan los vinculos y leyes
que á aquéllos, y hasta sus flaquezas y sus faltas se mitigan
embelleciéndolas. La veneración del poeta hacia el poder absoluto
era tan grande... que hasta las leyes del honor ha[bían] de ser
sacrificadas en su obsequio. [4:349])

Such a straightforward view of the honor plays prevailed until the early
1950s when British Hispanists led by Wilson and Parker laid bare the
works' ironies, and began to understand the historical fallibility of the
monarchs who were so quick to approve actions so offensive to Christian
sensibilities.[31]

Schack had also made the attempt to rehabilitate Lope's reputation,
which had suffered during the great Romantic movement for Calderón.
One of Lope's foremost virtues was his representation of all types of
characters, high and low. Of Lope's bucolic scenes, Schack rhapsodizes,

Now he offers us a rustic passion with inimitable freshness and
amiability; now the simplicity and sincerity of the countryside;
now, lastly, he delights us with the contrasts he traces between
unaffected rural life with that of the cities and courts.... One
breathes in these scenes a pure and cool air, a zephyr which
seems to waft from the incomparable valleys of the Sil and the
Genil [Rivers]; all the enchantments of the Southern [European]
sky, and of a nature as grandiose as lovely, seeming to spread
over them. Nobody, not even perhaps Cervantes himself, has
observed so many characteristics of the Spanish country people,
nor represented them with such seductive features.... To appre-
ciate in their merit the truth of these descriptions, it helps not to
forget that we are dealing with a Southern people, whose
liveliness, imagination and wit seem to belong to all, and whose
coarseness does not lack a certain intelligence.

(Ya nos ofrece una rústica pasión con inimitable frescura y
agrado; ya la sencillez y franqueza de los campos; ya, por
último, nos deleita por los contrastes que traza entre la vida
rural y sin afectación con la de ciudades y cortes.... Respírase
en estas escenas un aire puro y fresco, un céfiro que parece
soplar de los encantos del cielo meridional, y de una naturaleza

tan grandiosa como bella, parece que se extienden sobre ellos.
Ninguno, ni aun acaso el mismo Cervantes, ha observado todas
las propiedades del pueblo español de los campos, ni representá-
dolo con rasgos tan seductores. . . . Para apreciar en su valor la
verdad de estas descripciones, es conveniente no olvidar que se
trata de un pueblo meridional, cuya viveza, imaginación y agudeza
parecen ser patrimonio común de todos, y cuya grosería no
carece de cierto ingenio. [2:454-55])

Menéndez y Pelayo's disparagement of Calderón in 1881 in favor of
Lope served further to enhance the latter's reputation. Even Calderón's
exceptional *The Alcalde of Zalamea* was only made possible by Lope's
pioneering efforts:

It is . . . worthy of applause that Calderón has situated this vindi-
cation of injured honor not among noblemen, as happens in all
his other plays, but in an honorable *villano;* for which Lope had
already given the example in *The King, the Greatest Alcalde,*
Fuenteovejuna, and *Peribáñez,* which are three tragic dramas
having a great affinity with *The Alcalde of Zalamea.*

(Es . . . de aplaudir que Calderón haya puesto esta vindicación
de la honra mancillada, no entre caballeros, como en todas las
demás producciones suyas acontece, sino en un villano honrado;
de lo cual había ya dado ejemplo Lope en *El mejor alcalde, el*
rey, Fuenteovejuna, y *Peribáñez,* que son tres dramas trágicos
que tienen mucha afinidad con *El alcalde de Zalamea.* [*Calderón*
y su teatro, 227])

Although Lope's fortunes rose most rapidly in Western Europe with
the tercentenary commemorations of his death in 1935, through the
Germans in the nineteenth century, the Russians especially undertook
numerous adaptations of *Fuenteovejuna,* along with *The Alcalde of*
Zalamea. According to Jack Weiner, Lope was a favorite in Tsarist
Russia primarily because *Fuenteovejuna* was thought to promote the
alliance between the monarchy and the masses, whose common enemy
was the nobility.[32] Soviet scholars since the Bolshevik Revolution, Weiner
points out, regard the play as revolutionary, not monarchist, and
Fuenteovejuna has been mounted to convey that in Soviet Russia. By

1946, according to Weiner, *"Fuenteovejuna* had been translated into twelve Soviet languages" (167 n.2).

Ada M. Coe's catalogue of *comedia* productions announced in Madrid newspapers between 1661 and 1819 registers numerous stagings of both *The Alcalde of Zalamea* and *Life Is a Dream.*[33] While Lope's *The Greatest Alcalde* also proved a favorite, there is no record of a single production of *Fuenteovejuna* during these years in Spain. I have seen a reference to a 1903 mounting,[34] but according to Dougherty, this play was not staged (in Madrid at least) at all between 1920 and 1930.[35] The twenties were a period of dictatorship and monarchy in Spain, but a growing disaffection with both led to the establishment in 1931 of Spain's Second Republic, at which point King Alphonse XIII went into exile. Antimonarchical feeling was so strong that the names of all royal personages were expunged from Madrid's theater marquees.[36] The republic lasted until the outbreak of the Civil War in 1936. During its early phase, the government of Azaña made a relatively large amount of money available for the cultivation of the arts. Among other projects, the university theatrical troupe "La Barraca" was formed, headed by Federico García Lorca and Eduardo Ugarte. "La Barraca" was partly intended to promote cultural understanding among the populace, and developed a repertory of classical theater that it presented in Madrid and on tour in the provinces.[37] In the repertory, along with some of Cervantes's interludes and an *auto sacramental* by Calderón, were Lope's *The Knight of Olmedo* and *Fuenteovejuna.* This adaptation of *Fuenteovejuna,* specifically aimed to enlighten the people of Spain as to their democratic heritage, was also meant to relate to the lives of its current audience, and costuming was made contemporary. The fiendish Comendador Fernán Gómez became a symbol of *caciquismo,* clad in a business suit and, interestingly, given red hair and beard—to evoke the figure of Judas.[38]

Lorca claimed to be careful to respect the original text of *Fuenteovejuna,* adding almost nothing and only leaving out what he judged would confuse or be irrelevant to his audience. However, Lorca, who despised the Catholic Monarchs,[39] happened to decide that they, and the entire "second action," the national theme of Ciudad Real, were superfluous. Therefore the King and Queen, who in the original text preside over the final scenes, and who *withhold* approval of the popular uprising, were deleted.[40] The people were transformed into the triumphant, completely vindicated heroes, subjugated to no one. Lorca's adaptation of the play has a great deal in common with then-contemporary Soviet productions, which also eliminate the monarchs. During the early Second Republic many Spaniards traveled to Russia, including Rafael Alberti in 1932, who, Weiner writes, may well have been influenced by Russian versions of *Fuenteovejuna.*

> According to [the Soviet author Ovadii] Savich, Alberti wrote to the Soviet Hispanist F. V. Kel'in that during the summer of 1933 Federico García Lorca had told Alberti of his interest in traveling to the Soviet Union also. According to Kel'in, both Alberti and his wife [María Teresa León] wanted to do for the Spanish proletariat what the Soviets had done for theirs [with the adaptations of *Fuenteovejuna*]. . . . I would . . . suggest that Lorca's production of *Fuenteovejuna* with his jitney theater, called La Barraca, can be traced to Alberti's and León's trip to the Soviet Union. ("Lope de Vega's *Fuenteovejuna,*" 219-20)

Lorca's *Fuenteovejuna* was mounted in the summer of 1933. Lorca, who also eliminated King Juan II and his deus ex machina appearance at the end of *The Knight of Olmedo,* attempted to persuade Pura Ucelay, whose Club Anfistora put on *Peribáñez,* to leave out King Enrique "el Tercero" from that play.[41] In short, these modern adaptations, which were very well received, seethed with an antimonarchical sentiment thoroughly antithetical to the *comedias'* original political orientations.

With these "slight" revisions, Lorca invented a democratic heritage that had never existed. His changes coincided with and perhaps influenced contemporary criticism's view of *Fuenteovejuna* that the double plot, and the national theme, was a defect,[42] a notion the remnants of which persevered in a 1953 article by the British scholar Albert E. Sloman.[43] In *Fuenteovejuna* the national theme, "though linked to the main action in spirit and though providing emphasis for Lope's theme, . . . is by no means essential to the play. Indeed with but minor alterations, the play could stand with the secondary action removed."

Scholarship also continued to idealize the role of this play's *pueblo.* In 1955 Leo Spitzer wrote, "Fuenteovejuna itself is an idyllic island of Primitivism in which the values of the Golden Age are still miraculously preserved."[44] Furthermore, in both "*Peribáñez* and *Fuenteovejuna* . . . the communal conscience is itself a protagonist" (281 n.8). In 1971, Duncan Moir writes in *A Literary History of Spain,* "What is attacked in *Fuenteovejuna* is the aristocratic conviction that commoners are not entitled to a sense of honour. . . . When [the Comendador] dies, we feel an exultant religious triumph." The peasant honor plays are "not realistic or naturalistic, but markedly idealised" (63, 65). *Peribáñez* is a "double tragedy: the tragedy of the nobly spirited peasant, Peribáñez, *primus inter pares*, . . . and the tragedy of the basically honorable young Comendador" (66–67). *The Villano in His Corner* treats

> Juan Labrador, the dignified and sententious peasant who is content with his lot and so impressively virtuous that the King, who tests his loyalty in various ways and envies him his stoicism, his tranquility and integrity, finally summons him to a high place of honour at Court. (67)

According to Bruce W. Wardropper, in this play Lope paints "a rustic life of utmost beauty, of utmost goodness, of utmost truth" ("una vida campestre de suma belleza, de suma bondad, de suma verdad").[45]

If, as Moir and Ruiz Ramón state, Spain's *comedia* did show the rest of Europe that a humbly born man can be a tragic hero, it is true because Europeans interpreted the plays along democratic lines. Succeeding generations, from eighteenth-century middle-class Frenchmen, to nineteenth-century Russian tsarists, to twentieth-century Soviets, and Spaniards during the Second Republic, to our contemporaries today, continue to read tracts for democracy in works that in the beginning may very well have upheld the stratified social status quo.

Duncan Moir's view of these plays is essentially Lorca's, which at first may seem surprising since the Briton and his coauthor of *A Literary History of Spain,* Wilson, belonged to the "British School" of Hispanists so devoted to careful textual analysis.[46] But the idea of *avant la lettre* democratic sentiments in seventeenth-century plays must have been nearly irresistible to intellectuals in the years since Lorca for several reasons, mainly political and social.

During and after the Spanish Civil War (1936–39), a significant number of Spanish Republicans—primarily the humanists[47]—escaped Franco's Spain to exile in France, Great Britain, the United States, and Latin America, where the citizens of "la España Peregrina" ("Wandering Spain") joined their sympathetic anti-Falangist colleagues. In political exile, Paul Ilie writes, it is natural to maintain an idealized view of one's past in the forsaken homeland:

A commonplace of exile studies of all nations is that the exilic sensibility tends toward a universal limbo of immobile idealism. Consequently, its established ideas are more predictable than those of the resident citizens whose national contexts are evolving with respect to the moment of departure. . . . We already know, in the case of Spain, that the Republicans who left their authoritarian country by and large maintained their liberal beliefs. (11)

Both emigrant and resident ("inner") exiles tend to distort the past favorably. "Furthermore," according to Ilie, "foreign liberals after the Civil War detested Spain" (68). Many of the exiled intellectuals found their new homes in the universities of these foreign liberals. Therefore, a dramatic tradition that is seen to exalt the people over authoritarian interests in Spain would naturally appeal both to Spanish exiles and their hosts. Moreover, the influential British critic, Edward M. Wilson, may himself, together with Alexander A. Parker, have been an important conduit of this liberal view of the *comedia*. As a young man, Wilson studied in Madrid, living in the Residencia de Estudiantes with Dámaso Alonso[48] and other members of the "Generation of '27," including Federico García Lorca. Wilson then returned to England and began to write literary criticism. Susana Hernández Araico recalls Parker reminiscing in 1984 about his formative scholarly years: "Parker mentioned that in his first conversations with Edward M. Wilson about Calderón's theater, during walks through university gardens, both found a way of transcending the threat of war with Hitler" ("mencionó que en sus primeras conversaciones con Edward M. Wilson sobre el teatro de Calderón, durante paseos por jardines universitarios, ambos encontraban una forma de trascender la amenaza de la guerra con Hitler").[49] Wardropper has pointed out to me that, while Wilson and Parker were undoubtedly democrats, both, partly because of their religious leanings (the former being an Anglo-Catholic; the latter, a Roman Catholic), had some sympathy for some of Franco's policies, and inclined politically toward the right. "In the case of Wilson," Wardropper writes, "his conservatism led him to dignify not the working man but the tiller of the soil. . . . The farmer is seen as the maintainer of the social order."[50] It bears repeating that the farmers examined in previous chapters end expressly by abandoning the tilling of the soil. Neither Juan Labrador, nor Peribáñez, nor Pedro Crespo can be said truly to respect the social—or economic—order. Again, the heroic exception is the only aristocrat among them, Sancho de Roelas.

In any case, it is perfectly understandable that the British School of Hispanists should sport this pro-democratic, pro-bucolic bias, and that their British and American disciples (including, for example, Dunn and Wardropper) should also see in the "peasant" *comedias* an idealized view of the Spanish people. The latest generation of Hispanists for the most part continues to advance the liberal view. In his impressive examination of *comedia*-reception in northern Europe (*Calderón in the German Lands*, 1983), Henry W. Sullivan states that *The Alcalde of Zalamea* ends on an "implicitly subversive note" (150), and in Pedro Crespo's famous "patrimonio del alma" speech, "Calderón has . . . situated honor outside the tangible hierarchies of social rank and privileged birth, and equated it with an immanent dignity, a divine selfhood, inherited by every human soul at birth" (149). However, Anthony J. Cascardi begins to correct the extreme posture of critics who follow Spitzer in seeing a "Utopian dream" verging on Marxism in *Fuenteovejuna:* "the *comedia,*" he states, "consistently admits a vision of the 'modern' or the 'new,' yet with equal consistency it sacrifices that vision in favor of the stability to be achieved through the dominance of the 'old.'"[51]

In summary, the prevailing view of Lope and Calderón, which makes heroes of the peasants, is the result of centuries of social and economic change, and of productions aimed to make the plays relevant to contemporary audiences. Reception of these plays evolved toward liberal interpretations due to the influences of a rising middle class, of Romanticism, of egalitarian tendencies in the political philosophy of such important writers as Joaquín Costa, and of leftist adaptations of classical plays early in this century. The peasants became the heroes at the expense of all characters representing established authority.

The mass exodus of Republican intellectuals from Spain at the end of the Civil War in 1939 carried with it an anti-Falangist political orientation which joined with that of sympathetic scholars in the countries of refuge. This well-meaning communion of revulsion to fascism has helped perpetuate the perception of exceptionally democratic values in Lope de Vega and Calderón.

I hope that I have shown that it is defensible to find in these works a condemnation of the violent solutions chosen by the peasant protagonists. Consequently, plays like *Peribáñez* and *The Alcalde of Zalamea* may be considered ultimately far more artistically and ethically sensitive—if less revolutionary—than scholars have previously indicated. If this study results in a qualified unseating of the peasant as hero in the Golden Age *comedia*, then Hispanists will have to redefine their claim for Spanish theater's special role in the evolution of European drama. This step toward critical rigor will, I think, in the long run, help gain for Golden Age theater the respect it so richly deserves.

NOTES

ABBREVIATIONS

BAE   Biblioteca de Autores Españoles
BCom   *Bulletin of the Comediantes*
BH   *Bulletin Hispanique*
BHS   *Bulletin of Hispanic Studies*
BN   Biblioteca Nacional (Madrid)
CHA   *Cuadernos Hispanoamericanos*
CSIC   Consejo Superior de Investigaciones Científicas
CRCL   *Canadian Review of Comparative Literature*
FMLS   *Forum for Modern Language Studies*
HR   *Hispanic Review*
I & L   *Ideologies & Literature*
Ib   *Iberoromania*
JHP   *Journal of Hispanic Philology*

KRQ	*Kentucky Romance Quarterly*
MLN	*Modern Language Notes*
MLR	*Modern Language Review*
NBAE	Nueva Biblioteca de Autores Españoles
NRFH	*Nueva Revista de Filología Hispánica*
PCG	*Primera Crónica General*
PMC	*Poema de mio Cid*
PMLA	*Publications of the Modern Language Association*
Pol R	*Polish Review*
RABM	Revista de Archivos, Bibliotecas y Museos
RAE	Real Academia Española
RCEH	*Revista Canadiense de Estudios Hispánicos*
RF	*Romanische Forschungen*
RFE	*Revista de Filología Española*
RJ	*Romanistisches Jahrbuch*
RO	*Revista de Occidente*
RPh	*Romance Philology*
RQ	*Romance Quarterly*
RR	*Romanic Review*
SP	*Studies in Philology*

Prologue

1. "Popular Culture and Spanish Literary History," in *Literature Among Discourses: The Spanish Golden Age,* ed. Godzich and Spadaccini (Minneapolis: University of Minnesota Press, 1986), 41–61.

Chapter 1

1. " '*Don Juan* will be known, *by and by,* for what it is intended—a *satire* on *abuses* in the present states of society, and not an eulogy of vice' " (Byron's letter to John Murray, 22 December 1822, in *The Works of Lord Byron, Letters and Journals,* ed. R. E. Prothero [London, 1901], 5:242; cited in Alvin B. Kernan, *The Plot of Satire* [New Haven: Yale University Press, 1965], 208n; repr. in part as "The Perspective of Satire: *Don Juan,*" in *Twentieth-Century Interpretations of 'Don*

Juan', ed. Edward E. Bostetter [Englewood Cliffs, N.J.: Prentice-Hall, 1969], 93 n. 5). See also Paul G. Trueblood, *Lord Byron*, 2d ed. (Boston: Twayne, 1977), 139–47.

2. "Introduction: The Idea of the Hero," in Brombert's *The Hero in Literature* (*Major Essays on the Changing Concepts of Heroism from Classical Times to the Present*) (Greenwich, Conn.: Fawcett, 1969), 19, 16.

3. In *Anatomy of Criticism: Four Essays* (Princeton: Princeton University Press, 1971), 33–67.

4. "The Problem of the Hero in the Later Medieval Period," in *Concepts of the Hero in the Middle Ages and the Renaissance*, ed. Norman T. Burns and Christopher J. Reagan (Albany: State University of New York Press, 1975), 29.

5. Spanish authors are for the most part absent from Bloomfield's discussion, although Cervantes is held up as a writer in whose opus both trends in the "dialectical movement" (p. 32) function: antihero in *Don Quixote*; hero in the later romance published posthumously, the *Persiles*. But then, movement from realism to idealism or romance might well be an archetypal pattern characterizing the trajectory of many authors' works. Shakespeare evolves from the early history plays to the *Tempest*; Calderón from honor plays to court fantasies; Tolstoy from *The Cossacks*, to *War and Peace*, to *Resurrection*; Galdós from the *Episodios nacionales* to *Misericordia*. See Ruth El Saffar, *Novel to Romance: A Study of Cervantes's "Novelas ejemplares"* (Baltimore: Johns Hopkins University Press, 1974).

6. *The Hero and the King: An Epic Theme* (New York: Columbia University Press, 1982), 3.

7. In the words of Otis H. Green, *desengaño* is the "awakening to the nature of reality . . . to have the scales fall from one's eyes, to see things as they are" (*Spain and the Western Tradition: The Castilian Mind in Literature from "El Cid" to Calderón* [Madison: University of Wisconsin Press, 1966], 4:44). See 4:43–76.

8. See E. R. Dodds, *The Greeks and the Irrational* (Berkeley: University of California Press, 1951); and Bruno Snell, *The Discovery of the Mind: The Greek Origins of European Thought*, trans. T. G. Rosenmeyer (New York: Harper & Bros., 1960).

9. *Aethetics: Lectures on Fine Art*, trans. T. M. Knox (Oxford: Clarendon, 1975), 1:184–93.

10. Thomas McCrary, lecture presented at Columbia University, New York, December 1980.

11. *Hero and Saint: Shakespeare and the Graeco-Roman Heroic Tradition* (New York: Oxford University Press, 1971), 85.

12. See Ernst Robert Curtius, *European Literature and the Latin Middle Ages*, trans. Willard R. Trask (New York: Harper & Row, 1953), 173–76.

13. Bloomfield, "The Problem of the Hero," 43.

14. "The Concept of the Hero in the Early Middle Ages," in *Concepts of the Hero*, 21; see also 4–6 and 19–20.

15. *The Song of Roland*, trans. Frederick Goldin (New York: Norton, 1978), 162; the original quotation is from *La Chanson de Roland*, ed. Léon Gautier (Tours: Alfred Mame et Fils, 1872), *laisse* 289, 314.

16. See S. M. Stern, *Les chansons mozarabes: les verbs finaux (kharjas) en espagnol dans les muwashshahs arabes et hébreux* (Oxford: B. Cassirer, 1964); and Emilio García Gómez, ed., *Las jarchas romances de la serie árabe en su marco*, 2d ed. (Barcelona: Seix Barral), 1975.

17. See Colin Smith, *The Making of the "Poema de mio Cid"* (Cambridge: Cambridge University Press, 1983).

18. *A Literary History of Spain: The Middle Ages* (London: Ernest Benn, 1971), 41.

19. Jackson, *The Hero and the King,* 82–84.

20. See Thomas R. Hart's "Characterization and Plot Structure in the *Poema de Mio Cid,"* in *"Mio Cid" Studies,* ed. Alan D. Deyermond (London: Tamesis, 1977), 69–70.

21. *The Poem of the Cid,* trans. Lesley Byrd Simpson (Berkeley: University of California Press, 1975), 77. Quotations in the original will be from *Poema de mio Cid,* ed. Colin Smith (Oxford: Clarendon, 1972), where the Cid and the King meet at line 2025.

22. *Sophocles: A Study of Heroic Humanism* (Cambridge: Harvard University Press, 1951), esp. 142–46.

23. "Pero Vermúez and the Politics of the Cid's Exile," *MLR,* 78 (1983): 325–26.

24. Jerry R. Craddock, "Must the King Obey His Laws?" in *Florilegium Hispanicum: Medieval and Golden Age Studies Presented to Dorothy Clotelle Clarke,* ed. John S. Geary, Charles B. Faulhaber, and Dwayne E. Carpenter (Madison, Wisc.: Hispanic Seminary of Medieval Studies, 1983), 71–79.

25. Alan D. Deyermond, *Epic Poetry and the Clergy: Studies on the "Mocedades de Rodrigo"* (London: Tamesis, 1968), 19–20.

26. Antonio Pérez Gómez, Introduction to his edition of *Romancero de don Alvaro de Luna (1540-1800)* (Valencia: n.p., 1953), 12.

27. Colin Smith, Introduction to his edition of *Spanish Ballads* (Oxford: Pergamon, 1964), 39.

28. *Spanish Ballads,* 40.

29. See E. M. Wilson, "Tragic Themes in Spanish Ballads," in his *Spanish and English Literature of the 16th and 17th Centuries: Studies in Discretion, Illusion and Mutability* (Cambridge: Cambridge University Press, 1980, 220–33); repr. from *Diamante,* 8 (London: Hispanic and Luso Brazilian Council, 1958).

30. *La epopeya castellana a través de la literatura española* (Buenos Aires: Espasa-Calpe, 1945), 188.

31. Smith, *Spanish Ballads,* 22.

32. *Poesías castellanas completas,* ed. Elias L. Rivers (Madrid: Castalia, 1969), 119, line 1.

33. Bloomfield, "The Problem of the Hero," 36.

34. "The Myth of the Hero in Boccaccio," in *Concepts of the Hero,* 268–91.

35. First published in 1554; written as early as the 1520s.

36. In *An Exemplary History of the Novel: The Quixotic versus the Picaresque* (Chicago: University of Chicago Press, 1981), 54, Reed writes,

> The idea of beginning at the beginning rather than in the middle implicitly disclaims any epic ambitions on Lazarillo's part, yet the final phrase of his prologue ironically presents him as an ersatz Aeneas: "how much more they have accomplished who have had Fortune against them from the start, and who have nothing to thank but their own labor and skill at the oars for bringing them into a safe harbor" ("cuánto más hicieron los que, siéndoles [la Fortuna] contraria, con fuerza y maña remando, salieron a buen puerto").

(*The Life of Lazarillo de Tormes: His Fortunes and Adversities,* trans. M. S. Merwin [Garden City, N.Y.: Doubleday, 1962], 39; the original from *Lazarillo de Tormes,* ed. Francisco Rico, 4th ed. [Barcelona: Planeta, 1983], 7).

37. See Deyermond, *Lazarillo de Tormes: A Critical Guide* (London: Grant & Cutler, 1975), 52.

38. "El pícaro de nuevo," *MLN,* 100 (1985): 202.

39. A *converso* is either himself a forced convert to Christianity, or the descendent of one. *Converso*-status became a serious social handicap in Spain after the Reconquest. See Américo Castro, *De la edad conflictiva: El dráma de la honra en España y en su literatura* (Madrid: Taurus, 1961).

40. Alexander A. Parker, *Literature and the Delinquent: The Picaresque Novel in Spain and Europe, 1599-1753* (Edinburgh: University Press, 1967), 67.

41. See Bruce W. Wardropper, "El trastorno de la moral en el *Lazarillo,*" *NRFH,* 15 (1961): 441-47; and James Iffland, *Quevedo and the Grotesque* (London: Tamesis, 1983), 2:76-140.

42. P. Félix García, ed. (Madrid: "La Lectura," 1930), 1:60. These remarks on the picaresque in part draw on my article "The Critical Attitude in *Rinconete y Cortadillo,*" *Cervantes,* 3 (1983), esp. 141.

43. *Don Quixote of la Mancha,* trans. Walter Starkie (New York: Signet, 1957), chap. 22, 214-15; the original from *Don Quijote de la Mancha,* prepared by Martín de Riquer (Barcelona: Juventud, 1955), 1:208.

44. See Alban K. Forcione, *Cervantes, Aristotle, and the "Persiles"* (Princeton: Princeton University Press, 1970), 303-43; and Patricia Kenworthy, "The Character of Lorenza and the Moral of Cervantes' *El viejo celoso,*" *BCom,* 31 (1979): 105-7.

45. Dian Fox, "The Apocryphal Part One of *Don Quijote,*" *MLN,* 100 (1985): 406-16.

46. Thomas R. Hart, "Versions of Pastoral in Three *Novelas ejemplares,*" *BHS,* 58 (1981): 287-88.

47. The phrase "I am who I am" ("Soy quien soy"), probably derived from God's self-definition in Exod. 3:14, became in Spanish Golden Age literature a proverbial declaration of a character's awareness of the obligations concomitant with his own social rank. However, as Frank P. Casa explains, its literary invocation "is not an assumption of divinity but an affirmation of the necessity to act according to what one is or what [one] should be ideally. It is, in essence, the concept of playing out well one's role in life" ("Aspects of Characterization in Golden Age Drama," in *Studies in Honor of Everett W. Hesse,* ed. William C. McCrary and José A. Madrigal [Lincoln, Neb.: Society of Spanish and Spanish-American Studies, 1981], 41). See Leo Spitzer's seminal discussion of the phrase, " 'Soy Quien Soy,' " *NRFH,* 1 (1948): 113-27.

48. *The Oaten Flute: Essays on Pastoral Poetry and the Pastoral Ideal* (Cambridge: Harvard University Press, 1975), 167-74. See also Thomas R. Hart and Steven Rendall, "Rhetorical Persuasion in Marcela's Address to the Shepherds," *HR,* 46 (1978): 287-98.

49. *The Hero with a Thousand Faces,* 2d ed. (Princeton: Bollingen, 1972), 193-96.

50. Parker, *Literature and the Delinquent,* 75-137.

51. "The Isolation of the Renaissance Hero," in his *Prefaces to Renaissance Literature* (New York: Norton, 1965), 92; repr. from *Reason and Imagination,* ed. Joseph A. Mazzeo (New York: Columbia University Press, 1962).

52. Sebastián de Cobarruvias Orozco, *Tesoro de la lengua castellana o española* (Madrid: Turner, 1979), 531a.

53. *Diccionario de Autoridades,* Facsimile Edition (Madrid: Gredos, 1963), 4:145b.

54. "Among the ancient pagans, he whom they believed born of a god or goddess and of a human, for which they made him out more than a man and less than a god; such as Hercules, Achilles, Aeneas, etc." ("Entre los antiguos paganos, el que creían nacido de un dios o una diosa y de una persona humana, por lo cual le reputaban más que hombre y menos que dios; como Hércules, Aquiles, Eneas, etc."). 20th ed. (Madrid: Real Academia Española, 1984), 2:728b.

55. "Hero or Saint? Hagiographic Elements in the Life of the Cid," *JHP*, 7 (1983): 87–105.

56. See James Crapotta, "The Cid of Guillén de Castro: The Hero as Moral Exemplar," *REH*, 9 (1982): 39–46.

57. "Medieval Historiography Misconstrued: The Exile of the Cid, Rodrigo Díaz, and the Supposed *Invidia* of Alfonso VI," *Medium Aevum*, 52 (1983): 286–99.

58. "Death" ("La Muerte") speaks to Don Rodrigo in Henry Wadsworth Longfellow's rendering of stanza 38:

> "The eternal life beyond the sky
> Wealth cannot purchase, nor the high
> And proud estate;
> The soul in dalliance laid,—the spirit
> Corrupt with sin shall not inherit
> A joy so great.
> But the good monk in cloistered cell
> Shall gain it by his book and bell,
> His prayers and tears;
> And the brave knight, whose arm endures
> Fierce battle, and against the Moors
> His standard rears."

> ("El vivir que es perdurable
> No se gana con estados
> Mundanales;
> Ni con vida delectable
> Donde moran los pecados
> Infernales.
> Mas los buenos Religiosos
> Gánanla con oraciones
> Y con lloros:
> Los caballeros famosos
> Con trabajos y aflicciones
> Contra Moros.")

From *Coplas de Jorge Manrique, Translated from the Spanish; With an Introductory Essay on the Moral and Devotional Poetry of Spain.* By Henry W. Longfellow (Boston: Allen & Ticknor, 1833), 66–69.

59. See, for example, Calderón's two-part sacramental play celebrating the canonization of a thirteenth-century Castilian king who personally fights in the Reconquest, *The Saint-King Don Fernando* (*El Santo Rey Don Fernando*), in Calderón, *Obras completas*, vol. 3, ed. Angel Valbuena Prat, 2d ed. (Madrid: Aguilar, 1967).

60. "Honor in Spanish Golden-Age Drama: Its Relation to Real Life and Morals," *BHS*, 35 (1958): 204.

61. Ephesians 6:10–20; 2 Timothy 2:3–4.

62. See Branca, "The Myth of the Hero in Boccaccio," 283–89; and Eugene M. Waith, *The Herculean Hero in Marlowe, Chapman, Shakespeare, and Dryden* (New York: Columbia University Press, 1962), 54.

63. See Margherita Morreale's "Estudio preliminar" to L. Gracián Dantisco's *Galateo español* (Madison Wisc.: Clásicos Hispánicos, 1968), 1–63; and "El modelo ideal de caballero," in Elena Postigo Castellanos, *Honor y privilegio en la Corona de Castilla: El Consejo de las Ordenes y los caballeros de hábito en el siglo XVII* (Soria: Junta de Castilla y León, 1988), 255–59.

64. "Hero or Anti-Hero? The Genesis and Development of the *Miles Christianus,*" in *Concepts of the Hero,* 136.

65. Américo Castro, *De la edad conflictiva,* 24.

66. 5th ed., ed. José F. Montesinos (Madrid: Espasa-Calpe, 1971), 176–77.

67. *Summa,* Part 2, Section 2, Question 158, Article 1; noted by Waith, *The Herculean Hero,* 44.

68. See Jonathan Brown and J. H. Elliott, *A Palace for a King: The Buen Retiro and the Court of Philip IV* (New Haven: Yale University Press, 1980), 156–60.

69. Brower, *Hero and Saint,* 84.

70. Canto 32, lines 13–16, quoted by August J. Aquila, "Ercilla's Concept of the Ideal Soldier," *Hispania,* 60 (1977): 72b.

71. See Frank Pierce, *The Heroic Poem of the Spanish Golden Age: Selections* (New York: Oxford University Press, 1947).

72. See N. D. Shergold, *A History of the Spanish Stage* (Oxford: Clarendon, 1967); John J. Allen, *The Reconstruction of a Spanish Golden Age Playhouse: El Corral del Príncipe* (Gainesville: University Presses of Florida, 1983); and Brown and Elliott, *A Palace for a King,* 55–86.

73. The sole extant early text is the twelfth-century *Act of the Magi (Aucto de los Reyes Magos),* in Castilian but probably composed by a French monk. See Shergold, *A History of the Spanish Stage,* 5.

74. See Alan D. Deyermond, *The Petrarchan Sources of "La Celestina"* (London: Oxford University Press, 1961), esp. 52–57.

75. See George Shipley's series of articles on the linguistic subtleties of the work, including "Authority and Experience in *La Celestina,*" *BHS,* 62 (1985): 95–111.

76. Trans. Lesley Byrd Simpson (Berkeley: University of California Press, 1955), 43–44; the original from the edition introduced by Stephen Gilman and prepared by Dorothy S. Severin (Madrid: Alianza, 1979), 85–86.

77. See Shipley's *"Non erat hic locus;* the Disconcerted Reader in Melibea's Garden," *RPh,* 27 (1974): 286–303.

78. See Peter N. Dunn, "Pleberio's Lament," *PMLA,* 91 (1976): 406–19.

79. In the spring of 1978, I attended a version of the work adapted for the stage by Camilo José Cela and presented at Madrid's Teatro de la Comedia. Pleberio's lament was among the many passages deleted.

80. See Harry Sieber, "Dramatic Symmetry in Gómez Manrique's *La Representación del Nacimiento de Nuestro Señor,*" *HR,* 33 (1965): 118–35.

81. In his "Prohemio" (Prologue) to *Preceptiva dramática española del Renacimiento y Barroco,* ed. Federico Sánchez Escribano and Alberto Porqueras Mayo, 2d ed. (Madrid: Gredos, 1972), 64.

82. See E. M. Wilson and Duncan Moir, *A Literary History of Spain: The Golden Age: Drama, 1492–1700* (London: Ernest Benn, 1971), 29.

83. See Walter Cohen, *Drama of A Nation: Public Theater in Renaissance England and Spain* (Ithaca: Cornell University Press, 1985).

84. In *Preceptiva dramática española*, 155. William T. Brewster's prose translation, introduced by Brander Matthews, was published in 1914 in New York by the Dramatic Museum of Columbia University. It is available in *Papers on Playmaking*, ed. Brander Matthews, Preface by Henry W. Wells (New York: Hill & Wang, 1957).

85. "Cervantes' *Numancia* and Imperial Spain," *MLN*, 94 (1979): 200.

86. Carroll B. Johnson, "*La Numancia* and the Structure of Cervantine Ambiguity," *I & L*, 3 (1980): 75–94.

87. "The Classical Tradition in Spanish Dramatic Theory and Practice in the Seventeenth Century," in *Classical Drama and Its Influence: Essays Presented to H. D. F. Kitto*, ed. M. J. Anderson (London: Methuen, 1965), 225.

88. In the "Eclogue to Claudio" ("Egloga a Claudio"), noted by Hugo A. Rennert and Américo Castro in *Vida de Lope de Vega (1562–1635)*, 2d ed. (Salamanca: Anaya, 1968), 345.

89. (Bordeaux: Féret et Fils, 1965), xxiv. In 1985, Castalia (Madrid) published a Spanish translation, entitled *Lo villano en el teatro del Siglo de Oro*.

90. Trans. Allan Gilbert, in *Literary Criticism: Plato to Dryden* (New York: American Book, 1940), 293; cited in Waith, *The Herculean Hero*, 146.

91. In *Preceptiva dramática española*, 265.

Chapter 2

1. A version of this section, entitled "In Defense of Segismundo," appeared in *BCom*, 41 (1989): 141–54.

2. *Life Is a Dream*, in *The Classic Theater*, vol. 3, *Six Spanish Plays*, ed. Eric Bentley (Garden City, N.Y.: Doubleday, 1959). Quotations in the original Spanish are from the text edited by Augusto Cortina 5th ed. (Madrid, Espasa-Calpe, 1971), cited by act and line number. See Esther W. Nelson's "Ellipsis in *La vida es sueño*: The Lack of Feminine Perspectives," in *Texto y espectáculo: Selected Proceedings of the Symposium on Spanish Golden Age Theater*, ed. Barbara Mujika (Lanham, Md.: University Press of America, 1989): 99–116.

3. New York: Hill & Wang, 1970.

4. See Dian Fox, "*El médico de su honra*: Political Considerations," *Hispania*, 65 (1982): 28–38; revised and reprinted in *Kings in Calderón: A Study in Characterization and Political Theory* (London: Tamesis, 1986): 67–84.

5. "On *La vida es sueño*," in *Critical Essays on the Theatre of Calderón*, ed. Bruce W. Wardropper (New York: New York University Press, 1965), 88–89.

6. "Segismundo and the Rebel Soldier," *BHS*, 45 (1968): 197, 200. See also Hall's "Poetic Justice in *La vida es sueño*: A Further Comment," *BHS*, 46 (1969): 128–31.

7. "Segismundo y el soldado rebelde," in *Hacia Calderón: Coloquio Anglogermano Exeter, 1969*, ed. Hans Flasche (Berlin: Walter de Gruyter, 1970), 74–75.

8. "Calderón's Rebel Soldier and Poetic Justice Reconsidered," *BHS*, 62 (1985): 183.

9. "Authority and Subversion in Cervantes and Calderón," paper presented at

Columbia University, September 1980; "Reason's Unreason in *La vida es sueño*," paper presented at Columbia University, November 1983 and published in *I & L* (new series), 2 (1986): 103–18; and "Way Stations in the Errancy of the Word: A Study of *La vida es sueño*," paper presented at the Modern Language Association Convention, December 1986, New York, and published in *Renaissance Drama and Cultural Change*, ed. Mary Beth Rose (Evanston, Ill.: Northwestern University Press, 1986), 83–100.

10. "Thinking in *La vida es sueño*," *PMLA*, 100 (1985): 290b–91b.

11. See Melveena McKendrick, *Woman and Society in the Spanish Drama of the Golden Age* (Cambridge: Cambridge University Press, 1974); and Frederick A. de Armas, *The Invisible Mistress: Aspects of Feminism and Fantasy in the Golden Age* (Charlottesville, Virginia: Biblioteca Siglo de Oro, 1976).

12. But see de Armas, *The Return of Astraea: An Astral-Imperial Myth in Calderón* (Lexington: University Press of Kentucky, 1986), 106.

13. Mistaken for the Prince in the tower (458), Clarín decides he must play his (really Segismundo's) role: "fuerza es hacer mi papel" (3.61). But most of the self-referring theatrical language voices Basilio's principal error, that he has written a script in advance dooming his son. In the second act, he explains that Segismundo's horoscope "threatens a thousand tragedies and woes" (431) ("amenaza / mil desdichas y tragedias" [2.115–16]). In the third, dismayed, he surveys the civil war:

> The scene I set for swearing of allegiance
> Lends but added horror to this strife:
> It has become the back cloth to a funereal stage
> Where Fortune plays out her tragedies.
>
> (463)

> (El dosel de la jura, reducido
> a segundo intención, a horror segundo,
> teatro funesto es, donde importuna
> representa tragedias la fortuna.)
>
> (3.253–56)

Estrella sees everywhere woe and tragedies (464) ("todo es desdichas y tragedias todo" [3.280]); and Rosaura finally recounts to Segismundo her own "trágicas fortunas" (3.544). That in the end events belie this negative linguistic determinism underscores the fallacy in Basilio's deterministic treatment of his son, which in Counter-Reformation Spain would have been considered un-Catholic. If the play had indeed ended in a tyrannical act by Segismundo, not only would it have fulfilled the tragedy in Basilio's script; but it would have validated the King's heretical denial of free will.

14. *The Theater and the Dream: From Metaphor to Form in Renaissance Drama* (Baltimore: Johns Hopkins University Press, 1973). See Anthony J. Cascardi, *The Limits of Illusion: A Critical Study of Calderón* (Cambridge: Cambridge University Press, 1984).

15. "Kingship and Community in *La vida es sueño*," *BHS*, 58 (1981): 217–28; revised and reprinted in *Kings in Calderón*, 103–18.

16. See May, "Segismundo y el soldado rebelde," 72.

17. "The Tradition Behind the Punishment of the Rebel Soldier in *La vida es sueño*," *BHS*, 50 (1973): 1–17.

18. "Further Testimony in the Rebel Soldier Case," *BCom*, 24 (1972): 13b.

19. Respectively, in *Del rey y de la institución real* (*De Rege et Regis Institutione* (1599); and *Defensa de la fe* (*Defensio Fidei*) (1613).

20. *Del rey*, in *Obras de Padre Juan de Mariana*, ed. F. P[i] y M[argall], BAE, 31 (Madrid: Atlas, 1950), Book 1, chapter 6, 482b–83a. See Guenter Lewy, *Constitutionalism and Statecraft During the Golden Age of Spain: A Study of the Political Philosophy of Juan de Mariana, S.J.* (Geneva: E. Droz, 1960), 72–73; and C. Alan Soons, *Juan de Mariana* (Boston: Twayne, 1982).

21. See Roland Mushat Frye's admirable discussion in *The Renaissance Hamlet: Issues and Responses in 1600* (Princeton: Princeton University Press, 1984), esp. 38–75.

22. R. M. Frye, *The Renaissance Hamlet,* 66, 74.

23. See Bernice Hamilton, *Political Thought in Sixteenth-Century Spain: A Study of the Political Ideas of Vitoria, De Soto, Suárez, and Molina* (Oxford: Clarendon, 1963); and Fox, *Kings in Calderón,* esp. chap. 4.

24. Of unknown authorship.

25. "Calderón's Rebel Soldier and Poetic Justice," *BHS,* 46 (1969): 123.

26. *Idea de un príncipe político-cristiano representada en cien empresas,* ed. Vicente Carcía de Diego (Madrid: Espasa-Calpe, 1927), 2:200–201.

27. E. M. W. Tillyard, *The Elizabethan World Picture* (London: Chatto & Windus, 1952); S. K. Heninger, *Touches of Sweet Harmony: Pythagorean Cosmology and Renaissance Poetics* (San Marino, Calif.: Huntington Library, 1974).

28. "The Epic Hero Superseded," in *Concepts of the Hero,* 200–201.

29. See Jean Canavaggio, *Cervantes,* trans. J. R. Jones (New York: Norton, 1990), 144–76.

30. Molho, "El pícaro de nuevo," 204. See also Castro, *De la edad conflictiva.*

31. On *arbitristas* and the economic conditions that spawned them, see J. H. Elliott, *Imperial Spain: 1469–1716* (New York: New American Library, 1963), 281–316; and his "Self-Perception and Decline in Early Seventeenth-Century Spain," *Past and Present,* 74 (1977): 41–61. For literary renderings of the *arbitrista,* see, for example, Cervantes's exemplary novel *The Dogs' Colloquy* and Quevedo's *The Rogue.* See also Hart's "History, Epic, Novel: Camões and Cervantes," *RQ,* 34 (1987): 95–102 for a view of Don Quixote as *arbitrista.*

32. Cf. R. O. Jones, "Poets and Peasants," in *Homenaje a William L. Fichter: Estudios sobre el teatro antiguo hispánico y otros ensayos,* ed. A. David Kossoff and José Amor y Vázquez (Madrid: Castalia, 1971), 341–45.

33. The standard biography of Lope is Hugo A. Rennert and Américo Castro's *Vida de Lope de Vega (1562–1635),* 2d ed. (Salamanca: Anaya, 1968). The earliest version, by Rennert, was published in English and is available as *The Life of Lope de Vega (1562–1635)* (New York: Stechert, 1937).

34. See "Apéndice 2o: Función del 'vulgo' en la preceptiva dramática española de la Edad de Oro," in Sánchez Escribano and Porqueras Mayo, *Preceptiva dramática española,* 365–87.

35. Eight of the "Prólogos" are available in *Comedias escogidas de Frey Lope Félix de Vega Carpio,* ed. Juan Eugenio Hartzenbusch, BAE 52 (Madrid: Imprenta de los Sucesores de Hernando, 1910), 4:xxi–xxix.

36. Respectively, in *Teatro y literatura en la sociedad barroca* (Madrid: Seminarios y Ediciones, 1972), esp. 105–35; and *Sociología de la comedia española del siglo XVII* (Madrid: Cátedra, 1976), 163–80.

37. *Diccionario crítico etimológico de la lengua castellana* (Madrid: Gredos, 1954), 4:740b.

38. Rosaura: "Villain, you lie" (450) ("Villano, mientes" [2.969]); Estrella: "You are a crude, coarse suitor" (452) ("Eres / villano y grosero amante" [2.1021-22]).

39. *Recherches sur le "Refranero" Castellan* (Paris: Société d'Édition "Les Belles Lettres," 1971), 230.

40. It was published in Part 7 of Lope's *comedias* (Madrid, 1617). See Alonso Zamora Vicente's "Estudio preliminar" to his edition, *El villano en su rincón. Las bizarrías de Belisa* (Madrid: Espasa-Calpe, 1963), esp. xx.

41. On the date of composition, see esp. Marcel Bataillon, "*El villano en su rincón*," in his *Varia lección de clásicos españoles* (Madrid: Gredos, 1964), 332-39; Joaquín Casalduero, "Sentido y forma de *El villano en su rincón*," *Revista de la Universidad de Madrid*, 11 (1962): 547-49; Zamora Vicente, "Estudio preliminar," lii-lvi; and J. R. Andrews, S. G. Armistead, and J. H. Silverman, "Two Notes for Lope de Vega's *El villano en su rincón*," *BCom*, 18 (1966): 33a-34a.

42. See Zamora Vicente, "Estudio preliminar," xxiv.

43. Cecily Radford entitles her adapted translation of the play *The King and the Farmer: A Romantic Comedy* (London: H. W. F. Deane & Sons), 1948. Since Radford often departs significantly from the original text, I use my own translations, occasionally consulting her renderings, as well as those in the helpful notes to Wardropper's edition of the play, available in his anthology *Teatro español del Siglo de Oro* (New York: Charles Scribner's Sons, 1970), 258-364. Quotations in the original Spanish are from Wardropper's edition, where the epitaph appears in act 1, lines 735-43.

44. Fileto tells the King, "He is the humblest of men" ("[E]s el más humilde de los hombres" [1.809]).

45. Hesse, "*El villano en su rincón*," in his *Análisis e interpretación de la comedia* (Madrid: Castalia, 1970), 30-42; Wardropper, "La venganza de Maquiavelo: *El villano en su rincón*," in *Homenaje a William L. Fichter*, 765-72; Varey, "Towards an Interpretation of Lope de Vega's *El villano en su rincón*," in *Studies in Spanish Literature of the Golden Age Presented to E. M. Wilson*, (London: Tamesis, 1973), esp. 334-37.

46. "*Beatus . . . nemo: El villano en su rincón*, las 'Polianteas' y la literatura de emblemas," *Cuadernos de Filología* (Universidad de Valencia, Facultad de Filología), 3 (1981): 288.

47. Casalduero, "Sentido y forma," 558-60.

48. On the traditionally sexual connotations of footwear, see Sieber, *Language and Society in "Las vida de Lazarillo de Tormes"* (Baltimore: Johns Hopkins University Press, 1978), 51-53.

49. "*El villano en su rincón*: Lope's Rejection of the Pastoral Dream," *BHS*, 58 (1981): 113.

50. For example, Bataillon declares Juan Labrador "generoso" and emphasizes the peasant's wisdom (330, 331, 332). According to Moir in *A Literary History of Spain* (67), Juan Labrador is "the dignified and sententious peasant . . . and so impressively virtuous that the King . . . envies him his stoicism, his tranquility and integrity." For Varey, Lisarda is "the virtuous daughter of Juan Labrador" ("Towards an Interpretation," 323); she and Feliciano are, "by reason of their virtue and abilities, fitted" for courtly life (335).

51. See the third chapter (*tratado*) of *The Life of Lazarillo de Tormes;* and Cervantes's exemplary novel *The Deceitful Marriage* (*El casamiento engañoso*).

52. In the beginning, Finardo had warned Otón, "Mind it [the fact that Lisarda and Belisa may be married] doesn't lead you into trouble / because their clothes

proclaim them / folk of noble birth and prominence" ("No te resulte disgusto; / que en hábito parecen / gente noble y principal" [1.4–6]).

53. See John Lihani, ed., *Farsas y églogas de Lucas Fernández* (New York: Las Américas, 1969), 31.

54. See E. Templin, "The Mother in the Comedia of Lope," *HR*, 3 (1935): 219–44; and Arnold Rothe, "Padre y familia en el Siglo de Oro," *Ib*, 7 (1978): 146.

55. See Dixon, "*Beatus ... nemo*," 284–85.

56. For example, see the farmer's remarks to the disguised king, 2.712–15; 2.754–59. The Knight of the Green Cloak appears in *Don Quixote*, Part 2, chaps. 16–18.

57. Upon the summons of his children to court, he wails, "Who is that official who came / to my house that night, to my misery ... ?" ("¿Quién es aqueste alcaide que a mi casa / vino por mi desdicha aquella noche ... ?" [3.430–31]), adding,

> As far as money is concerned,
> I wouldn't be distressed; but, my children! ...
> Only a king could order this of me,
> and only my misfortune give him reason to.
> Now my good fortune declines.
>
> (Lo que es dinero
> no pudiera afligirme; mas ¡los hijos! ...
> Sólo un Rey me pudiera mandar esto,
> y sola mi desdicha darle causa.
> Ya declina conmigo la fortuna.)
> (3.433–34; 440–42)

The outburst provokes Otón to exclaim, "What sorrow!" ("¡Qué sentimiento!" [3.453]). When Juan Labrador arrives at court, he laments,

> I am so beset by unhappiness
> that it seems punishment from heaven. . . .
> Here at court are my children, which I don't regret
> as much as finding myself in person
> subjected to such harsh torture.
>
> ([T]anto mal poseo
> que parece del cielo este castigo. . . .
> Acá tengo mis hijos, que no siento
> tanto como el hallarme yo en persona
> en medio de tan áspero tormento.)
> (3.784–85; 790–92)

58. Ervin C. Brody, "Poland in Calderón's *Life Is a Dream:* Poetic Illusion or Historical Reality," *Pol R*, 14 (1969): 21–62; Hana Jehová, "Les motifs polonais ou tcheques dans *La vie est-un songe, CRCL*, 4 (1977): 179–85; Jack Weiner, "Un episodio de la historia rusa visto por autores españoles del Siglo de Oro: El pretendiente Demetrio," *JHP*, 2 (1978): 175–201.

59. Available in *Dramáticos posteriores a Lope de Vega*, ed. Ramón de Mesonero Romanos, BAE, 47, 2d ed. (Madrid: Gredos, 1966), 1:385–416.

60. *Ideas de los españoles del siglo XVII,* 2d ed. (Madrid: Gredos, 1966), 385–416.
61. In a letter cited by Herrero García, *Ideas,* 410.
62. Quoted by Herrero García, *Ideas,* 412.
63. Act 3, lines 365–92, ed. Juan María Marín (Madrid: Cátedra, 1983).
64. In the King's prose letters, between 3.166 and 167 and between 3.427 and 428; and twice more in lines 3.797 and 3.818.
65. Ed. Américo Castro (Madrid: Espasa-Calpe, 1973), 32. See Castro's note to line 14.
66. "Al doctor Salvador de León," in *Cartas filológicas del Licenciado Francisco Cascales,* in *Epistolario español,* ed. Eugenio de Ochoa, BAE, 62 (Madrid: RAE, 1965), 2:487b–89a.
67. "Los rasgos físicos y el carácter según los textos españoles del siglo XVII," *RFE,* 12 (1925): 160.
68. Cobarruvias, *Tesoro de la lengua castellana,* 311b.
69. Bataillon, *"El villano en su rincón,"* 332.
70. The King will not accompany his sister on her journey to meet her new husband in part "to avoid / such an excessive expense" ("por excusar / un gasto tan excesivo" [3:491–92]).
71. See Bataillon, *"El villano en su rincón,"* 336.
72. It appears in the *Veinte y una parte* (Madrid, 1635). In *Cronología de las comedias de Lope de Vega,* trans. María Rosa Cartes (Madrid: Gredos, 1968), S. Griswold Morley and Courtney Bruerton analyze versification to date the play's composition at 1620–23.
   My translations are based on the English rendering of John Garrett Underhill from his anthology *Four Plays by Lope de Vega* (New York: Charles Scribner's Sons, 1936), 103–87. The original Spanish is from Lope de Vega, *Comedias: El remedio en la desdicha. El mejor alcalde, el rey,* ed. J. Gómez Ocerín and R. M. Tenreiro (Madrid: Espasa-Calpe 1967), 1:175–272.
73. On the convention of a character's breaking the dramatic illusion at the end of the *comedia* to address the audience directly, see Wardropper, "The Dramatic Epilogue in Golden-Age Spain," *MLN,* 101 (1986): 205–19.
74. Available as the *Primera crónica general de España,* ed. Menéndez Pidal, NBAE, 5 (Madrid: Bailly-Bailliere é Hijos, 1906). See 1:659b–60b. Gómez Ocerín and Tenreiro include the relevant passage from the *PCG* at the conclusion of their edition of the play, 269–70.
75. Contained in Agustín Durán's *Romancero general, ó Colección de romances castellanos anteriores al siglo XVIII,* BAE, 16 (Madrid: Rivadeneyra, 1851), 2:3a.
76. "History and Poetry: A Re-Examination of Lope de Vega's *El mejor alcalde, el rey,"* *FMLS,* 16 (1980): 210.
77. See also Calderón's *To Know of Good and Evil (Saber del mal y del bien),* c. 1628.
78. On the structural coherence of the play, see Premraj R. K. Halkhoree, "El arte de Lope de Vega en *El mejor alcalde, el rey,"* *BHS,* 56 (1979): 33.
79. On the "love-hunt" in the ballad tradition, see Edith Randam Rogers, *The Perilous Hunt: Symbols in Hispanic and European Balladry* (Lexington: University Press of Kentucky, 1980), 15–20.
80. *El robo de Dina* is available in *Obras de Lope de Vega, Autos y coloquios,* II, ed. Marcelino Menéndez Pelayo, BAE, 159 (Madrid: Atlas, 1963), 7.2:7–53. See Edward Glaser, "Lope de Vega's *El robo de Dina,"* *RJ,* 15 (1964): esp. 322.
81. When Sancho jests that Nuño has arranged Elvira's marriage to a squire, she

answers in the same spirit: "Sancho, I don't weep over you, but over going off to a palace" (115) ("Sancho, no lloro por ti, / sino por ir a palacio" [1.253-54]). Later, Tello's offers of riches leave her unmoved.

82. "El arte de Lope de Vega," 37. Carter, in "History and Poetry," sees a sinister side to the lovers' teasing: "Lope is making a simple, basic, and benevolent human activity seem dependent on concealment, secrecy, dissimulation and deception." However, while it is dramatically ironic that Elvira really will be carried off to a palace, the lovers always treat one another with respect and affection—along with sharing a sense of humor.

83. "El servir" can mean "courtship" as well as "service."

84. After the wedding has been stopped, Elvira states, "You are now my husband, Sancho: / Come to my door tonight" (129) ("Ya eres, Sancho, mi marido: / ven esta noche a mi puerta" [1.715-16]). From then on they continue to refer to each other as husband and wife, although Sancho conscientiously makes it clear to the King that the ceremony has not taken place.

85. "Forms of Marriage," *New Catholic Encyclopedia* (New York: McGraw-Hill, 1967), 9:277a.

86. On Sancho's first visit to Tello after Elvira's abduction, the *labrador* speaks allegorically: taking his rusted sword from its worn sheath,

> I found the tallest tree—amain
> With stroke and blow I leveled it like grain.
> Not because the tree had robbed me of Elvira,
> But because it was so tall and arrogant
> That it gazed down in scorn on the others as if they were of little account:
> Such is the power of a ferocious giant.
>
> (141)

> (. . . llegué al árbol más alto, y a reveses
> y tajos igualé sus blancas mieses.
>   No porque el árbol fué tan alto y arrogante,
> que a los demás como a pequeños mira:
> tal es la fuerza de un feroz gigante.)
>   (2.1059-66)

Later, Pelayo describes the tapestry he saw hanging in Tello's hall. The clown heard that it was of "King Ball" ("el rey Baúl"):

> SANCHO.   Silly! He must have said "Saul."
> PELAYO.   Ball when he wanted to kill Badill.
> SANCHO.   David was his son-in-law.
> PELAYO.   Yes; the priest was preaching at church once
>   That he hit flat on the noggin
>   With one of Moses's hard tears [a stone]
>   The giant, a liar.
> SANCHO.   Goliath, you lout!
>   (153)

> (SANCHO.   ¡Necio!, Saúl diría.
> PELAYO.   Baúl cuando al Badil matar quería.

Sancho.   David, su yerno era.
Pelayo.   Sí, que en la igreja predicaba el cura
                 que le dió en la mollera
                 con una de Moisén lágrima dura
                 a un gigante que olía.
Sancho.   Golías, bestia.

                                    (2.1412-19)

87. In the Torres Naharro play, Himeneo and Febea are caught meeting at night in her room. Her infuriated brother and guardian, the Marqués, intends to murder them both until he learns to his pleasure that they have been secretly wed. Febea announces proudly, "I knew how to get married / with no help from relatives, / and very well, too" ("me supe casar / sin ayuda de parientes, / y muy bien"). See D. W. McPheeter's edition of Torres Naharro's *Comedias. Soldadesca, Tinelaria, Himenea* (Madrid: Clásicos Castalia, 1973), act 5, lines 273-75.

88. "Estructura social de la comedia de Lope. A propósito de *El mejor alcalde, el rey,*" *Arbor,* 85 (1973): 453-66.

89. Introduction to his edition of Lope de Vega, *La fábula de Perseo o La bella Andrómeda* (Kassel: Reichenberger, 1985), 32.

90. Sancho, worrying over Elvira, is singularly indifferent to Pelayo's gift of doubloons from the King (155; 2.1487-92).

91. See J. H. Elliott, *Richilieu and Olivares* (Cambridge: Cambridge University Press, 1984).

92. See Leicester Bradner, "The Theme of *Privanza* in Spanish and English Drama 1590-1625," in *Homenaje a William L. Fichter,* 97-106; and Raymond R. MacCurdy, *The Tragic Fall: Don Alvaro de Luna and Other Favorites in Spanish Golden Age Drama* (Chapel Hill: University of North Carolina Press, 1978).

93. On the enigmatic sister of Don Tello, see Sturgiss E. Leavitt, "A Maligned Character in Lope's *El mejor alcalde, el rey,*" *BCom,* 6 (1954): 1a-3a; and Albert E. Sloman, "Lope's *El mejor alcalde, el rey:* Addendum to a Note by Sturgiss E. Leavitt," *BCom,* 7 (1955): 17a-19b.

Chapter 3

1. Mikhail Bakhtin, "Epic and Novel," in *The Dialogic Imagination: Four Essays,* ed. Michael Holquist, trans. Caryl Emerson and Michael Holquist (Austin: University of Texas Press, 1981), 15.

2. For example, Díez Borque views the *comedia* as support for the social and political status quo, while Robert ter Horst sees at least in Calderón a sort of pre-Romantic rebel, anticipating the modern rejection of classical epistemology (*Calderón: The Secular Plays* [Lexington: University Press of Kentucky, 1982]).

3. The dates are suggested by Morley and Bruerton, *Cronología,* 550.

4. (Madrid: Alianza, 1968), 141-42.

5. In the Introduction to his edition of *El peregrino en su patria* (Madrid: Castalia, 1973), 34-35.

6. *The Honor Plays of Lope de Vega* (Cambridge: Harvard University Press, 1977), 3.

7. *The Idea of a Theatre: A Study of Ten Plays. The Art of Drama in Changing Perspective* (Princeton: Princeton University Press, 1972), 230.

8. See, for example, E. M. Wilson, "The Four Elements in the Imagery of Calderón," *MLR*, 31 (1936): 34–47; A. A. Parker, *The Approach to the Spanish Drama of the Golden Age* (London: The Hispanic & Luso-Brazilian Councils, 1957) and "Towards a Definition of Calderonian Tragedy," *BHS*, 39 (1962): 222–37.

9. Alix Zuckerman-Ingber's *"El bien más alto": A Reconsideration of Lope de Vega's Honor Plays* (Gainesville: University Presses of Florida, 1984), which recognizes the characteristic weakness in the kings of the honor plays, deserves more attention than it has received to date.

10. *Experience and Artistic Expression in Lope de Vega: The Making of "La Dorotea"* (Cambridge: Harvard University Press, 1974).

11. Larson, *The Honor Plays*, 28. Morley and Bruerton state that the play was written no later than 1595 (*Cronología*, 244).

12. See Larson, *The Honor Plays*, 24–30; Donald McGrady, "The Comic Treatment of Conjugal Honor in Lope's *Las ferias de Madrid*," *HR*, 41 (1973): 33–42; and Zuckerman-Ingber, *"El bien más alto,"* 62–66; 134–35. *Las ferias de Madrid* is available in *Obras de Lope de Vega, Nueva edición. Obras dramáticas*, (Madrid: RAE, 1918), 5:582–621.

13. The play is available in Lope de Vega, *Obras escogidas*, ed. Federico Carlos Sainz de Robles (Madrid: Aguilar, 1974), 3:1233–66.

14. The heroic lover, Lisardo, at one point writes a ballad to the wife, Laura, calling her "Belisa." This is the pseudonym Lope himself often used in poetry referring to his own lover, Isabel de Urbina. The story ends when, to cover up the dishonor and his own violent retribution, the methodical and unromantic husband Marcelo secretly kills a total of six people.

15. "Sobre el punto de honor castellano," *RO*, 2d series, 1, no. 5 (1963): 154.

16. From Part 2, vol. 13, law 4; cited by Castro in "Algunas observaciones acerca del concepto del honor en los siglos XVI y XVII," *RFE*, 3 (1916): 44.

17. *Shakespeare and the Renaissance Concept of Honor* (Princeton: Princeton University Press, 1960), 66.

18. See Robert J. Nelson, *Corneille: His Heroes and Their Worlds* (Philadelphia: University of Pennsylvania Press, 1963), 68–109.

19. Honig, "The Seizures of Honor in Calderón," *Kenyon Review*, 23 (1961): 430–31; Wilson and Moir, *A Literary History of Spain*, 62; Larson, *The Honor Plays*, 181n.

20. Larson, *The Honor Plays*, 3. See also Hymen Alpern, "Jealousy as a Dramatic Motive in the Spanish *Comedia*," *RR*, 14 (1923): 276–85.

21. "El doble aspecto de la honra en el teatro del siglo XVII," *HR*, 26 (1958): 188–99.

22. *El alcalde de Zalamea*, ed. Augusto Cortina, 5th ed. (Madrid: Espasa-Calpe, 1971), act I, lines 874–76.

23. In the Avalle-Arce edition of *El peregrino*, 60.

24. *Doze comedias de Lope de Vega Carpio familiar del Santo Oficio. Sacadas de sus originales. Quarta parte* (Madrid, 1614). Colección Azarque (Ocaña, 1983) has published a facsimile edition of the *princeps*, with an informative prologue by Felipe B. Pedraza Jiménez (epilogue by Padre Jesús Santos).

25. For a summary of the dating controversy, see Julián María Marín, Introduction to his edition of the play, 5th ed. (Madrid: Cátedra, 1983), 40–45. Spanish quotations of the play are from this edition; the English renderings are my own, with occasional reliance on Jill Booty's loose translation in *Lope de Vega (Five Plays)*, ed. R. D. F. Pring-Mill (New York: Hill & Wang, 1961), 1–56.

26. In an edition of *Parte IV* published in Barcelona in 1614 (BN R.23.467), the play appears on fols. 76r.–100v. The last lines are followed by "Aqui da fin la famosa Tragicomedia de Peribañez, y el Comendador de Ocaña."

27. For example, in Hartzenbusch's 1857 edition, in *Comedias escogidas de Frey Lope Félix de Vega Carpio*, BAE, 41 (Madrid: Rivadeneyra), 3:281–302, the play is entitled *Peribáñez y el Comendador de Ocaña, Tragicomedia*. Alberto Blecua's edition (for Alianza [Madrid 1981]) shortens the title to *Peribáñez*.

28. *Peribáñez and the Comendador of Ocaña*, in *Eight Spanish Plays of the Golden Age* (New York: Modern Library, 1968), 98.

29. *Crónica del Rey Don Enrique Tercero de Castilla é de Leon*, included in the *Crónicas de los reyes de Castilla*, ed. Cayetano Rosell, BAE, 68 (Madrid: Rivadeneyra, 1877), 2:261a–b.

30. The matter of time is confused, although it is clear that Peribáñez reached home and was waiting inside before Fadrique entered. In 3.439–42, the impatient Comendador, anticipating his second visit to Casilda in Pedro's absence, wishes it were ten o'clock; Luján comforts him that it is nearly nine. Shortly afterwards the Comendador wishes it were eleven; Luján replies that it is only eight o'clock (3.497–99). Soon Peribáñez enters his house through the back way (3.591–628). Later (3.991–92) the peasant tells the King and Queen that he was home by ten o'clock. When Inés welcomes Fadrique at the front door, the Comendador declares, "I'm in pain at eleven" ("En pena a las onze estoy" [3.645]), playing on the notion that souls in purgatory suffer at midnight.

31. See Salomon, *Recherches*, 23–25.

32. "Images et structure dans *Peribáñez*," *BH*, 51 (1945): 125–59, repr. in Spanish translation in *El teatro de Lope de Vega: Artículos y estudios*, 2d ed., ed. José Francisco Gatti (Buenos Aires: Eudeba, 1967), 50–90 and in *Calderón y la crítica: Historia y antología*, ed. Manuel Durán and Roberto González Echeverría (Madrid: Gredos, 1976), 1:277–99; and in English translation in Wilson's *Spanish and English Literature of the 16th and 17th Centuries*, 130–54.

33. The most important essays are Charles V. Aubrun and José F. Montesinos, "*Peribáñez*," in *El teatro de Lope de Vega*, ed. José Francisco Gatti, 13–49; originally the prologue to their edition of *Peribáñez y el Comendador de Ocaña* (Paris: Hachette, 1943), xv–xlviii; Victor F. Dixon, "The Symbolism of *Peribáñez*," *BHS*, 43 (1966): 11–24; Georges Güntert, "Relección del *Peribáñez*," *RFE*, 54 (1971): 37–52; J. E. Varey, "The Essential Ambiguity in Lope de Vega's *Peribáñez*: Theme and Staging," *Theatre Research International*, 1, (1976): 157–78; Mary Gaylord Randel, "The Portrait and the Creation of *Peribáñez*," *RF*, 85 (1973): 145–58; John Bryans, "Providence or Discretion in *Peribáñez*," *JHP*, 2 (1977): 121–33; José M. Ruano de la Haza, "Malicia campesina y la ambigüedad esencial de *Peribáñez y el Comendador de Ocaña* de Lope," *Hispanófila*, 84 (1985): 21–30.

Two studies that ought to cause serious reconsideration of Lope's attitudes toward peasant honor in this play and in general are Peter W. Evans's "*Peribáñez* and Ways of Looking at Golden Age Dramatic Characters," *RR*, 74 (1983): 136–51; and Robin Carter's "*Peribáñez*: Disorder Restored," in *What's Past Is Prologue: A Collection of Essays in Honour of L. J. Woodward*, ed. Salvador Bacarisse, Bernard Bentley, Mercedes Clarasó, and Douglas Gifford (Edinburgh: Academic Press, 1984), 17–27. Along these lines, see most recently William R. Blue, "*Peribáñez* and Economics," in *Teatro y espectáculo*, 47–53.

34. *The Libation Bearers*, trans. Richmond Lattimore (Chicago: University of Chicago Press, 1953), 124, line 899.

35. Arthur McGee, *The Elizabethan Hamlet* (New Haven: Yale University Press, 1987).

36. "The Uniqueness of the *Comedia,*" *HR,* 27 (1950): 306-7.

37. "Towards a Definition of Calderonian Tragedy."

38. "Tragic Themes in Spanish Ballads," 226, 230.

39. "*El pintor de su deshonra* and the Neo-Aristotelian Theory of Tragedy," in *Critical Essays on the Theatre of Calderón,* (New York: New York University Press, 1965), 216-19.

40. Pedro closely questions the painter, who informs him (incorrectly) that Casilda is unaware of the Comendador's interest (2.668-69). Having arrived back in Ocaña, he asks himself, "If Casilda isn't guilty, / why do I shrink / from seeing her?" ("Si no es culpada / Casilda, por qué rehúyo / el verla?" [2.828-30]). He is then "notably relieved" ("Notable aliento he cobrado" [2:880]) to hear the reapers' song that absolves Casilda of encouraging Fadrique. As he prepares to march off at the head of his hundred rustic soldiers, he and Casilda carry on an enigmatic conversation about their persistent mutual jealousy, their "zelos tan soldados" (3.282-342). In a later soliloquy, again returning to Ocaña from Toledo, Peribáñez apostrophizes his "reed of honor" ("caña, la del honor" [3.537]): "I will cut you short before / you break, weak reed" ("yo te cortaré primero / que te quiebres, débil caña [3.555-56]). Bryans points out that the play on "caña" is an allusion to Luke 7:24-28, which condemns "worldly honor" ("Providence or Discretion in *Peribáñez,*" 125).

41. *New Catholic Encyclopedia,* 12:540a.

42. Dixon, "The Symbolism," 12.

43. See Blue, "*Peribáñez* and Economics," 50.

44. On the concept of "discretion," see A. A. Parker, "The Meaning of *Discretion* in *No hay más fortuna que Dios:* The Medieval Background and Sixteenth- and Seventeenth-Century Usage," the Appendix to his edition of Calderón's *No hay más fortuna que Dios,* 2d ed. (Manchester: Manchester University Press, 1962), 77-92. For the term's specific application to *Peribáñez,* see Ruano de la Haza's article in *Hispanófila.*

45. Emphasis mine; Peribáñez will become the dishonorable "ladrón" in Casilda's lament. In " 'Tienen los celos pasos de ladrones': Silence in Calderón's *El médico de su honra,*" *HR,* 33 (1965): 273-89, Daniel Rogers has examined for Calderón's honor play the metaphor of the suspicious husband as thief sneaking into his own house. "Jealousy," Rogers writes of Don Gutierre, "has reduced an honorable man to behaving like a thief" (283). Rogers notes that this figure of speech may be a biblical allusion to John 10:1-2, where Christ speaks: "Verily, verily, I say unto you, He that entereth not by the door into the sheepfold, but climbeth up some other way, the same is a thief and a robber. But he that entereth in by the door is the shepherd of the sheep." Peribáñez's speech to the King later will travesty Christ's pastoral imagery:

> I ran him through with the sword, and then
> he let the white lamb go,
> for I, like a shepherd,
> figured out how to save her from the wolf.

> (passéle [al Comendador] el pecho, y entonces
> dexó la cordera blanca,
> porque yo, como pastor,
> supe del lobo quitarla.)
>
>   (3.1005-8)

46. According to Halkhoree, "The Dramatic Use of Place in Lope de Vega's *Peribáñez*," *BCom*, 30 (1978): 15, Casilda "with justification" approves the death of "her erstwhile intimate companion and cousin." José M. Ruano and J. E. Varey, in the Introduction to their edition of the play (London: Tamesis, 1980), 26, state that Inés "allows Leonardo to beguile her under promise of marriage (1224–31), and in the third act she betrays her cousin and thus deserves her death at the hands of Peribáñez 'por traidora' (2893)."

47. Zuckerman-Ingber, in "Honor Reconsidered: *Los comendadores de Córdoba*," *JHP*, 4 (1979): 59–75, reprinted, revised and expanded in her *"El bien más alto,"* 24–44; McKendrick, and "Celebration or Subversion? *Los comendadores de Córdoba* Reconsidered," *BHS*, 61 (1984): 352–60.

48. Zuckerman-Ingber, *"El bien más alto,"* 40.

49. "[T]hey both fell to the ground; it is said Don Henry being underneath, and with the assistance of Beltrán, who turned them over and put Henry on top, [Henry] succeeded in stabbing [Peter] many times, killing him, a horrible occasion" ("[C]ayeron ambos en el suelo; dicen que don Enrique debajo, y con ayuda de Beltran, que les dió vuelta y le puso encima, le pudo herir de muchas puñaladas, con que le acabó de matar, cosa que pone grima") (Mariana, *Historia general de España*, in *Obras del Padre Juan de Mariana*, Book 17, chap. 13, 2:519a).

50. In the *Romancero general*, ed. Durán, 2:43a.

51. Of Henry as a teenager:

> although a boy, every day the gifts of courage and all kinds of virtues in his good nature became more and more evident. It is true that the very high hopes held for this Prince soon dispelled like smoke because of his poor health, an affliction that lasted all his life. A great shame and a very serious decline; on account of the illness his face turned yellow and disfigured, his body feeble, and his judgment not always fit for such an important responsibility, with its many and diverse demands. Finally, in his later years, he did not live up to the promise of his youth that people had counted on.

> (aunque mozo, de cada dia descubria mas prendas de su buen natural en valor y todo género de virtudes. Verdad es que las esperanzas que deste Príncipe se tenian muy grandes en breve se regalaron y deshicieron como humo por causa de su poca salud, mal que le duró toda la vida. Grande lástima y daño muy grave; con la indisposicion traia el rostro amarillo y desfigurado, las fuerzas del cuerpo flacas, las del juicio á veces no tan bastantes para peso tan grande, tantos y tan diversos cuidados. Finalmente, los años adelante no continuó en las buenas muestras que antes daba y que las gentes se prometian de su buen natural [Book 19, chap. 6, 39b].)

52. See Aubrun and Montesinos, *"Peribáñez,"* 35.

53. *The Metamorphoses of Lope de Vega's King Pedro* (Madrid: Plaza Mayor Scholar, 1974).

54. See Peter N. Dunn, "Some Uses of Sonnets in the Plays of Lope de Vega," *BHS*, 34 (1957): 220–21.

55. The final tercets:

> Woe is me, who adore that ungrateful and green ivy
> hung on another wall,

whose hardness I try to soften!
Such is the only end that I can hope for,
but, since I am certain of dying,
may love change you to stone!

(¡Mísero yo, que adoro en otro muro
colgada aquella ingrata y verde hiedra,
cuya dureza enternecer procuro!
Tal es el fin que mi esperança medra:
mas, pues que de morir estoy seguro,
¡plega al amor que te convierta en piedra!)
                                                    (II, 802-7)

According to Dixon in *"Beatus . . . nemo"* (284), "the destructive ivy, if sometimes
for Lope as for some emblemists meant *ingratitude,* for others [like Aneau, Horozco,
and Cobarruvias] it was a symbol of *whoring"* ("la destructora hiedra, si bien alguna
vez para Lope como para algunos emblematistas significaba la *ingratitud,* para otros
[como Aneau, Horozco y Cobarruvias] era símbolo de la *ramera"*).
  56. See Ruano and Varey, *Peribáñez,* 183n.
  57. Before learning that Peribáñez had hired Luján, Fadrique actually decided to
abandon his pursuit of Casilda. He tells Leonardo that he has had her portrait
painted: "Since I can't live with the original, / I'll live with the painting of it" ("pues
con el vivo no puedo, / viviré con el pintado" [2.221-22]). It is, then, Peribáñez, who
by knowingly hiring the Comendador's lackey, resuscitates Fadrique's hope and
active assault on his honor.
  58. "The Hero," in Brombert, *The Hero in Literature,* 38; repr. with some
deletions from Bowra's *Heroic Poetry* (New York: St. Martin's Press, 1961), 91-131.
  59. "The Norms of Epic," in Brombert, *The Hero in Literature,* 56; repr. from
Greene's *The Descent from Heaven* (New Haven: Yale University Press, 1963), 8-25.
  60. See Cedric H. Whitman, *Sophocles.*
  61. Blas remonstrates with Peribáñez upon his tardy arrival at the meeting of the
brotherhood: "Your absence has been very hard on us" ("Gran falta nos habéis
hecho" [2.33]).
  62. English translations of *Fuenteovejuna* are my own, with occasional references to Roy Campbell's rendering of the play in *The Classic Theatre,* 161-231. The
Spanish is from the Francisco López Estrada edition, 4th ed., (Madrid: Castalia,
1983), act 2, line 1464.
  63. The first in-depth study of the collective protagonist is Perry J. Powers's
doctoral dissertation "The Concept of the City-State in the Dramas of Lope de Vega"
(Baltimore: Johns Hopkins University, 1947).
  64. "Los villanos filosóficos y políticos (La configuración de *Fuente Ovejuna* a
través de los nombres y 'apellidos')," *CHA,* 180 (1969): 539.
  65. Juan Manuel Rozas, *"Fuenteovejuna* desde la segunda acción," in *Actas del I.
Simposio de Literatura Española,* ed. Alberto Navarro González (Salamanca: Ediciones
Universidad de Salamanca, 1981), 185.
  66. The Orders of Calatrava, Santiago, and Alcántara were the three military-
religious organizations, each headed by Maestres, founded during Spain's Reconquest.
The Maestre's nearest subordinate was the Comendador.
  67. The relevant passage is printed by Menéndez y Pelayo in his edition of the
Obras de Lope de Vega for the RAE, 10:clix-clxvii.

68. Ribbans, "The Meaning and Structure of Lope's *Fuenteovejuna*," *BHS*, 31 (1954): 168–69; repr. in Spanish translation in *El teatro de Lope de Vega*, 91–123; and Carter, *"Fuenteovejuna* and Tyranny: Some Problems of Linking Drama with Political Theory," *FMLS*, 13 (1977): 330–31.

69. See William C. McCrary, *"Fuenteovejuna:* Its Platonic Vision and Execution," *SP*, 58 (1961): 179–92.

70. For example, according to López Estrada, "Lope created on stage, from the social point of view, a utopian Fuenteovejuna" ("Lope creó en la escena una Fuente Obejuna utópica desde el punto de vista social" ["Los villanos filosóficos," 530]). In *A Literary History of Spain: The Golden Age: Drama*, 65–66, Wilson and Moir write that the community is "markedly idealised" and that *Fuenteovejuna* counts among the *comedias* meant as propaganda to repopulate the countryside, exalting "the virtues of country life as opposed to the misery and vice of city life."

71. The entire exchange, which takes place immediately after Laurencia's and Pascuala's own successful appeal to Mengo for protective company, reads as follows:

JACINTA.	Help me, for God's sake,
	in the name of friendship!
LAURENCIA.	What's wrong, Jacinta dear?
PASCUALA.	We two are your friends.
JACINTA.	The Comendador's men
	on the way to Ciudad Real
	armed more with native infamy
	than with noble blades,
	want to drag me to him.
LAURENCIA.	Well, Jacinta, may God free you,
	for if [the Comendador] takes liberties with you,
	with me he will be cruel.

(She leaves.)

PASCUALA.	Jacinta, I'm not a man
	who can defend you.

(She leaves.)

(JACINTA.	¡Dadme socorro, por Dios,
	si la amistad os obliga!
LAURENCIA.	¿Qué es esto, Jacinta amiga?
PASCUALA.	Tuyas lo somos las dos.
JACINTA.	Del Comendador criados,
	que van a Ciudad Real,
	más de infamia natural
	que de noble acero armados,
	me quieren llevar a él.
LAURENCIA.	Pues, Jacinta, Dios te libre,
	que cuando contigo es libre,
	conmigo será crüel.

[Vase.]

PASCUALA.	Jacinta, yo no soy hombre
	que te puedo defender.

[Vase.])

Laurencia clearly does love her honor more than her friend. It is Mengo who stays to help and suffer.

72. Lope dedicated the *Triunfo de la fe en los reinos del Japón* to Mariana (Rennert and Castro, *Vida de Lope de Vega*, 242).

73. In his "*Fuenteovejuna* y el honor villanesco en el teatro de Lope de Vega," *CHA*, 161-62 (1963): 749, Alexey Almasov offers the following explanation for the King's leniency with the Maestre:

> In medieval thought, by taking Ciudad Real and killing the King's faithful vassals, the Maestre . . . was not committing an act of high treason, but exercising one of the legitimate rights of the feudal lord, namely, that of carrying on "private war" against the king. Therefore, the pardon of [the Maestre] was logical.

> (Para el pensamiento medieval, el Gran Maestre al tomar a Ciudad Real y matar a fieles vasallos del rey . . . no cometía un acto de alta traición, sino que ejercía uno de sus derechos legítimos del señor feudal, a saber, el de llevar la "guerra privada" contra el rey. Por eso, el otorgarle el perdón a Rodrigo Téllez fué un acto lógico.)

74. There is the case of Bamba's sonnet in the *Comedia de Bamba* (available in *Obras de Lope de Vega*, vol. 16, *Crónicas y leyendas dramáticas de España*, ed. Menéndez y Pelayo, BAE, 195 [Madrid: Atlas, 1966], 295-342). However, the peasant dies apotheosized, and Menéndez y Pelayo writes that because of this play's religious character, "we have decided to include it among the saints' plays" ("por su carácter religioso, hemos preferido ponerla entre las comedias de santos" ["Observaciones preliminares," 10]). See Walter Cohen, *Drama of a Nation: Public Theater in Renaissance England and Spain* (Ithaca: Cornell University Press, 1985), 239-54.

75. "Two Historical *Comedias* and the Question of *Manierismo*," *RF*, 73 (1961): 340.

76. "Los villanos filosóficos," 531.

77. *The Childhood of Saint Isidro* (*La niñez de San Isidro*) (1622), *The Youth of Saint Isidro* (*La juventud de San Isidro*) (1622), *Saint Isidro, Labrador of Madrid* (*San Isidro Labrador de Madrid*) (before 1600). See Salomon, *Recherches*, 216-21.

78. In Lope de Vega, *Obras escogidas*, vol. 3, *Teatro*, ed. Federico Carlos Sainz de Robles (Madrid: Aguilar), 354a. Later (356a), María succeeds in convincing Isidro of her innocence by walking on water.

79. Letter of 22 March 1982, quoted with the permission of the writer of the letter.

Chapter 4

1. Gonzalo Correas, *Vocabulario de refranes y frases proverbiales*, ed. Miguel Mir, 2d ed. (Madrid: RABM, 1924), 221, 54.

2. Available in Calderón, *Autos sacramentales*, ed. Angel Valbuena Prat, 5th ed. (Madrid: Espasa-Calpe, 1967), 1:67-124; and in English as *The Great Stage of the World*, trans. George W. Brandt (Manchester: Manchester University Press, 1976).

3. Not having exercised free will, in Catholic doctrine the Unborn Child is condemned by original sin. See canto 2 of Dante's *Inferno*.

4. Shergold, *A History of the Spanish Stage*, 426.

5. "Apéndice 2o: Función del 'vulgo' en la preceptiva dramática de la Edad de Oro," in their *Preceptiva dramática española*, 365–87.

6. "Some Early Calderón Dates," *BHS*, 38 (1961), 280–81.

7. *Luis Pérez, el gallego*, in Calderón, *Obras completas*, ed. Valbuena Briones, 5th ed. (Madrid: Aguilar, 1969), 1:299b. English translations are my own.

8. *Rinconete y Cortadillo*, in *Novelas ejemplares*, ed. Harry Sieber, 12th ed. (Madrid: Cátedra, 1989), 1:230.

9. In his "Nota preliminar" to the play, in Calderón, *Obras completas*, 279a.

10. Valbuena lists them in the Bibliography of his edition of the *comedia*, 280b. Among them are *Gil Pérez, the Gallician*, in *Six Dramas of Calderón*, trans. Edward Fitzgerald (London, 1853), 103–42 (a very free translation); *Louis Pérez de Galice*, trans. A. de la Beaumelle, in *Chefs-d'oeuvre des théâtres étrangers*, (Paris, 1822), 2:117–217; and a German version in *Ausgewählte Schauspiele*, trans. Konrad Pasch (Freiburg im Breisgau, 1891).

11. In the five-act *Don Juan Tenorio*.

12. *Vida de Don Quijote y Sancho, según Miguel de Cervantes Saavedra. Explicada y comentada por Miguel de Unamuno* (1905).

13. "Bandits and Saints in the Spanish Drama of the Golden Age," in *Critical Studies of Calderón's "Comedias,"* ed. J. E. Varey, of *The "Comedias" of Calderón* (London: Gregg and Tamesis, 1973), 19:167. This article (slightly revised) is a translation of Parker's "Santos y bandoleros en el teatro español del Siglo de Oro," *Arbor*, 13 (1949): 395–416.

14. *Imperial Spain 1469–1716* (New York: Penguin, 1981), 250, 268.

15. See Ralph E. Giesey, *If Not, Not: The Oath of the Aragonese and the Legendary Laws of Sobrarbe* (Princeton: Princeton University Press, 1968).

16. See C. Alan Soons, *Juan de Mariana*, 50, 56; Gregorio Marañón, *Antonio Pérez (El hombre, el drama, la época)* (Buenos Aires: Espasa-Calpe, 1947), 2:524–30; and Alfredo Hermenegildo, "Adulación, ambición e intriga: Los cortesanos en la antigua tragedia española," *Segismundo*, 25–26 (1977): 80–87.

17. On the significance of Sebastian's military policies for *Secret Vengeance*, see Fox, *Kings in Calderón*, 37–49. On implied criticism of Philip II in *The Three Justices in One*, see 85–96 of the same book.

18. Weiner, "Un episodio de la historia rusa."

19. See 291b, 293b, and 305a.

20. *Imperial Spain*, 288.

21. "Carta de Rivadeneira para un privado de Su Majestad sobre las causas de la pérdida de la Armada," in Rivadeneira, *Historias de la Contrarreforma*, ed. Eusebio Rey (Madrid: Biblioteca de Autores Cristianos, 1945), 1353–54.

22. See Soons, *Juan de Mariana*, 56.

23. "Lope de Vega's Urban Comedy," *Hispanófila Especial*, no. 1 (1974): 56–57.

24. On veiled criticism of Philip II in Juan de la Cueva's theater, see Anthony Watson, *Juan de la Cueva and the Portuguese Succession* (London: Tamesis, 1971).

25. The following discussion draws on and expands my remarks in " 'Quien tiene al padre alcalde . . .' ": The Conflict of Images in Calderón's *El alcalde de Zalamea*," *RCEH*, 6 (1982): 262–68. My approach to the play is indebted to José M. Aguirre's *"El alcalde de Zalamea: ¿Venganza o justicia?" Estudios Filológicos*, 7 (1971): 119–32; and Peter W. Evans's "Pedro Crespo y el Capitán," in *Hacia Calderón:*

Quinto Coloquio Anglogermano, Oxford 1978, ed. Hans Flasche and Robert D. F. Pring-Mill (Wiesbaden: Franz Steiner, 1982), 48–54. For the possible political significance of the play for an audience in the 1640s see Fox, *Kings in Calderón,* 97–101.

26. "Self-Perception and Decline," 47.

27. See Shergold and Varey, "Some Early Calderón Dates," 275–76; Albert E. Sloman, *The Dramatic Craftsmanship of Calderón: His Use of Earlier Plays* (Oxford: Dolphin, 1958), 218; and C. A. Jones, "Honor in *El alcalde de Zalamea,*" in *Critical Essays on the Theatre of Calderón,* 195.

28. Calderón, *El alcalde de Zalamea,* in *La vida es sueño. El alcalde de Zalamea,* ed. Cortina, act 2, line 767. All references to the original Spanish will be to this edition. English translations are my own.

29. Aguirre was the first to note the Captain's attack of conscience.

30. Correas, *Vocabulario de refranes,* 428.

31. Correas, *Vocabulario de refranes,* 428. E. Inman Fox has suggested to me that Crespo's close collaboration with an *escribano,* a member of a profession popularly associated with *conversos,* would intimate to the audience that the peasant's own ancestry may be tainted.

32. *The Prodigious Magician/El mágico prodigioso,* ed. and trans. Bruce W. Wardropper (Potomac, Md.: Studia Humanitatis, 1982), 173, lines 1727–35.

33. It is possible that the Captain dies in part as a surrogate for Don Mendo, a nobleman who has exasperated Crespo so much in the past. The useless, impoverished hidalgo's Quixote-like part in this play has puzzled critics, as the character and his woeful sidekick vanish after the midpoint.

34. The source play has been attributed to Lope de Vega and appears in *Obras escogidas,* ed. Sainz de Robles (Madrid: Aguilar, 1955), 3:1399–1426.

35. See Salomon, *Recherches,* 755, 769, 777.

36. *Tratado de la religion y virtudes que debe tener el príncipe cristiano para gobernar y conservar sus estados, contra lo que Nicolas Maquiavelo y los políticos deste tiempo enseñan,* in *Obras escogidas del Padre Pedro de Rivadeneira,* ed. D. Vicente de la Fuente, BAE, 60 (Madrid: Librería y Casa Editorial Hernando, 1927), 538b.

37. *Tratado,* 521a.

Chapter 5

1. "*El arte nuevo* y la nueva biografía," in his *De Cervantes y de Lope de Vega,* 7th ed. (Madrid: Austral, 1973), 76.

2. *Memorial de la politica necessaria, y vtil restauracion á la Republica de España, y estados de ella, y del desempeño vniversal de estos Reynos* (Valladolid, 1600), fol. 56r.–v.

3. "Self-Perception and Decline," 56.

4. See Bruce W. Wardropper, "Comic Illusion: Lope de Vega's *El perro del hortelano,*" *KRQ,* 14 (1967): 101–11.

5. "Cervantes y la picaresca: Notas sobre dos tipos de realismo," *NRFH,* 11 (1957): 314–42.

6. Dunn, "Cervantes De/Reconstructs the Picaresque," *Cervantes,* 2 (1982): 115–16n.

7. Luzán, *La Poética. Reglas de la poesía en general y de sus principales especies,* ed. Russell P. Sebold (Barcelona: Textos Hispánicos Modernos Editorial Labor, 1977), originally published in 1737 and revised in 1789; Menéndez y Pelayo, *Calderón y su teatro,* ed. Carlos Marfani (Buenos Aires: Emecé, 1911), originally published in 1881.

8. *The Approach to the Spanish Drama of the Golden Age* (London: Hispanic & Luso-Brazilian Councils, 1957), 3-4, 27.

9. "*El alcalde de Zalamea* y el sub-género," in *Hacia Calderón: Quinto Coloquio Anglogermano. Oxford 1978,* ed. Hans Flasche and Pring-Mill (Wiesbaden: Franz Steiner, 1982), 43.

10. The play is available in *Obras de Lope de Vega,* new ed., ed. Cotarelo y Mori, (Madrid: RAE, 1930), 7:1-30.

11. In "Prólogos de ocho tomos de comedias de Lope de Vega," xxii.

12. See Cotarelo y Mori, *Bibliografía de las controversias sobre la licitud del teatro en España* (Madrid: RABM, 1904); Sánchez Escribano and Porqueras Mayo, *Preceptiva dramática española;* and Wilson, "Las 'dudas curiosas' a la aprobación del Maestro Fray Manuel de Guerra y Ribera," *Estudios Escénicos,* 6 (1960): 47-63.

13. "Aprobación del quinto tomo de comedias de Calderón," 14 April 1682, in "Artículos biográficos y críticos acerca de Don Pedro Calderón de la Barca y su teatro," in *Obras de Don Pedro Calderón de la Barca,* ed. Hartzenbusch, BAE, 7 (Madrid: RAE, 1944), xlii.

14. *Historia del teatro español (Desde sus orígenes hasta 1900),* 2d ed. (Madrid: Alianza, 1971), 1:186.

15. The play was also known as *The Garrotting Most Smartly [or Strategically] Given (El garrote más bien dado),* a title that reeks with irony.

16. Cioranescu, "Calderón y el teatro clásico francés," in his *Estudios de literatura española y contemporánea* (Universidad de la Laguna, 1954), 137-95, and *Le masque et le visage: Du baroque espagnol au classicisme français* (Geneva: Droz, 1983); Franzbach, *El teatro de Calderón en Europa* (Madrid: Fundación Universitaria Española, 1982); Sullivan, *Calderón in the German Lands and the Low Countries: His Reception and Influence, 1654-1980* (Cambridge: Cambridge University Press, 1983), esp. 68-100. See also de Armas, "The Dragon's Gold: Calderón and Boisrobert's *La vie n'est qu'un songe,*" KRQ, 30 (1983): 335-48.

17. See the table in Franzbach, *El teatro de Calderón,* 225-26.

18. Emilie Bergmann, "The Epic Vision of Cervantes's *Numancia,*" *Theatre Journal* (March, 1984): 85-96.

19. Enrique Centeno, "Miguel Narros: Una coherente trayectoria," in the program to the production of *El castigo sin venganza* directed by Narros at Madrid's Teatro Español, 1985-86, 17.

20. Interview with Ignacio Amestoy, associate director of the Teatro Español, Madrid, 30 September 1985.

21. Frederick Schlegel, *Lectures on the History of Literature, Ancient and Modern. Translated from the German,* (London: George Bell and Sons, 1896; originally published in German in 1815), 267, 270.

22. Spanish translation by Eduardo de Mier (Madrid: M. Tello, 1886-87), 4:375-76.

23. See Rafael Pérez de la Dehesa, *El pensamiento de Costa y su influencia en el 98* (Madrid: Sociedad de Estudios y Publicaciones, 1966); and Manuel Tuñón de Lara, *Costa y Unamuno en la crisis de fin de siglo* (Madrid: Edicusa, 1974), esp. 207-31.

24. *La Edad de Plata (1902-1939): Ensayo de interpretación de un proceso cultural,* 2d ed. (Madrid: Cátedra, 1983), 34.

25. "El legado vanguardista de Tirso de Molina," in the proceedings of the *V Jornadas de Teatro Clásico Español, Almagro, 1982: El trabajo con los clásicos en el teatro contemporáneo,* ed. Juan Antonio Hormigón (Madrid: Ministerio de Cultura, Dirección General de Música y Teatro, 1983), 2:16; and "The Spanish *Comedia* on Stage, 1920-1930," paper presented at the Instituto Internacional, Madrid, October 1985.

26. Dougherty, "El legado vanguardista," 16.

27. "The 'world-historical individual' has a dramatic character. He is destined by life itself to be a hero, to be the central figure in drama. . . . The important thing in [*The Alcalde of Zalamea* and other plays] is that the inner social substance of the collision [in this case, between Pedro Crespo and the Captain] makes it a decisive event, historically and socially; and that the heroes of such plays have within themselves that combination of individual passion and social substance which characterizes the 'world-historical individuals' " (*The Historical Novel,* trans. Hannah and Stanley Mitchell, introd. Fredric Jameson [Lincoln: University of Nebraska Press, 1983], 104-5).

28. "Honour and the Christian Background in Calderón," in *Critical Essays on the Theatre of Calderón,* 46-47.

29. "*La vida es sueño* y *El alcalde de Zalamea:* Para una sociología del texto calderoniano," *Ib,* 14 (1981): 29, 30.

30. See Demetrio Estébanez Calderón, "El tema del honor calderoniano en el teatro de Galdós," in *Actas del Congreso Internacional sobre Calderón y el Teatro Español del Siglo de Oro,* ed. Luciano García Lorenzo (Madrid: CSIC, 1983), 3:1392-93.

31. See esp. Wilson, "Gerald Brenan's Calderón," *BCom,* 6 (1952): 6-8.

32. "Lope de Vega's *Fuenteovejuna* under Tsars, Commissars, and the Second Spanish Republic (1931-1939)," *Annali, Istituto Universitario Orientale, Sezione Romanza,* Naples, 24 (1982), 172.

33. *Catálogo bibliográfico y crítico de las comedias anunciadas en los periódicos de Madrid desde 1661 hasta 1819* (Baltimore: Johns Hopkins University Press, 1935), 103-4, 231-33, 149.

34. John Lyon, *The Theatre of Valle-Inclán* (Cambridge: Cambridge University Press, 1983), 3.

35. "The Spanish *Comedia* on Stage, 1920-1930."

36. McGaha, *The Theatre in Madrid During the Second Republic: A Checklist* (London: Grant & Cutler, 1979), 9-10.

37. Suzanne Wade Byrd, *García Lorca: "La Barraca" and the Spanish National Theater* (New York: Abra, 1975); Luis Sáenz de la Calzada, *"La Barraca": Teatro Universitario,* Prologue by Rafael Martínez Nadal (Madrid: RO, 1976).

38. Sáenz de la Calzada, 65.

39. See Ian Gibson's remarks on Lorca's last interview before his death, in *The Assassination of Federico García Lorca* (Harmondsworth, Middlesex, England, 1983), 55.

40. See Byrd's reconstruction of Lorca's version in *La "Fuenteovejuna" de Federico García Lorca* (Madrid: Pliegos, 1984).

41. Francisco García Lorca, *Federico y su mundo,* ed. Mario Hernández, 2d ed. (Madrid: Alianza, 1981), 446.

42. For example, in "The Historical Elements of Lope de Vega's *Fuenteovejuna,*" *PMLA,* 49 (1934): 664, Claude E. Anibal complains that the Ciudad Real and Fuenteovejuna episodes of the play have "little in common," and that "the *Reyes*

Católicos [Fernando and Isabel], accorded attention quite out of proportion to their minor function in the drama—the administration of justice from the horizon—are themselves a distracting element" (657).

43. "The Structure of Calderón's *La vida es sueño*," *MLR*, 48 (1953): 299–300.

44. "A Central Theme and Its Structural Equivalent in Lope's *Fuenteovejuna*," *HR*, 23 (1955): 275 n.1.

45. "La venganza de Maquiavelo: *El villano en su rincón*," in *Homenaje a William L. Fichter*, 767.

46. See Pring-Mill, "Los calderonistas de habla inglesa y *La vida es sueño*: Métodos del análisis temático-estructural," in *Litterae Hispanae et Lusitanae: Festschrift zum Fünfzigjahrigen Bestehen des Iberoamerikanischen Forschungsinstituts der Universität Hamburg*, ed. Hans Flasche (Munich: Max Hueber, 1968), 369–413.

47. Paul Ilie, *Literature and Inner Exile: Authoritarian Spain, 1939–1975* (Baltimore: Johns Hopkins University Press, 1980), 80.

48. Manuel Durán and Roberto González Echevarría, *Calderón y la crítica: Historia y antología*, (Madrid: Gredos, 1976), 1:95.

49. Susana Hernández Araico, *Ironía y tragedia en Calderón* (Potomac, Md.: Scripta Humanistica, 1986), 9 n.14.

50. Letter of 9 July 1987, quoted with permission of the writer.

51. "The Old and the New: The Spanish *Comedia* and the Resistance to Historical Change," *Renaissance Drama*, 17 (1986): 4.

SELECTED BIBLIOGRAPHY

Frequently cited collections of essays and plays are listed herein by title.

Aeschylus. *The Libation Bearers.* Trans. Richmond Lattimore. Chicago: University of Chicago Press, 1953.

Aguirre, José M. "*El alcalde de Zalamea:* ¿Venganza o justicia?" *Estudios Filológicos,* 7 (1971): 119–32.

Alfonso X. *Primera crónica general de España.* Vol. 1. Ed. Ramón Menéndez Pidal. NBAE, 5. Madrid: Bailly-Bailliere é Hijos, 1906.

Allen, John J. *The Reconstruction of a Spanish Golden Age Playhouse: El Corral del Príncipe.* Gainesville: University Presses of Florida, 1983.

Alpern, Hymen. "Jealousy as a Dramatic Motive in the Spanish *Comedia.*" *RR,* 14 (1923): 276–85.

Aníbal, Claude E. "The Historical Elements of Lope de Vega's *Fuenteovejuna.*" *PMLA,* 49 (1934): 657–718.

Aquila, August J. "Ercilla's Concept of the Ideal Soldier." *Hispania,* 60 (1977): 68–75.

Aubrun, Charles V., and José F. Montesinos. "*Peribáñez.*" In *El teatro de Lope de Vega,* 13–49.

Avalle-Arce, Juan Bautista. Introduction to Lope de Vega, *El peregrino en su patria.* Madrid: Castalia, 1973.

Ayala, Francisco. "Sobre el punto de honor castellano." *RO,* 2d series, 1, no. 5 (1963): 151–74.

Bakhtin, Mikhail M. "Epic and Novel." In *The Dialogic Imagination: Four Essays.* Ed. Michael Holquist. Trans. Caryl Emerson and Michael Holquist, 3–40. Austin: University of Texas Press, 1981.

Bataillon, Marcel. "*El villano en su rincón.*" In his *Varia lección de clásicos españoles,* 329–72. Madrid: Gredos, 1964.

Bergmann, Emilie. "The Epic Vision of Cervantes' *Numancia.*" *Theatre Journal* (March 1984): 85–96.

Bloomfield, Morton W. "The Problem of the Hero in the Later Medieval Period." In *Concepts of the Hero,* 27–48.

Blue, William R. "*Peribáñez* and Economics." In *Texto y espectáculo,* 47–53.

Bolgar, Raymond R. "Hero or Anti-Hero? The Genesis and Development of the *Miles Christianus.*" In *Concepts of the Hero,* 120–46.

Bowra, C. M. "The Hero." In *The Hero in Literature,* ed. Victor Brombert, 22–52. Repr. with some deletions from Bowra's *Heroic Poetry,* 91–131. New York: St. Martin's Press, 1961.

Bradner, Leicester. "The Theme of *Privanza* in Spanish and English Drama 1590–1625." In *Homenaje a William L. Fichter,* 97–106.

Branca, Vittore. "The Myth of the Hero in Boccaccio." In *Concepts of the Hero,* 168–91.

Brody, Ervin C. "Poland in Calderón's *Life Is a Dream:* Poetic Illusion or Historical Reality." *Pol R,* 14 (1969): 21–62.

Brombert, Victor. "Introduction: The Idea of the Hero." In *The Hero in Literature,* 168–91.

Brower, Reuben A. *Hero and Saint: Shakespeare and the Graeco-Roman Heroic Tradition.* New York: Oxford University Press, 1971.

Brown, Jonathan, and J. H. Elliott. *A Palace for a King: The Buen Retiro and the Court of Philip IV.* New Haven: Yale University Press, 1980.

Bryans, John V. "*El alcalde de Zalamea* y el sub-género." In *Hacia Calderón: Quinto Coloquio Anglogermano. Oxford 1978,* ed. Hans Flasche and R. D. F. Pring-Mill, 42–47. Wiesbaden: Franz Steiner, 1982.

———. "Providence or Discretion in *Peribáñez.*" *JHP,* 2 (1977): 121–33.

Bush, Douglas. "The Isolation of the Renaissance Hero." In his *Prefaces to Renaissance Literature,* 91–106. New York: Norton, 1965. Repr. from *Reason and Imagination,* ed. Joseph A. Mazzeo. New York: Columbia University Press, 1962.

Byrd, Suzanne Wade, ed. La *"Fuenteovejuna" de Federico García Lorca.* Madrid: Pliegos, 1984.

———. *García Lorca: "La Barraca" and the Spanish National Theater.* New York: Abra, 1975.

Byron, Lord George. Letter to John Murray, 22 December 1822. In *The Works of Lord Byron, Letters and Journals,* ed. R. E. Prothero, 5:242. London, 1901. Cited in Alvin B. Kernan, *The Plot of Satire,* 208n. New Haven: Yale University Press, 1965. Repr. in part as "The Perspective of Satire: *Don Juan.*" In *Twentieth-Century Interpretations of Don Juan,* ed. Edward E. Bostetter, 93, n. 5. Englewood Cliffs, N.J.: Prentice-Hall, 1969.

Calderón de la Barca, Pedro. *El alcalde de Zalamea.* In *La vida es sueño. El alcalde de Zalamea.* 5th ed. Ed. Augusto Cortina. Madrid: Espasa-Calpe, 1971.
——. *El gran teatro del mundo.* In *Autos sacramentales.* Vol. 1. Ed. Valbuena Prat.
——. *The Great Stage of the World.* Trans. George W. Brandt. Manchester: Manchester University Press, 1976.
——. *Luis Pérez, el gallego.* In *Obras completas.* Vol. 1. 5th ed. Ed. Angel Valbuena Briones. Madrid: Aguilar, 1969.
——. *The Prodigious Magician / El mágico prodigioso.* Ed. and trans. Bruce W. Wardropper. Madrid: Porrúa Turanzas, 1982.
——. *El Santo Rey don Fernando.* In *Obras completas.* Vol. 3. 2d ed. Ed. Angel Valbuena Prat. Madrid: Aguilar, 1967.
——. *La vida es sueño.* In *La vida es sueño. El alcalde de Zalamea.* 5th ed. Ed. Augusto Cortina. Madrid: Espasa-Calpe, 1971.
——. *Life Is a Dream.* Trans. Edwin Honig. New York: Hill and Wang, 1970.
——. *Life Is a Dream.* In *The Classic Theater.* Vol. 3, *Six Spanish Plays.* Ed. Eric Bentley. Trans Roy Campbell. Garden City, N.Y.: Doubleday, 1959.
Campbell, Joseph. *The Hero with a Thousand Faces.* 2d ed. Princeton: Bollingen, 1972.
Canavaggio, Jean. *Cervantes.* Trans. J. R. Jones. New York: Norton, 1990.
Carter, Robin. "*Fuenteovejuna* and Tyranny: Some Problems of Linking Drama with Political Theory." *FMLS,* 13 (1977): 313–35.
——. "History and Poetry: A Re-Examination of Lope de Vega's *El mejor alcalde, el rey.*" *FMLS,* 16 (1980): 193–213.
——. "*Peribáñez:* Disorder Restored." In *What's Past Is Prologue: A Collection of Essays in Honour of L. J. Woodward,* ed. Salvador Bacarisse, Bernard Bentley, Mercedes Clarasó, and Douglas Gifford, 17–27. Edinburgh: Scottish Academic Press, 1984.
Casa, Frank P. "Aspects of Characterization in Golden Age Drama." In *Studies in Honor of Everett W. Hesse,* ed. William C. McCrary and José A. Madrigal, 37–47. Lincoln, Neb.: Society of Spanish and Spanish-American Studies, 1981.
Casalduero, Joaquín. "Sentido y forma de *El villano en su rincón.*" *Revista de la Universidad de Madrid,* 11 (1962): 547–64.
Cascales, Francisco. "Al doctor Salvador de León." In *Cartas filológicas del Licenciado Francisco Cascales.* In vol. 2 of *Epistolario español,* ed. Eugenio de Ochoa, 487b–89a. BAE, 62. Madrid: RAE, 1965.
Cascardi, Anthony J. *The Limits of Illusion: A Critical Study of Calderón.* Cambridge: Cambridge University Press, 1984.
——. "The Old and the New: The Spanish *Comedia* and the Resistance to Historical Change." *Renaissance Drama,* 17 (1986): 1–28.
Castro, Américo. "Algunas observaciones acerca del concepto del honor en los siglos XVI y XVII." *RFE,* 3 (1916): 1–50; 357–86.
——. *De la edad conflictiva: El drama de la honra en España y en su literatura.* Madrid: Taurus, 1961.
Centeno, Enrique. "Miguel Narros: Una coherente trayectoria." In the program to Lope de Vega, *El castigo sin venganza.* Madrid: Teatro Español, 1985–86, 16–19.
Cervantes, Saavedra, Miguel de. *Don Quijote de la Mancha.* 2 vols. Ed. Martin de Riquer, Barcelona: Juventud, 1955.

———. *Don Quixote de la Mancha.* Trans. Walter Starkie. New York: Signet, 1957.

———. *Rinconete y Cortadillo.* In *Novelas ejemplares.* Vol. 1. 12th ed. Ed. Harry Sieber, 189–240. Madrid: Cátedra, 1989.

La chanson de Roland. Ed. León Gautier. Tours: Alfred Mame et Fils, 1872.

Cobarruvias Orozco, Sebastián de. *Tesoro de la lengua castellana o española.* Madrid: Turner, 1979.

Cohen, Walter. *Drama of a Nation: Public Theater in Renaissance England and Spain.* Ithaca: Cornell University Press, 1985.

Combet, Louis. *Recherches sur le "Refranero" castillan.* Paris: Société "Les Belles Lettres," 1971.

Concepts of the Hero in the Middle Ages and the Renaissance. Ed. Norman T. Burns and Christopher J. Reagan. Albany: State University of New York Press, 1975.

Connolly, Eileen. "Further Testimony in the Rebel Soldier Case." *BCom,* 24 (1972): 13b.

Cope, Jackson. *The Theater and the Dream: From Metaphor to Form in Renaissance Drama.* Baltimore: Johns Hopkins University Press, 1973.

Corominas, Joan de. *Diccionario crítico etimológico de la lengua castellana.* Madrid: Gredos, 1954.

Correa, Gustavo. "El doble aspecto de la honra en el teatro del siglo XVII." *HR,* 26 (1958): 188–99.

Correas, Gonzalo. *Vocabulario de refranes y frases proverbiales.* 2d ed. Ed. Miguel Mir. Madrid: RABM, 1924.

Costa, Joaquín. "Oligarquía y caciquismo como la forma actual de gobierno de España." In *Oligarquía y caciquismo, Colectivismo agrario, y otros escritos,* ed. Rafael Pérez de la Dehesa, 15–46. Madrid: Alianza, 1967.

Cotarelo y Mori, Emilio. *Bibliografía de las controversias sobre la licitud del teatro en España.* Madrid: RABM, 1904.

Craddock, Jerry R. "Must the King Obey his Laws?" In *Florilegium Hispanicum: Medieval and Golden Age Studies Presented to Dorothy Clotelle Clarke,* ed. Charles B. Faulhaber, Dwayne E. Carpenter, and John S. Geary, 71–79. Madison, Wisc.: Hispanic Seminary of Medieval Studies, 1983.

Crapotta, James. "The Cid of Guillén de Castro: The Hero as Moral Exemplar." *RCEH,* 9 (1982): 39–46.

Critical Essays on the Theatre of Calderón. Ed. Bruce W. Wardropper. New York: New York University Press, 1965.

Crónica del Rey Don Enrique Tercero de Castilla é de León. In *Crónicas de los reyes de Castilla,* 2:161–271. Ed. Cayetano Rosell. BAE, 68. Madrid: Rivadeneyra, 1877.

Curtius, Ernst Robert. *European Literature and the Latin Middle Ages.* Trans. Willard R. Trask. New York: Harper & Row, 1953.

de Armas, Frederick A. *The Invisible Mistress: Aspects of Feminism and Fantasy in the Golden Age.* Charlottesville, Va.: Biblioteca Siglo de Oro, 1976.

———. *The Return of Astraea: An Astral-Imperial Myth in Calderón.* Lexington: University Press of Kentucky, 1986.

Deyermond, Alan D. *Epic Poetry and the Clergy: Studies on the "Mocedades de Rodrigo."* London: Tamesis, 1968.

———. *"Lazarillo de Tormes": A Critical Guide.* London: Grant & Cutler, 1975.

———. *A Literary History of Spain: The Middle Ages.* London: Ernest Benn, 1971.

———. *The Petrarchan Sources of "La Celestina."* London: Oxford University Press, 1961.

Diccionario de Autoridades. Facsimile Edition. Madrid: Gredos, 1963.

Diccionario de la langua española. 2 vols. 20th ed. Madrid: RAE, 1984.

Díez Borque, José María. "Estructura social de la comedia de Lope. A propósito *El mejor alcalde, el rey," Arbor,* 85 (1973): 453-66.

———. *Sociología de la comedia española del siglo XVII.* Madrid: Cátedra, 1976.

Dixon, Victor. *"Beatus . . . nemo: El villano en su rincón,* las 'Polianteas' y la literatura de emblemas," *Cuadernos de Filología* (Universidad de Valencia, Facultad de Filologia), 3 (1981): 279-300.

———. "The Symbolism of *Peribáñez." BHS,* 43 (1966): 11-24.

Dodds, E. R. *The Greeks and the Irrational.* Berkeley: University of California Press, 1951.

Dougherty, Dru. "El legado vanguardista de Tirso de Molina." In the proceedings of the *V Jornadas de Teatro Clásico Español, Almagro, 1982: El trabajo con los clásicos en el teatro contemporáneo,* 2:13-28. Ed. Juan Antonio Hormigón. Madrid: Ministerio de Cultura, Dirección General de Música y Teatro, 1983.

———. "The Spanish *Comedia* on Stage, 1920-1930." Paper presented at the Instituto Internacional. Madrid, 24 October 1985.

Dunn, Peter N. "Cervantes De/Reconstructs the Picaresque." *Cervantes,* 2 (1982): 109-31.

———. "Honour and the Christian Background in Calderón." In *Critical Essays on the Theatre of Calderón,* 24-60.

———. Letter to the author, 22 March 1982.

———. "Pleberio's Lament." *PMLA,* 91 (1976): 406-19.

———. "Some Uses of Sonnets in the Plays of Lope de Vega." *BHS,* 34 (1957): 213-22.

Durán, Agustín, ed. *Romancero general, ó Colección de romances castellanos anteriores al siglo XVIII.* Vol. 2. BAE, 16. Madrid: Rivadeneyra, 1851.

Durán, Manuel and Roberto González Echevarría. *Calderón y la crítica: Historia y antología.* 2 vols. Madrid: Gredos, 1976.

El Saffar, Ruth S. "Authority and Subversion in Cervantes and Calderón." Paper presented at Columbia University, September 1980.

———. *Novel to Romance: A Study of Cervantes's "Novelas ejemplares."* Baltimore: Johns Hopkins University Press, 1974.

———. "Reason's Unreason in *La vida es sueño," I & L* (new series), 2 (1986): 103-18.

———. "Way Stations in the Errancy of the Word: A Study of *La vida es sueño."* Paper presented at the Modern Language Association Convention, December 1986, New York. Published in *Renaissance Drama and Cultural Change,* ed. Mary Beth Rose, 83-100. Evanston, Ill.: Northwestern University Press, 1986.

Elliott, J. H. *Imperial Spain: 1469-1716.* New York: New American Library, 1963.

———. *Richilieu and Olivares.* Cambridge: Cambridge University Press, 1984.

———. "Self-Perception and Decline in Early Seventeenth-Century Spain." *Past and Present,* 74 (1977): 41-61.

Estébanez Calderón, Demetrio. "El tema del honor calderoniano en el teatro de Galdós." In *Actas del Congreso Internacional sobre Calderón y el Teatro Español del Siglo de Oro.* Vol. 3. Ed. Luciano García Lorenzo, 1389-1404. Madrid: CSIC, 1983.

Evans, Peter W. "Pedro Crespo y el Capitán." In *Hacia Calderón: Quinto Coloquio Anglogermano, Oxford 1978,* ed. Hans Flasche and R. D. F. Pring-Mill, 48–54. Wiesbaden: Franz Steiner, 1982.

———. "*Peribáñez* and Ways of Looking at Golden Age Dramatic Characters." *RR,* 74 (1983): 136–51.

Exum, Frances. *The Metamorphoses of Lope de Vega's King Pedro.* Madrid: Plaza Mayor Scholar, 1974.

Fergusson, Francis. *The Idea of a Theatre: A Study of Ten Plays. The Art of Drama in Changing Perspective.* Princeton: Princeton University Press, 1972.

Forcione, Alban K. *Cervantes, Aristotle, and the "Persiles."* Princeton: Princeton University Press, 1970.

"Forms of Marriage." In *New Catholic Encyclopedia,* 9:276–80. New York: McGraw-Hill, 1967.

Fox, Dian. "The Apocryphal Part One of *Don Quijote.*" *MLN,* 100 (1985): 406–16.

———. "The Critical Attitude in *Rinconete y Cortadillo.*" *Cervantes,* 3 (1983): 135–47.

———. "In Defense of Segismundo." *BCom,* 41 (1989): 141–54.

———. Interview with Ignacio Amestoy, associate director of the Teatro Español. Madrid, 30 September 1985.

———. *Kings in Calderón: A Study in Characterization and Political Theory.* London: Tamesis, 1986.

———. "Pero Vermúez and the Politics of the Cid's Exile." *MLR,* 78 (1983): 319–27.

———. "'Quien tiene al padre alcalde . . .'": The Conflict of Images in Calderón's *El alcalde de Zalamea.*" *RCEH,* 6 (1982): 262–68.

Franzbach, Martin. *El teatro de Calderón en Europa.* Madrid: Fundación Universitaria Española, 1982.

Frye, Northrop. *Anatomy of Criticism: Four Essays.* Princeton: Princeton University Press, 1971.

Frye, Roland Mushat. *The Renaissance Hamlet: Issues and Responses in 1600.* Princeton: Princeton University Press, 1984.

García Lorca, Francisco. *Federico y su mundo.* 2d ed. Ed. Mario Hernández. Madrid: Alianza, 1981.

Gibson, Ian. *The Assassination of Federico García Lorca.* Harmondsworth, Middlesex, England, 1983.

Giesey, Ralph E. *If Not, Not: The Oath of the Aragonese and the Legendary Laws of Sobrarbe.* Princeton: Princeton University Press, 1968.

Glaser, Edward. "Lope de Vega's *El robo de Dina.*" *RJ,* 15 (1964): 315–34.

Godzich, Wlad, and Nicholas Spadaccini. "Popular Culture and Spanish Literary History." In *Literature among Discourses: The Spanish Golden Age,* ed. Wlad Godzich and Nicholas Spadaccini, 41–61. Minneapolis: University of Minnesota Press, 1986.

González de Cellorigo, Martín. *Memorial de la política necessaria, y vtil restauracion à la Republica de España, y estados de ella, y del desempeño vniversal de estos Reynos.* Valladolid, 1600.

Green, Otis H. *Spain and the Western Tradition: The Castilian Mind in Literature from "El Cid" to Calderón.* 4 vols. Madison: University of Wisconsin Press, 1966.

Greene, Thomas M. "The Norms of Epic." In *The Hero in Literature,* 53–60. Repr. from Greene's *The Descent from Heaven,* 8–25. New Haven: Yale University Press, 1963.

Guerra y Ribera, Manuel. "Aprobación del quinto tomo de comedias de Calderón," 14 April 1682. In "Artículos biográficos y críticos acerca de Don Pedro Calderón de la Barca y su teatro." In *Obras de Don Pedro Calderón de la Barca*, ed. Juan Eugenio Hartzenbusch, xlii–xliii. BAE, 7. Madrid: RAE, 1944.

Güntert, Georges. "Relección del *Peribáñez*." *RFE*, 54 (1971): 37–52.

Halkhoree, Premraj R. K. "El arte de Lope de Vega en *El mejor alcalde, el rey*." *BHS*, 56 (1979): 31–42.

——. "The Dramatic Use of Place in Lope de Vega's *Peribáñez*." *BCom*, 30 (1978): 13–18.

Hall, H. B. "Poetic Justice in *La vida es sueño*: A Further Comment." *BHS*, 45 (1968): 128–31.

——. "Segismundo and the Rebel Soldier." *BHS*, 45 (1968), 189–200.

Hamilton, Bernice. *Political Thought in Sixteenth-Century Spain: A Study of the Political Ideas of Vitoria, De Soto, Suárez, and Molina.* Oxford: Clarendon, 1963.

Hart, Thomas R. "Characterization and Plot Structure in the *Poema de Mio Cid*." In *"Mio Cid" Studies*, 63–72.

——. "History, Epic, Novel: Camões and Cervantes." *RQ*, 34 (1987): 95–102.

——. "Versions of Pastoral in Three *Novelas ejemplares*." *BHS*, 58 (1981): 283–91.

——, and Steven Rendall. "Rhetorical Persuasion in Marcela's Address to the Shepherds." *HR*, 46 (1978): 287–98.

Hegel, Georg Wilhelm Friedrich. *Aesthetics: Lectures on Fine Art.* 2 vols. Trans. T. M. Knox. Oxford: Clarendon, 1975.

Heiple, Daniel L. "The Tradition Behind the Punishment of the Rebel Soldier in *La vida es sueño*." *BHS*, 50 (1973): 1–17.

Heninger, S. K. *Touches of Sweet Harmony: Pythagorean Cosmology and Renaissance Poetics.* San Marino, Calif.: Huntington Library, 1974.

The Hero in Literature (Major Essays on the Changing Concepts of Heroism from Classical Times to the Present). Ed. Victor Brombert. Greenwich, Conn.: Fawcett, 1969.

Herrero García, Miguel. *Ideas de los españoles del siglo XVII.* 2d ed. Madrid: Gredos, 1966.

——. "Los rasgos físicos y el carácter según los textos españoles del siglo XVII." *RFE*, 12 (1925): 157–77.

Hesse, Everett W. "*El villano en su rincón*." In his *Análisis e interpretación de la comedia*, 30–42. Madrid: Castalia, 1970.

Homenaje a William L. Fichter: Estudios sobre el teatro antiguo hispánico y otros ensayos, ed. A. David Kossoff and José Amor y Vázquez. Madrid: Castalia, 1971.

Homer. *The Iliad of Homer.* Trans. Richmond Lattimore. Chicago: University of Chicago Press, 1961.

Honig, Edwin A. "The Seizures of Honor in Calderón." *Kenyon Review*, 23 (1961): 430–31.

Huppé, Bernard F. "The Concept of the Hero in the Early Middle Ages." In *Concepts of the Hero*, 1–26.

Iffland, James. *Quevedo and the Grotesque.* Vol. 2. London: Tamesis, 1982.

Ilie, Paul. *Literature and Inner Exile: Authoritarian Spain, 1939–1975.* Baltimore: Johns Hopkins University Press, 1980.

Jackson, W. T. H. *The Hero and the King: An Epic Theme.* New York: Columbia University Press, 1982.

Jehová, Hana. "Les motifs polonais ou tcheques dans *La vie est-un songe.*" *CRCL,* 4 (1977): 179-85.

Johnson, Carroll B. *"La Numancia* and the Structure of Cervantine Ambiguity." *I & L,* 3 (1980): 75-94.

Jones, C. A. "Honor in *El alcalde de Zalamea.*" In *Critical Essays on the Theatre of Calderón,* 193-202.

——. "Honor in Spanish Golden-Age Drama: Its Relation to Real Life and Morals." *BHS,* 35 (1958): 199-210.

Jones, R. O. "Poets and Peasants." In *Homenaje a William L. Fichter,* 341-55.

Kenworthy, Patricia. "The Character of Lorenza and the Moral of Cervantes' *El viejo celoso.*" *BCom,* 31 (1979): 105-7.

King, Willard F. "Cervantes' *Numancia* and Imperial Spain." *MLN,* 94 (1979): 200-21.

Larson, Donald R. *The Honor Plays of Lope de Vega.* Cambridge: Harvard University Press, 1977.

Lazarillo de Tormes. 4th ed. Ed. Francisco Rico. Barcelona: Planeta, 1983.

Leavitt, Sturgiss E. "A Maligned Character in Lope's *El mejor alcalde, el rey.*" *BCom,* 6 (1954): 1a-3a.

Lewy, Guenter. *Constitutionalism and Statecraft During the Golden Age of Spain: A Study of the Political Philosophy of Juan de Mariana, S.J.* Geneva: E. Droz, 1960.

The Life of Lazarillo de Tormes: His Fortunes and Adversities. Trans. M. S. Merwin. Garden City, N.Y.: Doubleday, 1962.

Lihani, John. *Farsas y églogas de Lucas Fernández.* New York: Las Américas, 1969.

López Estrada, Francisco. "Los villanos filosóficos y políticos (La configuración de *Fuenteovejuna* a través de los nombres y 'apellidos')," *CHA,* 180 (1969): 518-42.

Lukács, Georg. *The Historical Novel.* Trans. Hannah and Stanley Mitchell. Introduction by Fredric Jameson. Lincoln: University of Nebraska Press, 1983.

Luzán, Ignacio de. *La Poética. Reglas de la poesía en general y de sus principales especies,* ed. Russell P. Sebold. Barcelona: Textos Hispánicos Modernos Editorial Labor, 1977.

Lyon, John. *The Theatre of Valle-Inclán.* Cambridge: Cambridge University Press, 1983.

McCrary, Thomas. Lecture presented at Columbia University, New York, December 1980.

McCrary, William C. *"Fuenteovejuna:* Its Platonic Vision and Execution." *SP,* 58 (1961): 179-92.

MacCurdy, Raymond R. *The Tragic Fall: Don Alvaro de Luna and Other Favorites in Spanish Golden Age Drama.* Chapel Hill: University of North Carolina Press, 1978.

McGaha, Michael D. Introduction to his edition of Lope de Vega, *La fábula de Perseo o La bella Andrómeda,* 3-58. Kassel: Reichenberger, 1985.

——. *The Theatre in Madrid During the Second Republic: A Checklist.* London: Grant & Cutler, 1979.

McGee, Arthur. *The Elizabethan Hamlet.* New Haven: Yale University Press, 1987.

McGrady, Donald. "Calderón's Rebel Soldier and Poetic Justice Reconsidered." *BHS,* 62 (1985): 181-84.

——. "The Comic Treatment of Conjugal Honor in Lope's *Las ferias de Madrid.*" *HR*, 41 (1973): 33–42.

McKendrick, Melveena. "Celebration or Subversion? *Los comendadores de Córdoba* Reconsidered." *BHS*, (1984): 352–60.

——. *Woman and Society in the Spanish Drama of the Golden Age.* Cambridge: Cambridge University Press, 1974.

Mainer, José-Carlos. *La Edad de Plata (1902–1939): Ensayo de interpretación de un proceso cultural.* 2d ed. Madrid: Cátedra, 1983.

Malón de Chaide, Pedro. *La conversión de la Magdalena.* Vol. 1. Ed. P. Félix García. Madrid: "La Lectura," 1930.

Manrique, Jorge. *Coplas de Jorge Manrique, Translated from the Spanish; With an Introductory Essay on the Moral and Devotional Poetry of Spain,* by Henry W. Longfellow. Boston: Allen & Ticknor, 1833.

Maravall, José Antonio. *Teatro y literatura en la sociedad barroca.* Madrid: Seminarios y Ediciones, 1972.

Mariana, Juan de. *Del rey y de la institución real (De Rege et Regis Institutione).* In *Obras del Padre Juan de Mariana.* Vol. 2. Ed. F. P[i] y M[argall]. BAE, 31. Madrid: Atlas, 1950.

——. *Historia general de España.* In *Obras del Padre Juan de Mariana.* Vols. 1 and 2.

May, T. E. "Segismundo y el soldado rebelde." In *Hacia Calderón: Coloquio Anglogermano. Exeter 1969,* ed. Hans Flasche, 71–75. Berlin: Walter de Gruyter, 1970.

Menéndez Pidal, Ramón. "*El arte nuevo* y la nueva biografía." In his *De Cervantes y de Lope de Vega,* 69–143. 7th ed. Madrid: Austral, 1973.

——. *La epopeya castellana a través de la literatura española.* Buenos Aires: Espasa-Calpe, 1945.

Menéndez y Pelayo, Marcelino. *Calderón y su teatro,* ed. Carlos Marfani. Buenos Aires: Emecé, 1911.

"*Mio Cid*" *Studies,* ed. Alan D. Deyermond. London: Tamesis, 1977.

Moir, Duncan W. "The Classical Tradition in Spanish Dramatic Theory and Practice in the Seventeenth Century." In *Classical Drama and Its Influence: Essays Presented to H. D. F. Kitto,* ed. M. J. Anderson, 191–228. London: Methuen, 1965.

Molho, Maurice. "El pícaro de nuevo." *MLN* 100 (1985): 199–222.

Morley, S. Griswold, and Courtney Bruerton. *Cronología de las comedias de Lope de Vega.* Trans. María Rosa Cartes. Madrid: Gredos, 1968.

Morón Arroyo, Ciriaco. "*La vida es sueño* y *El alcalde de Zalamea:* Para una sociología del texto calderoniano." *Ib,* 14 (1981): 27–41.

Morreale, Margherita. "Estudio preliminar" to *Galateo español,* by L. Gracián Dantisco, 1–63. Madison, Wisc.: Clásicos Hispánicos, 1968.

Nelson, Esther W. "Ellipsis in Calderón's *La vida es sueño:* The Lack of Feminine Perspectives." In *Texto y espectáculo,* 99–116.

Nelson, Robert J. *Corneille: His Heroes and Their Worlds.* Philadelphia: University of Pennsylvania Press, 1963.

Parker, Alexander A. *The Approach to the Spanish Drama of the Golden Age.* London: Hispanic & Luso-Brazilian Councils, 1957.

——. "Bandits and Saints in the Spanish Drama of the Golden Age." In *Critical Studies of Calderón's Comedias,* Vol. 19 of *Pedro Calderón de la Barca. Comedias,* ed. J. E. Varey, 151–68. London: Gregg and Tamesis, 1973.

——. "Calderón's Rebel Soldier and Poetic Justice." *BHS,* 46 (1969): 120–27.
——. *Literature and the Delinquent: The Picaresque Novel in Spain and Europe, 1599–1753.* Edinburgh: University Press, 1967.
——. "The Meaning of *Discreción* in *No hay más fortuna que Dios:* The Medieval Background and Sixteenth- and Seventeenth-Century Usage." Appendix to his edition of Calderón, *No hay más fortuna que Dios,* 77–92. 2d ed. Manchester: Manchester University Press, 1962.
——. "Towards a Definition of Calderonian Tragedy." *BHS,* 39 (1962): 222–37.
Pérez de la Dehesa, Rafael. *El pensamiento de Costa y su influencia en el 98.* Madrid: Sociedad de Estudios y Publicaciones, 1966.
Pérez Gómez, Antonio. Introduction to his edition of *Romancero de don Alvaro de Luna (1540–1800).* Valencia: n.p., 1953.
Pierce, Frank. *The Heroic Poem of the Spanish Golden Age: Selections.* New York: Oxford University Press, 1947.
Poema de mio Cid. Ed. Colin Smith. Oxford: Clarendon, 1972.
The Poem of the Cid. Trans. Lesley Byrd Simpson. Berkeley: University of California Press, 1975.
Poggioli, Renato. *The Oaten Flute: Essays on Pastoral Poetry and the Pastoral Ideal.* Cambridge: Harvard University Press, 1975.
Postigo Castellanos, Elena. *Honor y privilegio en la corona de Castilla: El Consejo de las Ordenes y los Caballeros de Hábito en el siglo XVII.* Junta de Castilla y León, 1988.
Powers, Perry J. "The Concept of the City-State in the Dramas of Lope de Vega." Ph.D. diss., Johns Hopkins University, 1947.
Preceptiva dramática española del Renacimiento y el Barroco. 2d ed. Ed. Federico Sánchez Escribano and Alberto Porqueras Mayo. Madrid: Gredos, 1972.
Pring-Mill, R. D. F. "Los calderonistas de habla inglesa y *La vida es sueño:* Métodos del análisis temático-estructural." In *Litterae Hispanae et Lusitanae: Festschrift für Fünfzigjährigen Bestehen des Iberoamerikanischen Forschungsinstituts der Universität Hamburg,* 369–413. Munich: Max Hueber, 1968.
Quevedo y Villegas, Francisco de. *El buscón.* Ed. Américo Castro. Madrid: Espasa-Calpe, 1973.
Randel, Mary Gaylord. "The Portrait and the Creation of *Peribáñez." RF,* 85 (1973): 145–58.
Reed, Walter L. *An Exemplary History of the Novel: The Quixotic versus the Picaresque.* Chicago: University of Chicago Press, 1981.
Reichenberger, Arnold G. "The Uniqueness of the *Comedia." HR,* 27 (1959): 303–16.
Rennert, Hugo A. *The Life of Lope de Vega (1562–1635).* New York: Stechert, 1937.
——, and Américo Castro. *Vida de Lope de Vega (1562–1635).* 2d ed. Salamanca: Anaya, 1968.
Ribbans, Geoffrey. "The Meaning and Structure of Lope's *Fuenteovejuna." BHS,* 31 (1954): 150–70. Repr. in Spanish translation in *El teatro de Lope de Vega,* 91–123.
Rivadeneira, Pedro de. "Carta de Rivadeneira para un privado de Su Majestad sobre las causas de la perdida de la Armada." In *Historias de la Contrarreforma,* ed. Eusebio Rey, 1351–55. Madrid: Biblioteca de Autores Cristianos, 1945.
——. *Tratado de la religion y virtudes que debe tener el príncipe cristiano para*

gobernar y conservar sus estados, contra lo que Nicolas Maquiavelo y los políticos deste tiempo enseñan. In *Obras escogidas del Padre Pedro de Rivadeneira,* ed. D. Vicente de la Fuente, 449–587. BAE, 60. Madrid: Librería y Casa Editorial Hernando, 1927.

Rogers, Daniel. "'Tienen los celos pasos de ladrones': Silence in Calderón's *El médico de su honra.*" *HR,* 33 (1965): 273–89. Repr. in *Critical Studies of Calderón's Comedias,* 1–16.

Rojas, Fernando de. *La Celestina.* Ed. Dorothy S. Severin. Introduction by Stephen Gilman. Madrid: Alianza, 1979.

———. *La Celestina.* Trans. Lesley Byrd Simpson. Berkeley: University of California Press, 1955.

Rothe, Arnold. "Padre y familia en el Siglo de Oro." *Ib,* 7 (1978): 120–67.

Rozas, Juan Manuel. "*Fuenteovejuna* desde la segunda acción." In *Actas del I Simposio de Literatura Española,* ed. Alberto Navarro González, 173–92. Salamanca: Ediciones Universidad de Salamanca, 1981.

Ruano de la Haza, José M. "Malicia campesina y la ambigüedad esencial de *Peribáñez y el Comendador de Ocaña* de Lope." *Hispanófila,* 84 (1985): 21–30.

———, and J. E. Varey. Introduction to Lope de Vega, *Peribáñez.* London: Tamesis, 1980.

Ruiz Ramón, Francisco. *Historia del teatro español.* Vol. 1, *Desde sus orígenes hasta 1900.* 2d ed. Madrid: Alianza, 1971.

Saavedra Fajardo, Diego de. *Idea de un príncipe político-cristiano representada en cien empresas.* 3 vols. Ed. Vicente García de Diego. Madrid: Espasa-Calpe, 1927.

Sáenz de la Calzada, Luis. "*La Barraca*": *Teatro Universitario.* Prologue by Rafael Martínez Nadal. Madrid: RO, 1976.

Salomon, Noël. *Recherches sur le thème paysan dans la comedia au temps de Lope de Vega.* Bordeaux: Féret et Fils, 1965. Translated as *Lo villano en el teatro del Siglo de Oro.* Madrid: Castalia, 1985.

Schack, Adolf Friedrich von. *Historia de la literatura y del arte dramática en España.* 5 vols. Trans. Eduardo de Mier. Madrid: M. Tello, 1886–87.

Schlegel, Frederick. *Lectures on the History of Literature, Ancient and Modern. Translated from the German.* London: George Bell and Sons, 1896.

Shergold, N. D. *A History of the Spanish Stage.* Oxford: Clarendon, 1967.

———, and J. E. Varey. "Some Early Calderón Dates." *BHS,* 38 (1961): 274–86.

Shipley, George. "Authority and Experience in *La Celestina.*" *BHS,* 62 (1985): 95–111.

———. "*Non erat hic locus;* the Disconcerted Reader in Melibea's Garden," *RPh,* 27 (1974): 286–303.

Sieber, Harry. "Dramatic Symmetry in Gómez Manrique's *La Representación del Nacimiento de Nuestro Señor.*" *HR,* 33 (1965): 118–35.

———. *Language and Society in "La vida de Lazarillo de Tormes."* Baltimore: Johns Hopkins University Press, 1978.

Sloman, Albert E. *The Dramatic Craftsmanship of Calderón: His Use of Earlier Plays.* Oxford: Dolphin, 1958.

———. "Lope's *El mejor alcalde, el rey:* Addendum to a Note by Sturgiss E. Leavitt." *BCom,* 7 (1955): 17a–19b.

———. "The Structure of Calderón's *La vida es sueño.*" *MLR,* 48 (1953): 293–300.

Smith, Colin. Introduction to his edition of *Spanish Ballads.* Oxford: Pergamon, 1964.

——. *The Making of the "Poema de mio Cid."* Cambridge: Cambridge University Press, 1983.

Snell, Bruno. *The Discovery of the Mind: The Greek Origins of European Thought.* Trans. T. G. Rosenmeyer. New York: Harper & Bros., 1960.

The Song of Roland. Trans. Frederick Goldin. New York: Norton, 1978.

Soons, C. Alan. *Juan de Mariana.* Boston: Twayne, 1982.

Soufas, C. Christopher. "Thinking in *La vida es sueño.*" *PMLA,* 100 (1985): 287–99.

Spitzer, Leo. "A Central Theme and Its Structural Equivalent in Lope's *Fuenteovejuna.*" *HR,* 23 (1955): 274–92.

——. "'Soy Quien Soy.'" *NRFH,* 1 (1948): 113–27.

Stewart, Douglas. *The Disguised Guest: Rank, Role and Identity in the "Odyssey."* Lewisburg, Pa.: Bucknell University Press, 1976.

Sullivan, Henry W. *Calderón in the German Lands and the Low Countries: His Reception and Influence, 1654–1980.* Cambridge: Cambridge University Press, 1983.

El teatro de Lope de Vega: Artículos y estudios. Ed. José Francisco Gatti. Buenos Aires: Eudeba, 1967.

Templin, E. "The Mother in the Comedia of Lope." *HR,* 3 (1935): 219–44.

ter Horst, Robert. *Calderón: The Secular Plays.* Lexington: University Press of Kentucky, 1982.

Texto y espectáculo: Selected Proceedings of the Symposium on Spanish Golden Age Theater. Ed. Barbara Mujika. Lanham, Md.: University Press of America, 1989.

Tillyard, E. M. W. *The Elizabethan World Picture.* London: Chatto & Windus, 1952.

Torres Naharro, Bartolomé de. *Comedia Himenea.* In *Comedias. Soldadesca, Tinelaria, Himenea,* ed. D. W. McPheeter. Madrid: Castalia, 1973. 181–237.

Trueblood, Alan S. *Experience and Artistic Expression in Lope de Vega: The making of "La Dorotea."* Cambridge: Harvard University Press, 1974.

Trueblood, Paul G. *Lord Byron.* 2d ed. Boston: Twayne, 1977.

Tuñón de Lara, Manuel. *Costa y Unamuno en la crisis de fin de siglo.* Madrid: Edicusa, 1974.

Valbuena Briones, Angel. Preliminary note to *Luis Pérez, el gallego.* In Calderón, *Obras completas,* 1:279–80.

Valdés, Alfonso de. *Diálogo de Mercùrio y Carón.* 5th ed. Ed. José F. Montesinos. Madrid: Espasa-Calpe, 1971.

Varey, J. E. "The Essential Ambiguity in Lope de Vega's *Peribáñez:* Theme and Staging." *Theatre Research International,* 1 (1976): 157–78.

——. "Towards an Interpretation of Lope de Vega's *El villano en su rincón.*" In *Studies in Spanish Literature of the Golden Age Presented to E. M. Wilson,* 315–37. Ed. R. O. Jones. London: Tamesis, 1973.

Vega, Garcilaso de la. *Poesías castellanas completas.* Ed. Elias L. Rivers. Madrid: Castalia, 1969.

Vega Carpio, Lope Félix de. *El arte nuevo de hacer comedias en este tiempo.* In *Preceptiva dramática española,* 154–65.

——. *The New Art of Writing Plays,* Trans. William T. Brewster. New York: Dramatic Museum of Columbia University, 1914. Repr. in *Papers on Playmaking,* ed. Brander Matthews. Preface by Henry W. Wells. New York: Hill & Wang, 1957.

——. *Comedia de Bamba.* In *Obras de Lope de Vega.* Vol. 16, *Crónicas y leyendas dramáticas de España,* ed. Marcelino Menéndez Pelayo, 295–342. BAE, 195. Madrid: Atlas, 1966.

——. *Los comendadores de Córdoba.* In *Obras escogidas,* 3:1233–66. Ed. Federico Carlos Sainz de Robles. Madrid: Aguilar, 1974.

——. *Doze comedias de Lope de Vega Carpio familiar del Santo Oficio. Sacadas de sus originales. Quarta parte.* Barcelona, 1614.

——. *Doze comedias de Lope de Vega Carpio familiar del Santo Oficio. Sacadas de sus originales. Quarta parte.* Madrid, 1614.

——. *Las ferias de Madrid.* In *Obras de Lope de Vega. Nueva Edición. Obras dramáticas.* Vol. 5. Madrid: RAE, 1918.

——. *Fuenteovejuna.* 4th ed. Ed. Francisco López Estrada. Madrid: Castalia, 1983.

——. *Fuenteovejuna.* Trans. Roy Campbell. In *The Classic Theater,* 161–231.

——. *La juventud de San Isidro.* In *Obras escogidas,* 3. Ed. Federico Carlos Sainz de Robles. Madrid: Aguilar, 1974.

——. *The King and the Farmer: A Romantic Comedy.* Trans. Cecily Radford. London: H. W. F. Deane & Sons, 1948.

——. *The King, the Greatest Alcalde.* In *Four Plays by Lope de Vega,* 103–87. Trans. John Garrett Underhill. New York: Charles Scribner's Sons, 1936.

——. *El Labrador del Tormes.* In *Obras de Lope de Vega,* 3:1–30. New ed. Ed. Cotarelo y Mori. Madrid: RAE, 1930.

——. *El mejor alcalde, el rey.* In *Comedias.* Vol. 1, *El remedio en la desdicha. El mejor alcalde, el rey,* ed. J. Gómez Ocerín and R. M. Tenreiro, 175–272. Madrid: Espasa-Calpe, 1967.

——. *El peregrino en su patria.* Ed. Juan Bautista Avalle-Arce. Madrid: Castalia, 1973.

——. *Peribáñez y el Comendador de Ocaña.* Ed. Felipe B. Pedraza. Facsimile Edition. Ocaña: Colección Azarque, 1983.

——. *Peribáñez y el Comendador de Ocaña, Tragicomedia.* In *Comedias escogidas de Frey Lope Félix de Vega Carpio,* 3:281–302. Ed. Juan Eugenio Hartzenbusch. BAE, 41. Madrid: Rivadeneyra, 1857.

——. *Peribáñez.* Ed. Alberto Blecua. Madrid: Alianza, 1981.

——. *Peribáñez.* Trans. Jill Booty. In *Lope de Vega (Five Plays),* ed. R. D. F. Pring-Mill, 1–56. New York: Hill & Wang, 1961.

——. "Prólogos." In *Comedias escogidas de Frey Lope Félix de Vega Carpio,* 4:xxii–xxix. Ed. Juan Eugenio Hartzenbusch. BAE, 52. Madrid: Imprenta de los Sucesores de Hernando, 1910.

——. *El robo de Dina.* In *Obras de Lope de Vega.* Vol. 7, *Autos y coloquios,* Part 2. Ed. Marcelino Menéndez y Pelayo. BAE, 159. Madrid: Atlas, 1963.

——. *El villano en su rincón.* In *Teatro Español del Siglo de Oro,* ed. Bruce W. Wardropper, 258–364. New York: Charles Scribner's Sons, 1970.

Waith, Eugene M. *The Herculean Hero in Marlowe, Chapman, Shakespeare, and Dryden.* New York: Columbia University Press, 1962.

Wardlaw, Frances Day. "*El villano en su rincón:* Lope's Rejection of the Pastoral Dream." *BHS,* 58 (1981): 113–19.

Wardropper, Bruce W. "Comic Illusion in *El perro del hortelano,*" *KRQ,* 14 (1967): 101–11.

——. "The Dramatic Epilogue in Golden Age Spain." *MLN,* 101 (1986): 205–19.

——. "The Epic Hero Superseded." In *Concepts of the Hero,* 63–89.

——. Letter to the author, 9 July 1987.

——. "Lope de Vega's Urban Comedy." *Hispanófila Especial,* 1 (1974): 47–61.

——. "El trastorno de la moral en el *Lazarillo.*" *NRFH,* 15 (1961): 441–47.

——. "La venganza de Maquiavelo: *El villano en su rincón.*" In *Homenaje a William L. Fichter,* 765–72.

Watson, A. Irvine. "*El pintor de su deshonra* and the Neo-Aristotelian Theory of Tragedy." In *Critical Essays on the Theatre of Calderón,* 203–23.

Watson, Anthony. *Juan de la Cueva and the Portuguese Succession.* London: Tamesis, 1971.

Watson, Curtis Brown. *Shakespeare and the Renaissance Concept of Honor.* Princeton: Princeton University Press, 1960.

Weiner, Jack. "Un episodio de la historia rusa visto por autores españoles del Siglo de Oro: El pretendiente Demetrio." *JHP,* 2 (1978): 175–201.

——. "Lope de Vega's *Fuenteovejuna* under Tsars, Commissars, and the Second Spanish Republic (1931–1939)." *Annali, Istituto Universitario Orientale, Sezione Romanza* (Naples), 24 (1982): 167–223.

West, Geoffrey. "Hero or Saint? Hagiographic Elements in the Life of the Cid." *JHP,* 7 (1983): 286–99.

——. "Medieval Historiography Misconstrued: The Exile of the Cid, Rodrigo Díaz, and the Supposed *Invidia* of Alfonso VI." *Medium Aevum,* 52 (1983): 286–99.

Whitman, Cedric. *Sophocles: A Study of Heroic Humanism.* Cambridge: Harvard University Press, 1951.

Wilson, E. M. "Las 'dudas curiosas' a la aprobación del Maestro Fray Manuel de Guerra y Ribera." *Estudios Escénicos,* 6 (1960): 47–63.

——. "The Four Elements in the Imagery of Calderón." *MLR,* 31 (1936): 34–47.

——. "Gerald Brenan's Calderón." *BCom,* 6 (1952): 6–8.

——. "Images et structure dans *Peribáñez.*" *BH,* 51 (1945), 125–59. Repr. in Spanish translation in *El teatro de Lope de Vega,* 50–90; and in *Calderón y la crítica: Historia y antología.* Vol. 1. Ed. Manuel Durán and Roberto González Echeverría. Madrid: Gredos, 1976, 277. Repr. in English translation in Wilson's *Spanish and English Literature of the 16th and 17th Centuries: Studies in Discretion, Illusion and Mutability,* 130–54. Cambridge: Cambridge University Press, 1980.

——. "On *La vida es sueño.*" In *Critical Essays on the Theatre of Calderón,* 63–89.

——. "Tragic Themes in Spanish Ballads." In his *Spanish and English Literature of the 16th and 17th Centuries,* 220–33. Repr. from Diamante, 8. London: Hispanic and Luso Brazilian Council, 1958.

——, and Duncan Moir. *A Literary History of Spain. The Golden Age: Drama, 1492–1700.* London: Ernest Benn, 1971.

Zamora Vicente, Alonso. "Estudio preliminar" to Lope de Vega, *El villano en su rincón. Las bizarrías de Belisa,* vii–lxxvi. Madrid: Espasa-Calpe, 1963.

Zuckerman-Ingber, Alix. *"El bien más alto": A Reconsideration of Lope de Vega's Honor Plays.* Gainesville: University Presses of Florida, 1984.

INDEX